DATE DUE

APR 11 1998

MARRIAGE AND MENTAL ILLNESS
A SEX-ROLES PERSPECTIVE

THE GUILFORD FAMILY THERAPY SERIES
ALAN S. GURMAN, EDITOR

Marriage and Mental Illness: A Sex-Roles Perspective
R. JULIAN HAFNER
Living through Divorce: A Developmental Approach to Divorce Therapy
JOY K. RICE AND DAVID G. RICE
Generation to Generation: Family Process in Church and Synagogue
EDWIN H. FRIEDMAN
Failures in Family Therapy
SANDRA B. COLEMAN, EDITOR
Casebook of Marital Therapy
ALAN S. GURMAN, EDITOR
Families and Other Systems: The Macrosystemic Context of Family Therapy
JOHN SCHWARTZMAN, EDITOR
The Military Family: Dynamics and Treatment
FLORENCE W. KASLOW AND RICHARD I. RIDENOUR, EDITORS
Marriage and Divorce: A Contemporary Perspective
CAROL C. NADELSON AND DEREK C. POLONSKY, EDITORS
Family Care of Schizophrenia: A Problem-Solving Approach to the Treatment
of Mental Illness
IAN R. H. FALLOON, JEFFREY L. BOYD, AND CHRISTINE W. McGILL
The Process of Change
PEGGY PAPP
Family Therapy: Principles of Strategic Practice
ALLON BROSS, EDITOR
Aesthetics of Change
BRADFORD P. KEENEY
Family Therapy in Schizophrenia
WILLIAM R. McFARLANE, EDITOR
Mastering Resistance: A Practical Guide to Family Therapy
CAROL M. ANDERSON AND SUSAN STEWART
Family Therapy and Family Medicine: Toward the Primary Care of Families
WILLIAM J. DOHERTY AND MACARAN A. BAIRD
Ethnicity and Family Therapy
MONICA McGOLDRICK, JOHN K. PEARCE, AND JOSEPH GIORDANO,
EDITORS

Patterns of Brief Family Therapy: An Ecosystemic Approach
STEVE DE SHAZER
The Family Therapy of Drug Abuse and Addiction
M. DUNCAN STANTON, THOMAS C. TODD, AND ASSOCIATES
From Psyche to System: The Evolving Therapy of Carl Whitaker
JOHN R. NEILL AND DAVID P. KNISKERN, *EDITORS*
Normal Family Processes
FROMA WALSH, *EDITOR*
Helping Couples Change: A Social Learning Approach to Marital Therapy
RICHARD B. STUART

MARRIAGE
AND
MENTAL ILLNESS
A SEX-ROLES PERSPECTIVE

R. JULIAN HAFNER

Copyright © 1986 The Guilford Press
A Division of Guilford Publications, Inc.
200 Park Avenue South, New York, N.Y. 10003

Printed in the United States of America

Library of Congress Cataloging in Publication Data

Hafner, R. Julian.
  Marriage and mental illness.

  (Guilford family therapy series)
  Bibliography: p.
  Includes index.
  1. Marriage—Psychological aspects.   2. Sex role—
Psychological aspects.   3. Mental illness—Etiology—
Social aspects.   I. Title.   II. Series.
RC455.4.M37H34   1986   155.6′45   85-17693
ISBN 0-89862-064-3

TO DORINDA, JAMES, AND NUALA

Acknowledgments

My sincerest thanks go to those colleagues in the Department of Psychiatry at Flinders Medical Center who encouraged me to persevere with this book and gave me invaluable support. Ross Kalucy, Peter Gilchrist, Sandy Mac-Farlane, and John Condon were particularly patient and understanding.

Special thanks to Andrew Badenoch and Jill Fisher for sharing their ideas with me so generously, and for their helpful comments on the manuscript. My gratitude also to Janine Judd and Sandra Gay, who typed the manuscript.

I am grateful to the editor of the *Australian and New Zealand Journal of Psychiatry* for permission to reproduce a substantial part of my article "Marital Interaction in Persisting Obsessive Compulsive Disorders" (Hafner, 1982b).

Finally, I am deeply indebted to my wife and children for their support and encouragement and for their patience during my absence while writing.

Preface

Countless books and articles have been written about marriage. Anthropologists and sociologists have placed marriage in its historical and environmental context; demographers have analyzed the statistics of marriage; marriage therapists have illuminated its pathology. As much or more has been written about mental illness, again by authors from a wide range of professional backgrounds. However, very little has been written about the relationship between marriage and mental illness. It is this relationship that is the main focus of this book, a perspective engendered by the rapid and extensive changes in the institution of marriage that have occurred over the past 30 years.

Much of my energy over the past dozen years has been channeled into writing in scientific and professional journals about the relationship between marriage and mental illness. Although this is a necessary and rewarding pursuit for an academic psychiatrist, it is fairly limited in scope. Scientific papers are written for a restricted readership within tight constraints on structure and content; there is little room for speculation or for integrating material from different scientific disciplines. This book is a departure from such an approach. Although it is written primarily for those with a professional or scientific interest in marriage and mental illness, it should be of value to anyone who seeks to understand more clearly the nature of these two institutions and their relationship. I have placed much emphasis on detailed clinical examples, in the belief that these will provide a basis for anyone, at whatever level of professional or personal endeavor, to recognize and modify patterns of marital interaction that are contributing to psychological symptoms or psychiatric disorder. Naturally, the names and personal details of those described have been altered to protect their privacy.

R. Julian Hafner

Introduction

There has been a great increase over the past 30 years in the provision of mental health services in North America and other English-speaking countries. To a growing army of psychiatrists has been added an increasing number of clinical psychologists, mental health nurses and psychiatrically trained social workers, all of whom are paid primarily to provide mental health care.

That this expansion of services reflects in part an increased prevalence of psychological and psychiatric disorders is suggested by recent research (Hagnell, Lanke, Rorsman, & Öjesjö, 1982) showing that the amount of depression in the community has risen threefold over the past 25 years. Since depression is one of the most common psychological disorders, these findings suggest a significant increase in psychological distress and disability within a single generation.

Even if there has been no recent increase, the current point prevalence of psychiatric disorder in the United States is at least 15% (Weissman, Myers, & Thompson, 1981). Many factors contribute to this major public health problem. It is the aim of this book to focus on modern marriage and its contribution to the development and maintenance of psychological symptoms in married people.

In today's rapidly changing world, we have clung to marriage as an institution: Although the divorce rate has increased greatly over the past 20 years, this increase has been paralleled by the remarriage rate. If this is taken into account, it is clear that people are getting married more than ever before. Marriage has become an enduring, universally accessible institution in a changing, uncertain world. Onto marriage are projected hopes, dreams, and expectations that are the obverse of fears of abandonment, aloneness, and insignificance. However, clinging to the idea of marriage as a solution to the personal problems and conflicts of living in today's complex and changing world has become unhealthy and destructive for many people. By expecting the impossible of marriage and by preserving it as a symbol of personal salvation, human conflicts are often created or amplified: Out of this may emerge mental illness.

In order to develop this viewpoint, the first chapter outlines those changes that have occurred in the institution of marriage over the past two centuries. The next four chapters discuss: sex-role stereotyping and sex-role conflict within marriage; selection of marriage partner in relation to psychological adjustment; ways in which marital interaction leads to the development of psychological symptoms; and the labeling of psychological symptoms as mental illness and their unwitting reinforcement and consolidation by physicians and psychiatrists. Chapters 6, 7, and 8 deal with marital interaction in the more common psychiatric disorders. The final chapter suggests ways of avoiding or reversing unhelpful or pathological marital interactions as a means of creating more enriching and fulfilling relationships within marriage.

Contents

1. The Changing Institution of Marriage   **1**

MARRIAGE IN PREINDUSTRIAL ENGLAND   1
THE EFFECTS OF THE INDUSTRIAL REVOLUTION   7
THE EFFECTS OF TECHNOLOGY   11

2. Sex-Role Stereotyping and Conflict   **16**

ORIGINS OF THE MALE SEX-ROLE STEREOTYPE   18
SEX-ROLE STEREOTYPES AND MENTAL ILLNESS IN MEN   21
ORIGINS OF THE FEMALE SEX-ROLE STEREOTYPE   25
THE MUTUAL DEPENDENCE OF MALE AND
    FEMALE STEREOTYPES   32
SEX-ROLE CONFLICT   36
THE IMPACT OF SEX-ROLE RESEARCH ON
    CLINICAL THEORY AND PRACTICE   43

3. Choice of Marriage Partner   **47**

PERSONAL AND GENDER IDENTITY   47
MATE SELECTION   59
SUMMARY AND CONCLUSIONS   67

4. Psychological Symptoms Resulting from Marital Interaction   **69**

STATUS-ORIENTED MARRIAGES   70
SYMBIOTIC MARRIAGES   82
DENIAL OF MARITAL CONFLICT   98

5. Marriage, the Medical Model, and Psychiatry   **100**

STEREOTYPING THE MENTALLY ILL   100
PSYCHIATRY AND MEDICINE   103
HOW THE INTERACTION OF PSYCHIATRIC AND
    MARITAL SYSTEMS MAINTAINS SYMPTOMS   105
THE LACK OF RESEARCH INTO THE MARITAL CONTEXT
    OF PSYCHIATRIC DISORDER   111
INTERACTION OF MEDICAL AND MARITAL SYSTEMS
    IN SYMPTOM FORMATION   114

6. Marriage and Affective Disorders   **122**

    COMMUNITY STUDIES OF DEPRESSION   122
    MARRIAGE AND DEPRESSION   124
    MARITAL INTERACTION AND DEPRESSED WOMEN   126
    MARITAL INTERACTION AND DEPRESSED MEN   143
    MARRIAGE AND MANIA   149

7. Marriage and Anxiety Disorders   **152**

    PHOBIC DISORDERS   153
    AGORAPHOBIA   153
    AGORAPHOBIA IN MEN   160
    PHOBIAS IN MEN AND ALCOHOL DEPENDENCY   164
    ANXIETY STATES   164
    OBSESSIVE COMPULSIVE DISORDERS   168
    OBSESSIVE COMPULSIVE DISORDERS IN MEN   176

8. Marriage and Psychosis   **184**

    SEX DIFFERENCES   184
    RESEARCH ON SEX-ROLE ISSUES IN
      SCHIZOPHRENIC DISORDER   186
    MARRIAGE AND MEN WITH SCHIZOPHRENIA   187
    MARRIAGE AND WOMEN WITH SCHIZOPHRENIA   194
    CONCLUSIONS   204

9. Spouse-Aided Therapy and Beyond   **206**

    INDIVIDUAL THERAPY FOR MARRIED PATIENTS   207
    SPOUSE-AIDED THERAPY   214
    SPOUSE-AIDED AND INDIVIDUAL THERAPY COMPARED   222
    THE FINDINGS OF COMPARABLE STUDIES   225
    FUTURE DIRECTIONS   227

References   **231**

Author Index   **241**

Subject Index   **247**

CHAPTER ONE

The Changing Institution of Marriage

To comprehend the very recent changes in an institution as ancient and enduring as marriage a historical perspective is essential. English-speaking societies have changed profoundly over the past two centuries and marriage customs and attitudes have adapted and evolved accordingly. During this time, the single most powerful influence on Western culture has been the Industrial Revolution, which historians generally agree took place in England mainly between 1760 and 1830 (Seaman, 1981). Subsequently, the entire way of life of a majority of people in English-speaking nations and elsewhere changed fundamentally over a mere two or three generations. At the start of the 19th century, more than three quarters of the working population of England were employed on the land; by the end of that century, less than 10% were so employed. Instead, they worked in the mines and factories that had flourished in the wake of the Industrial Revolution. Similar changes had occurred in North America and northern Europe, and were associated with the creation and growth of the towns and cities in which a large majority of Westerners live today.

Because the transition from a rural preindustrial to an urban industrial way of life occurred relatively suddenly, many marriage customs and attitudes that originated in a rural context persisted, and persist today, in an urban setting. It is therefore difficult or impossible to comprehend modern marriage and its vicissitudes without understanding its origins in preindustrial society. Although many different cultures have contributed to the richness and diversity of today's English-speaking nations, derivatives of Anglo-Saxon culture remain among the most potent influences on contemporary English-speaking societies. Thus, marriage in the Anglo-Saxon-based culture of 17th- and 18th-century England will be used as a paradigm of marriage in preindustrial Western society.

MARRIAGE IN PREINDUSTRIAL ENGLAND

By the start of the 17th century, a large part of England had been divided into parishes. These geographical and administrative units ranged in size from a

1

single village to areas comprising a large town with surrounding manors, farms, and villages. The parishes provided a basis for the assessment and collection of taxes, for the administration of the Poor Law Act (promulgated in 1601 as a basic welfare facility), for the control and documentation of population movements, for dealing with certain crimes and misdemeanors, and for the dispensation of spiritual and moral guidance and welfare.

Conscientious senior parish officials (rectors) often kept detailed records in relation to these and other matters, so that a study of surviving parish registers has yielded an extraordinarily rich and consistent account of the structure and function of society and of marriage and family life in 17th- and 18th-century England (Laslett, 1977).

The Economics of Marriage

It has been established that the nuclear rather than the extended family was the basic social unit in 17th- and 18th-century England, and probably for at least the preceding millenium (Laslett, 1977). The average household size during the 17th century was about 4.8 persons (excluding servants), which is not greatly different from the mean of 3.7 persons per household in contemporary America. Less than 7% of the population lived in extended or multiple-family households. These findings are important because they show that the nuclear family is a longstanding rather than a recent feature of English-speaking societies.

Household size in preindustrial England was determined mainly by economics. Few married couples could afford to support economically unproductive people other than their own young offspring. The elderly and others who could not maintain themselves were generally forced to rely on parish welfare, which provided help at the margins of subsistence.

It is difficult to comprehend the economic harshness of preindustrial England and comparable areas of western Europe. For at least half the population, life was a constant struggle to secure sufficient food, clothing, and shelter to maintain life for themselves and any dependents. This is clearly documented in parish registers, which reveal that about 50% of people applied for or received poor relief during the course of their lives in the parish. Such people were usually unmarried, although de facto liaisons were common. Essentially, the choice of formal marriage was restricted to that proportion of the male population (about one-half) who had sufficient financial or occupational status and stability to provide for themselves and their dependents (Seaman, 1981).

Marriages were contracted for economic rather than for personal psychological reasons. Inheritance was determined by the principal of "primogeniture": On the death of the husband, the family's wealth was transferred to the oldest surviving son. In the absence of sons, daughters could inherit, but on marriage their assets were automatically transferred to the husband. Although there were exceptions, the rule of primogeniture was almost universally applied and had the official sanction of Church and State as a fundamental aspect of both Anglo-Saxon and Norman culture and tradition. Thus was perpetuated a patriarchal system within which married women were systematically denied any significant economic power or status.

Where patriarchs had modest assets or trades or occupations that could absorb only the oldest son, younger sons and daughters were generally confronted in early adulthood with major problems of survival. Thus, daughters were usually willing to enter marriage on a purely economic basis, even if they perceived as unsavoury the personal attributes of their husbands-to-be. Once married, their welfare and happiness depended in theory on the whim of their husbands, although in practice a wife could appeal to her family of origin or to the churchwarden, rector or parish constable if she was grossly or systematically mistreated. However, gross abuse of wives by husbands seems to have been rare, at least according to parish records and related sources. The following factors contributed to this.

In most families, marriages were arranged to provide for a mutually beneficial extension, consolidation, or redistribution of assets, particularly of agricultural land and its improvements. Such families were required to preserve a good working relationship as administrators of shared or contiguous assets. In such a situation, the husband avoided mistreating his wife in ways that would offend her family of origin. Wives of less wealthy husbands were protected by the fact that the couples' respective families almost always lived in the same parish, so that it was highly desirable for them to preserve a good relationship. This placed a powerful constraint upon husbands' maltreatment of their wives.

A further factor encouraging at least a civil relationship between husband and wife was the presence of servants. About one-third of those men who could afford to marry could also afford one or more resident domestic servants. Many others could afford to regularly employ servants on a nonresident basis. Thus, even domestic life was rarely entirely private, and any obvious abuse of wives by husbands (or, indeed, the reverse) would have been detected by servants and doubtless rapidly and widely disseminated through gossip.

Added to the family and community constraints on wife abuse was the need for husband and wife to maintain a good practical working relationship. Economic factors largely determined not only when and whom to marry, but the conduct of marriage itself. Larger, wealthier households had to be run efficiently, or they drained the family income. Indeed, many wealthy families went into financial decline after they had built or purchased a large family residence. Opportunities for petty theft and administrative inefficiency abounded in these complex households. It was the wife's duty to organize the servants and the general running of the household, the overall domestic budget, and details of social life and entertainment, together with many other duties and commitments. A wife who strongly resented her husband was unlikely to conduct her various roles with efficiency, and may have been

3

deliberately inefficient as a means of expressing indirectly her frustration and resentment. Most husbands could not afford this, and therefore took pains to preserve good relationships with their wives.

In smaller households, an efficient and harmonious division of labor between husband and wife was essential to economic survival. If, as was commonly the case, the husband owned a small farm, his wife's efficient contribution to the overall management and day-to-day function was vital. When the husband was an artisan, mutual cooperation was equally necessary. For example, cloth manufacture was a very common rural industry in the 17th and 18th centuries. Children carded the wool, the wife spun it into yarn, and the husband undertook the weaving and finishing processes. Major conflicts between husband and wife could not be sustained without undermining or destroying the family's economic base. Since this might lead to a dependence on parish welfare, which often meant an enforced breakup of the family and near starvation for its members, disruptive conflict was feared and avoided by both partners.

Expectations of Marriage

Since both marriage itself and choice of mate were determined largely by economics, personal characteristics and attributes were not prominent in the process of mate selection. Virtually all marriages were arranged by parents and senior family members rather than by the participants themselves. Wives-to-be were rarely in a position to object to a proposed partnership for their survival often depended on it. Although men had more chance than women of surviving in the unmarried state, their future prospects often depended on their capacity to marry a woman with some economic assets, or whose family could offer a substantial dowry. In any event, since most people lived in or nearby fairly isolated villages and small towns ranging in population from 150–1200, choice of broadly eligible marriage partners was generally limited to less than a dozen or so.

The modern concept of romantic love as a prelude to marriage was virtually absent in England at this time. Since marriage was mainly a path to economic survival or improvement, notions of romance and personal attraction were largely redundant. Sex within marriage was widely regarded as a duty required for procreation rather than an exercise in pleasure. The general level of physical attractiveness was much less than it is today. Light, cotton clothing was rare and expensive, and most people dressed in heavy, functional, and unattractive woolen garments. Wood for heating was expensive, and coal was not yet available as an alternative except in a few localized areas adjacent to coal mines. Water had to be carried by hand to most households. Thus, the use of water in most dwellings was restricted to cooking and drinking. Bathing and regular washing of clothes were unusual, and soap was a rare and expensive luxury. General hygiene and nutrition were poor. Lice and skin diseases (often related to chronic skin infections and vitamin deficiencies) were endemic, even among the wealthy. Since the weather was cold or wet for most of the year, and few could afford separate nightclothes, most people wore the same set of clothes night and day for months on end. Strong body odors were accepted as inevitable, except among the wealthy, who usually attempted to disguise them with perfumes and essences rather than to undertake more vigorous personal hygiene. Thus, at least during the colder months, there was little incentive or opportunity for most people to indulge in the sexually idealized and romantic liaisons that are a characteristic of today's English-speaking societies.

The prevailing poor hygiene and nutritional status, together with little understanding of infectious diseases, preventive medicine, and public health, contributed to high levels of mortality. Average life expectancy was less than 40 years. Very high perinatal and infant mortality were the major contributors to this low figure: Married couples of average economic status expected to lose about half their offspring before adulthood, and children born out of wedlock or to poor parents had an even lower survival rate. However, once adulthood was achieved, average life expectancy was about 65 years, so that most young adults could plan ahead on the assumption that they had a good chance of surviving for another 40–45 years. This expectation was altered only during major epidemics such as the Black Death or Great (Bubonic) Plague of 1665, or in time of famine or war.

However, just as the likelihood of survival to adulthood was strongly related to economic factors, so was the likelihood of subsequent life and health. The well-off were constantly aware of the disastrous consequences of loss of economic status, and the poor were constantly preoccupied with their daily struggle for survival. Against such a harsh background, the qualities of personal relationships were probably very different from those that prevail today. Unfortunately, parish registers and similar official records preserve facts rather than direct observations about the qualities of human relationships; These, therefore, must be inferred from available data, including the literature of the time. Rogers (1969) has suggested that preindustrial personal relationships among rural workers were characterized by mutual suspicion and distrust and low levels of empathy. These attitudes were accompanied by a strongly ambivalent dependence on authoritarian government, a restricted and mainly pessimistic world view, fatalism and a lack of innovativeness, and very limited personal aspirations. Such attitudes and expectations appear fully commensurate with the harsh and unpredictable environment that then prevailed.

The Religious Context

The Test Act of 1673 excluded from universities, schools, the armed forces, the Church, and municipal and public office all those who were not communicant members of the Anglican church. In 1677, an act of Parliament banned work on Sunday except for the morning and evening collection and delivery of milk. These acts of Parliament illustrate the strength of the relationship that developed between State and Church as part of their attempts to influence and control the beliefs and behavior of the populace.

These attempts were technically successful: Parish registers of the 18th century show that a majority of people took the sacrament and became communicants of the Anglican church when, at the age of 16, they were considered sufficiently mature. Admission to the Church required an explicit and enduring commitment to its spiritual, moral, and ethical standards. Thus, whatever occurred in private, in public a majority of people strictly adhered to the tenets and dogmas of the Anglican church. As attendance at school was voluntary and rarely without charge (only 25,000 received free education in 1714), formal education was restricted to the children of the financially secure. Educational curricula were determined largely by the Church, so that schools generally reinforced traditional Anglican values. Presumably, therefore, the beliefs, attitudes, and expectations of a great majority of people were determined by the Church, folklore, and local and family tradition, with the former exerting the greatest influence on many—an influence reinforced by the promise of hellfire and eternal damnation for those who fell seriously short of requirements. Given its power to influence conduct and beliefs in general, and its monopoly on conferring legal marital status, the attitudes of the Church to marriage were clearly of central importance.

The Christian church in England has a history of ambivalence to women and human sexuality, an ambivalence that owes much to the apparent asexuality of Christ, to the attitudes of such early theologians as Saint Thomas Aquinas, with their emphasis on celibacy, chastity, and asceticism as ideals, and to the misogyny of Saint Paul: "To the unmarried I say that it is well for them to remain single as I do. But if they cannot exercise self-control, they should marry. For it is better to marry than to be aflame with passion." (1 Cor. 7:8–9, Lindsell Edition, 1971)

The official English church of the 17th and 18th centuries was a strictly male institution (as it has remained until very recent moves to admit women to the clergy). It issued guidelines, *inter alia,* concerning sexual intercourse within marriage. If these were strictly adhered to, there were very few occasions when sexual intercourse was permissable.

The Anglican church also firmly supported the economically dependent position of women within marriage. This support was based on a long-standing theological consensus about the natural inferiority of women, which Saint Thomas Aquinas had attributed to a mysterious prenatal defect (Kay, 1972). Earlier, women had been degraded to such an extent that bishops assembling at Macon in A.D. 585 seriously and at length debated whether women were human. These basic assumptions were reinforced by references in the Bible to the naturally inferior position of women, as exemplified by parts of 1 Corinthians: "For a man ought not to cover his head, since he is the image and

6

glory of God; but woman is the glory of man. For man was not made from woman, but woman from man. Neither was man created for woman, but woman for man" (11:7–9). "The women should keep silence in the Churches. For they are not permitted to speak, but should be subordinate, as even the law says. If there is anything they desire to know, let them ask their husbands at home" (14:34–35).

These powerful official constraints upon the emancipation of women were almost universally accepted without question. Patriarchy and the economic powerlessness of married women were such embedded features of Anglo-Saxon and Norman culture that the Church was simply reinforcing the *status quo*.

The extent of extramarital sexual liaisons in 17th- and 18th-century England is difficult to assess, for obvious reasons. Such matters rarely appeared in official parish records. Official rates of illegitimate birth were very low, ranging from 1.0–3.0% between 1600 and 1750 (Laslett, 1977). Doubtless, many illegitimate births went unrecorded. However, given the comprehensive nature of parish control and documentation, a record was probably kept of most surviving illegitimate offspring who were acknowledged as such. It is of interest that the percentage of illegitimate births varied directly with the mean age at first marriage, which for women varied from 26.8 to 29.6 between 1647 and 1770. Men on average married 2–3 years later (Laslett, 1977). The fact that people married much later than they do today is a reminder of the essentially economic nature of the institution as it then was: Few men could afford to marry until their early 30s, and they tended to marry women who had had the opportunity to accumulate some personal economic assets.

THE EFFECTS OF THE INDUSTRIAL REVOLUTION

The initial benefits of the Industrial Revolution were patchy and limited mainly to those entrepreneurs who were able to profit from a juxtaposition of cheap labor, innovative technology, and an adequate supply of appropriate raw materials and fuel. That millions of industrial workers and their families endured almost unbearably squalid lives during the two to three generations after the Industrial Revolution has been abundantly documented and discussed: The theme of worker versus capitalist has been kept alive in the works of Marx and Engels. It is clear that for most people, the initial effects of the Industrial Revolution comprised mainly a move from a harsh and uncertain rural environment to a squalid and miserable life in a large town or city. The plight of very large numbers of people in the larger cities of the second half of the 19th century is starkly illustrated by the following description of a public churchyard in the London of the 1880s: "On the benches on either side arrayed a mass of miserable and distorted humanity . . . a welter of rags, and filth, of all manner of loathsome skin diseases, open sores, bruises, grossness, indecency, leering monstrosities and bestial faces. A chill, raw wind was blowing, and these creatures huddled there in their rags, sleeping for the most part, or trying to sleep" (Harrison, 1977, p. 212).

Even those who had dwellings and regular employment often lacked the financial means to afford adequate food and fuel. It has been estimated that over 30% of Londoners in the last quarter of the 19th century lived below basic levels of subsistence (Harrison, 1977). However, there emerged in 19th-century England, for the first time in English history, a sizable population whose lives were free of an exhausting daily physical struggle for survival, who lived a reasonably secure and predictable existence in fairly warm and comfortable dwellings, and whose nutritional and hygiene status was sufficient to allow sustained good health. Such people were employed in the upper and middle echelons of industrial organizations, or the fast-expanding public service, or had unearned incomes. The latter became increasingly common as entrepreneurial capitalistic families steadily accumulated assets that were subject to minimal taxation. Low levels of taxation were possible because government-funded welfare and health services barely existed. The growth of industry and the public service led also to the employment of an increasing number of clerical workers, and the more senior of these could afford to support themselves and their families in reasonable comfort.

The emergence in the cities and larger towns of a substantial group of people with the energy, money, and motivation for pleasurable and entertaining activities beyond the purely domestic led, among other things, to the beginnings of the modern entertainment industry. It led also to the rapid and enormous growth of prostitution (Harrison, 1977). There is a consensus that in mid-19th-century London, about 1 in every 60 houses was a brothel and 1 in every 15 women a full-time prostitute, yielding a total of about 80,000 prostitutes in a population of some 2.5 million. Similar ratios existed in many of the larger English industrial towns and cities. The situation was not greatly different in parts of America: The chief of police in New York City estimated in 1856 that the city contained 5,000 prostitutes and nearly 500 brothels, and by the 1890s, the number of prostitutes had risen to around 40,000. Concurrent with this flourishing of prostitution, for which the Victorian Era is renowned, was a change in the institution of marriage.

Increasingly, wealth was determined by profits from mining and industry rather than by ownership of agricultural land. Industrial wealth could be greatly increased by the entrepreneurial zeal of individuals or single families. It was therefore no longer always necessary to increase wealth by redistributing agricultural land through marriage. Husbands employed within industry and the public service were able to support their wives and children without enlisting them as direct collaborators in their work. Thus, for the first time, marriage ceased to be an arrangement almost entirely based on economic considerations. In their choice of mates, husbands began taking into account factors such as physical attractiveness; psychological compatibility; and artistic, literary, and social skills, although financial and social status remained major considerations. Wives continued to have little freedom in their choice of marriage partner, since partriarchy and the rule of primogeniture continued almost unchallenged until the rise of feminine protest in the 1880s. Even as late as 1869, John Stuart Mill concluded in his famous work *The Subjection of Women,* that "the wife is the actual bond-servant of her husband, no less so, as far as legal obligation goes, than slaves commonly so called. . . . However brutal a tyrant she may unfortunately be chained to . . . he can claim from her and enforce the lowest degradation of a human being, that of being the instrument of an animal function contrary to her inclinations" (cited in Harrison, 1977, p. 7).

It was not until the Married Women's Property Act of 1882 that a married woman was given absolute ownership of any economic assets that belonged to her before marriage, or that she obtained afterward. Only in 1919 were women given the right to vote, and this privilege was restricted to those over 30.

The Idealization of Married Women

Although in preindustrial England sex roles were often clearly defined, they were based on a necessary division of labor. Since most married couples and their children managed between them small, barely viable, farms or cottage industries, it was vital that tasks be optimally divided between family members. Thus, wives and husbands developed complementary skills, the nature of which was partly determined by gender and related traditions. Most couples and their young children were in regular daily contact. For example, the average size of farms was only 10–15 acres, since plowing, seeding, and gathering had to be done manually or with the aid of draft animals, using simple tools and equipment. Small farms could be adequately managed by one couple working efficiently together. Even young children generally made important contributions to the work required to maintain these small family businesses.

There was a matching division of labor regarding child rearing. Although young infants were supervised mainly by mothers and older children, once children reached the age of 4 or 5, they were as likely to be supervised by fathers and older children, who were therefore required to exercise nurturing roles in addition to their other duties. The idea that the nurturing of children was essentially a maternal role did not exist. Where a division of labor occurred in relation to child rearing, it concerned the transmission of traditional gender-related skills and knowledge from father to son and from mother to daughter.

The Industrial Revolution rapidly removed the essentially economic basis for shared family life. Husbands left home to work and were entirely removed from the daily life of the family, except on Sundays. Wives were left with sole responsibility for the management of domestic affairs, including child rearing.

There were few guidelines for the conduct of this new type of family life, which hitherto had been conducted only by the very wealthy in the context of large, complex, households. The ability to maintain a wife, home, and children rapidly became an important measure of social status in towns and cities, where status could no longer be determined on a traditional rural basis. Choice of wife, and desirable wifely behavior, was increasingly determined by husbands' needs to demonstrate social status. A physically attractive, well-mannered, cultured, educated, and musically and artistically talented wife emerged as an ideal status symbol.

A new division of labor appeared. The wife became the repository of nurturing attitudes and behavior, of domestic skills such as sewing and embroidery, and of certain limited artistic abilities. Husbands were required to display complementary traits such as competitiveness, aggressiveness, worldliness, and an indifference to the emotional needs of others. Since husbands had all the economic power and were almost invariably the instigators of marriage, wives had to adhere to their husbands' idealized view of wifeliness. Protest was futile and divorce virtually impossible. Thus, to avoid intrapsychic and intramarital conflict, wives often came to identify with their husbands' ideals of wifeliness, making a virtue of necessity. For example, a "lady of distinction" in 19th-century England suggested that "the most perfect and implicit faith in the superiority of a husband's judgement, and the most absolute obedience to his desire, is not only the conduct that will ensure the greatest success, but will give the most entire satisfaction" (Lederer & Jackson, 1968).

The ideal Victorian wife did, however, lack one important attribute: Sexuality. Sex within marriage remained as limited and ritualized by social custom as it had been earlier by religious influence. Victorian women were regarded as worthy (and wifely) only if their sexuality remained hidden, suppressed, or denied. Overt displays of sexuality indicated moral decadence, and occurred only in women unsuitable for marriage, or in prostitutes. Thus, a profoundly ambivalent view of female sexuality emerged as a central cultural theme in Victorian England and in 19th-century urban North America: It was impossible for a woman to be both respectable and sexual. Such beliefs had a profoundly inhibiting effect on sex within marriage. However, it was tacitly acknowledged that married men were permitted the regular use of prostitutes. This was regarded as a business transaction, totally devoid of personal or emotional commitment, and therefore could be pursued as a natural extension of the masculine approach to life beyond the domestic. These themes, in attenuated form, occur in modern marriage and contribute to the development of psychological symptoms in ways that will be discussed in later chapters.

In a more general sense, marriage practices in 19th-century England provided the basis for attitudes to marriage in contemporary English-speaking societies. However, throughout most of that century, married women were essentially powerless. It is, then, not surprising that the institution of marriage is adapting only with great difficulty to modern trends towards the equality of women.

THE EFFECTS OF TECHNOLOGY

Victorian women identified with the stereotyped, ambivalent male view of them primarily because they were powerless and had no real choice. Since women could not change matters, they buried their frustration and resentment deeply within themselves and strove to live up to the expectations of the men in their lives—whether husband or clients.

For affluent married women, this was not altogether difficult. Servants carried out all routine or menial domestic tasks and, perhaps together with a governess, cared for their children. Such women led busy lives organizing their servants and domestic affairs and arranging social engagements that were often highly elaborate and required an adherence to customs and rituals of great complexity. If these activities did not entirely fulfill them, they were permitted by their husbands to develop limited literary, musical, and artistic skills and interests. But the world beyond the domestic was strictly denied them.

Wives of less affluent husbands, who had no domestic servants, were no less busy. Gradual improvement in personal and public hygiene and nutritional standards meant that more children survived infancy. However, average family size increased only slightly; the average number of surviving children per married couple remained between 3 and 4, and few couples had more than 5 children (Gordon, 1973). This suggests that the Victorian constraints upon sex within marriage may have had an important birth control function before the widespread use of contraceptives that emerged in the 20th century.

Because marriage had acquired an additional function as a status symbol, it was important for houses to be clean, tidy, and well decorated, and for family members to be clean and neatly dressed. In the absence of modern domestic labor-saving devices and refrigeration, wives of average financial status were kept fully occupied by the demands of running a household without servants. Food purchase and preparation, and the making, repairing and washing of clothes, were particularly time consuming. Wives of less affluent husbands often took in extra sewing and washing to supplement the family income. Less than 10% of married women worked outside the home, partly because this implied the husband's inability to adequately support them, which sharply reduced his social status (Harrison, 1977).

The importance of marriage to social status is underlined by the fact that in mid-19th century, the marriage rate was similar to that of the 17th and 18th centuries: Only about 50% of the adult population was formally married, although many cohabited on an informal basis. Marriage was an unequivocal statement of comparative affluence, since barely half the adult male population could afford it. Although in preindustrial England social status had been determined largely by social class at birth, this was much less so in the larger towns and cities of the 19th century, where inhabitants' social origins were often unknown, or could be disguised. Thus, status symbols were an early and fundamental requirement of urban life, and it is not surprising that marriage was modified to help meet this need. The possession of children had the added benefit of demonstrating the husband's virility as well as his financial status.

Birth Control

An important effect of improved industrial technology was the introduction of effective, inexpensive, contraceptive devices. Although manufactured contraceptives had become available by the end of the 19th century, they were too expensive for most married couples. It was price, not ambivalence, that prevented their more widespread use. By the 1920s, reliable sheaths (condoms) for men and diaphragms for women had become affordable by even the poorer families. The later introduction of oral contraceptives consolidated this, and was accompanied by a gradual fall in the average number of children per family to the contemporary Western figure of about 2.2.

The ability of couples to regulate the number and timing of their children has been probably the most important single factor in determining contemporary marriage practices and attitudes. It has meant that women can omit or restrict child bearing as an aspect of married life. Traditionally, child rearing has been the essence of married life, and its absence or restriction requires a fundamental reappraisal of the meaning and purpose of marriage. The failure of a couple to undertake such a reappraisal of their marriage may contribute to the development of psychological symptoms in ways that will be discussed in later chapters.

Labor-Saving Devices

Because labor-saving devices are universal in contemporary Western homes, their historical impact on domestic life is not sufficiently appreciated. The possession of a refrigerator and freezer allows the purchasing of food for a family of 4 to be achieved within an average of 2 hours a week or less: For basics, a single weekly visit to a supermarket is generally sufficient. The purchase of frozen, precooked, or otherwise prepared and processed foods can reduce time spent on food preparation to less than is required to eat it. If full advantage is taken of modern cooking technology, nutritious meals for an average family can be produced in an hour a day or less. Regular use of fast-food outlets can reduce this time even further. Vacuum cleaners, washing machines, and tumble driers allow household cleaning and washing to be done in 3–4 hours per week, since other domestic tasks can be carried out while machines wash and dry. A well-organized person can adequately manage and maintain an average household and feed and clothe an average family in 12–14 hours a week. In its essence, managing a family is no longer a full-time job; it is a part-time job that, if carried out efficiently, leaves most of the week free for other activities.

I am not suggesting that it is necessarily desirable to spend only 12–14 hours a week managing and maintaining a household and providing basic physical care for its occupants. But I believe it is important to establish clearly that it is possible to provide such *basic* services, at an adequate level, within a small proportion of the total weekly time available. This great reduction in the time required to manage a household has occurred over only the past 30 years: a single generation. Never before has society undergone such a profound change in one of its major institutions in such a short time. Not surprisingly, attitudes and expectations of many people concerning family life and household management remain rooted in the previous generation. They have failed to acknowledge the rapid and fundamental changes in domestic life that have been made possible by modern technology.

Shorter Working Hours

Just as the burden of managing a home has been greatly reduced by recent technological developments, so has the burden of earning enough money to support a family. We have seen how preindustrial life in England and elsewhere in Europe and North America was for most people a constant struggle to survive. It was generally accepted that some form of work occupied the waking hours of most adults, to be interrupted only by the sleep of exhaustion, a Sunday of rest, and occasional religious festivals.

Although the Industrial Revolution released most people from relentless toil in the fields, it uprooted them into a new urban environment that required a new social structure. Here, although the lives of many became more affluent, leisured, and predictable, a majority continued to work throughout most of their waking hours: the men in mines, factories, and offices, the women mainly at home. Only in the past 30 years has work ceased to be the central theme of most peoples' lives. Today, the standard working week is 40 hours or less throughout the English-speaking world. For the first time in history, most people have the time, energy, and money to expand and develop their lives and interests beyond work. This is a new opportunity, a new challenge, and a new problem. It has had a profound effect on the institution of marriage.

Traditionally, both partners in a marriage believed that work and child rearing were the essence of their lives, and that any respites from the daily struggle to survive or to improve living standards were to be used for restoring energy and, perhaps, for capturing a few moments of pleasure and fun. Thus, there could be few fundamental differences between husband and wife about the conduct, meaning, and purpose of married life. If serious differences did emerge, they could be resolved by adherence to the authority or the advice of the Church. This is true no longer. A large, mainly hidden, agenda has been introduced recently into marriage: namely, the problem of deciding the correct balance between work and its usually more pleasurable alternatives. In a domestic context, even the definition of work may be problematical.

These are problems that are difficult enough for single, unattached people to resolve: Their resolution within marriage is far more difficult, since this requires a broad measure of agreement between two people who may not have dealt with such problems at a personal level, or who may have married in order to avoid confronting them.

It is impossible to determine the correct balance between work and alternative activities without considering many other aspects of life. Perhaps the most important of these is personal fulfillment. The idea and expectation of personal fulfillment have only very recently emerged as a major theme in the English-speaking world and other Western societies. As long as life consisted mainly of a struggle for physical survival, concerns about personal fulfillment and satisfaction were largely irrelevant. But in contemporary Western nations, almost everyone has been released from the struggle for physical survival. Although pockets of severe poverty still exist in the United States, England, and western Europe, and many people live at or below the poverty line, modern welfare concepts and facilities permit few to actually starve or freeze to death through poverty. The right of every citizen to basic food, clothing, shelter, and health-care facilities is almost universally acknowledged.

The removal of the struggle for physical survival from our daily lives has left us with a new set of problems that are just as challenging, and for which few guidelines have so far emerged: These are the problems of personal fulfillment and the development and maintenance of a sense of personal integrity and self-esteem. Closely linked to these personal needs is a sense of identity. Modern marriage is used by many people as a way of acquiring a sense of personal fulfillment and identity. But, just as there are few systematic or generally accepted guidelines for the acquisition of personal fulfillment in today's world, so there are few such guidelines for marital fulfillment. When two personally unfulfilled people marry in the hope of achieving both marital and personal fulfillment—and when few guidelines exist for either—the likelihood of success appears remote. Yet today very many people marry in precisely these circumstances. Some couples do achieve the personal and marital fulfillment they hoped for, but at least as many end up in divorce. Often, psychological symptoms emerge in one or both partners as part of their attempts to preserve their marriage. The mechanisms by which this occurs are the main focus of later chapters.

CHAPTER TWO

Sex-Role Stereotyping and Conflict

A "stereotype" is a relatively inflexible and oversimplified way of perceiving a person that is based not on his or her *individual* characteristics, but on the characteristics attributed to the group or class of people to which the person belongs. The two most widespread stereotypes are related to race or ethnic group and to sex role.

The civil-rights movement in America has done much to challenge the habitual and unquestioned use of racial and ethnic stereotypes, at least in public. It is no longer acceptable to publicly refer to racial minorities in terms of stereotypes. The private use of racial stereotypes will doubtless continue for much longer.

Although the women's movement has been at least as active and vigorous as the civil-rights endeavor, negative stereotyping of women has only recently been challenged on a significant scale, and remains widespread in public and private (Ruble, 1983; Stolk & Brotherton, 1981). This is mainly because sex-role stereotypes are so deeply ingrained in English-speaking society, and so widely and unconsciously accepted by both men and women, that it is difficult for many people to recognize that their use is questionable or problematic. The following anecdote illustrates this.

A boy and his father had a major automobile accident. The father was killed on impact, but the son survived with severe injuries and was taken by ambulance to the nearest hospital with facilities for major surgery. The senior traumatic surgeon was called to examine the boy, and upon doing so said "I cannot operate on this boy because he is my son."

Most people, when asked to explain this, refer to stepfathers or adoptive fathers, but rarely arrive without help at the correct answer: The surgeon is the boy's *mother*. So ingrained is the idea that surgery—especially traumatic surgery—is a male occupation that almost everyone makes the unconscious assumption that the surgeon is a man.

This occupational stereotype is just one aspect of sex-role stereotyping. Women's maternal and nurturing roles are other attributes that are widely seen in stereotyped terms. Idealized mothers are generally regarded as patient, self-sacrificing, warm, affectionate, and responsive to the emotional needs of their children and others. They are not aggressive or overly assertive, are guided by intuition and emotion rather than logic, and depend on their husbands for advice, guidance, and protection in areas beyond the domestic. They are altruistic and live for and through their children and husbands.

In contrast, idealized fathers are seen as adventurous, competitive, and assertive, as well as aggressive if this is required to protect their own or their family's interests. They are ruled by logic rather than emotion and are required to suppress or deny feelings of weakness, helplessness, and timidity. They avoid the overt display of emotions indicating a distressed, sad, or fearful state. The expression of tender, loving feelings is not required of them, and they are not expected to be sensitive to the emotional needs of others or to publicly reveal their own personal worries, fears, and doubts. This stereotype is richly demonstrated by the following letter written by a 17-year-old American youth in 1984:

A father is a person who is forced to endure childbirth without an anesthetic.

A father growls when he feels good and laughs when he's scared half to death.

Fathers are supposed to have the strength of an ox, the endurance of a camel, the shrewdness of a fox, the patience of an elephant, the industriousness of a beaver, the cheerfulness of a robin, and the speed of a cheetah.

A father is also required to be a jack-of-all-trades who can fix anything on the face of the earth. He must also have accurate knowledge of the best places to catch the whopping fish limits in three hours or before the fishing crew gets discouraged, whichever comes first.

Fathers must mow it, paint it, spade it, grease it, hang it, steer it, trim it, weed and feed it, find it, and even pay for it.

Fathers often sit at the head of the table. A father is well-known for the wear and tear he puts on maternity waiting room carpets.

Fathers are known to stubbornly stick by their convictions—even when they know they're wrong.

A father is never quite the hero his daughter thinks, never quite the man his son believes him to be. This worries him sometimes.

So he works too hard trying to smooth the rough places in the road for those of his own who will follow him.

A father is a thing who gets angry when school grades aren't as good as he thinks they should be. He comes down hard on the one who gets a check mark in front of "disrupts class and annoys others."

A father goes to war sometimes, he also learns to swear and cuss and even spit through his teeth. A father always wants more for his children than he has.

Fathers fight dragons almost daily. They hurry away from the table and take off to the arena, which is sometimes called an office or a workshop, or a place of employment. There, with calloused and practiced hands, they tackle the dragon with the three heads: weariness, work, and monotony.

Fathers, as a general rule, are not the tidiest of persons. They do, however, like their newspaper just as it comes from the paper box, not with crumpled pages, with sections mismatched or missing, with spots of Coke or smudges of spaghetti and, above all, do not wish to find the paper in a rumpled, disheveled heap in some corner of the house, before they've had a chance to read it.

By their very nature, fathers are dominant, domesticated, daydreamers, debators, deliberators, and often demanding. Most of the time fathers are dependable, sometimes they are distant and even difficult. Fathers are not often diplomatic or dissatisfied; they're never disloyal or dishonest.

A father is a person who will understand when you've struck out.

A father can be a friend if you meet him halfway.

A father never copies anyone else.

A father never lies. . . . (V. Knight, personal communication, 1984).

Research has clearly demonstrated that sex-role stereotyping in America is largely independent of educational or occupational status (Broverman, Broverman, Clarkson, Rosenkrantz, & Vogel, 1972). Such professionals as psychologists and psychiatrists are just as likely to have a stereotyped view of sex roles as are construction workers, truck drivers, or sales assistants. Although there is some variation, English-speaking countries other than America show a similar level of adherence to sex-role stereotypes (Goldman & Goldman, 1983). The pervasive and persistent nature of sex-role stereotyping in English-speaking societies is best understood from a historical perspective.

ORIGINS OF THE MALE SEX-ROLE STEREOTYPE

The male sex-role stereotype is derived from the fact that in general men are heavier, taller, and stronger than women. This substantial physical difference emerged in humankind's hominid ancestors as an early and fundamental aspect of the struggle for existence. Our hominid ancestors lived predominantly in cohesive social groups of 10–20 adults together with their young. Food supplies were composed of mainly fruit, berries, nuts, edible roots and other plants, eggs, grubs, and insects. However, animal meat was an essential nutritional supplement. Hence, social groups who were most successful at hunting were those most likely to survive. This was particularly true of hominid groups in northern Europe, where the harsh winters greatly reduced the availability of plant foods, making a group's hunting skill a major determinant of its survival.

Successful hunting required at least 3–4 group members who were able to travel rapidly over long distances, if necessary; who could run very fast over shorter distances; and who had sufficient physical strength and coordination to overcome their prey, to dismember it, and to carry the pieces back to the larger group or guard them while waiting its arrival. Such attributes in hominids were largely incompatible with advanced pregnancy or the care of suckling babies and infants. Thus, hunting became a specialized male task and, through the struggle for existence and survival of the fittest, men gradually evolved the size and strength characteristics that distinguish them from women.

As humankind's hominid ancestors adapted increasingly successfully to their various environments, their enlarging numbers threatened to outstrip the available food supply. Once again, this was most likely to occur in northern Europe, where winter regularly reduced the availability of basic foods. Thus, groups began to compete with each other for sufficient territory to sustain them. Those males who had physical and psychological attributes most suited to hunting were also those who were most able to challenge and fight males from competing groups. Thus, physical strength, size, speed and agility, and a psychological preparedness for intraspecific fighting (that is, fighting between members of the same species) became male characteristics that favored the survival of the group.

Fighting between small groups of men over territory and chattels remained a central feature of human evolution until recently. It was a prominent feature of early Anglo-Saxon culture. As social groups became larger and more complex, the defense and acquisition of territory became a specialized function carried out by trained men. The need to sustain an army for territorial defense and expansion was the basis of the English feudal system, which enshrined the principles of patriarchy and primogeniture within Anglo-Saxon culture.

Under the feudal system, a baron (war-lord) or lord of the manor leased land to peasants on his territory in return for the various goods and services required to sustain an army. The goods were composed mainly of food, clothes, and weaponry, and the services mainly of the taking up of arms when required. These arrangements were sealed by an oath of obedience and loyalty to the baron. Great importance was attached to this oath, which was also binding on the peasant's family. Thus, the baron was the ultimate patriarch, with complete authority over all peasants and their families. This authority even extended to the well-known *droit de seigneur*—the right of the feudal Lord to have intercourse with a peasant's bride on her wedding night.

The prosperity of many families and individuals under the feudal system depended largely on their capacity to supply the feudal lord with effective fighting men, or to fight themselves. Such services, if outstanding, were likely to be rewarded with increased land holdings and other privileges, or a share in the spoils of war. Thus, fighting prowess was very highly valued in Anglo-Saxon England, and was retained as a central aspect of myth, legend, and folklore as well as daily life. This veneration and glorification of warfare and individual fighting prowess in the service of territorial defense or acquisition continued as a central theme of English-speaking nations until very recently.

The extreme male sex-role stereotype on "macho man" image is, of course, based on the idea of man as a warrior. For successful combat, a man must suppress or exert ruthless control over any feelings of fear and self-doubt within himself, and over any feelings of compassion toward his foe. Therefore, the ideal fighting man must be capable of either totally dehumanizing his enemies, or of ruthlessly eliminating any human feelings toward them. One way of dehumanizing an enemy is to stereotype him. Thus, effective warfare requires two complementary stereotypes: one of an invincible, fearless warrior fighting a justifiable war; the other of an enemy so debased, evil, and barbaric as to be subhuman.

The rise of nationalism in the 18th, 19th, and 20th centuries required such stereotypes to be elaborated and reinforced. Government propaganda in the 19th and 20th centuries became an increasingly effective means of persuading men and women alike that honor and loyalty required all able-bodied men to volunteer to fight for their country against barbaric, subhuman enemies. So effective was this propaganda that in England during the First World War, able-bodied young men not wearing uniforms in public were openly abused and even mobbed by women who assumed they were not doing their duty as fighting men. The Germans were portrayed in government propaganda as bestial and nonhuman.

This veneration of warfare and dehumanization of enemies persisted in spite of the slaughter of millions of young men during World War I. Only after this slaughter was repeated, and widely extended to civilians, in the Second World War, was there a significant change in popular attitudes to warfare. This change has been shown clearly in America, Australia, and other English-speaking nations who sent fighting men to Vietnam in the late 1960s and early 1970s. The survivors returned not always to the glory that they anticipated, but instead to public ambivalence and even vilification.

In America, the media were largely responsible for this change of attitude. In Europe, during the Second World War, civilians had been subjected to widespread bombing and had thus experienced at first hand the realities of modern warfare. Americans had escaped bombing of their own country (except for Pearl Harbor). However, daily exposure to television pictures of the grim, ghastly reality of the Vietnam War gradually eroded American ideas about warfare. For the first time, there was widespread public debate about whether war was *ever* justifiable. Hitherto, although the desirability of joining or starting a war had often been widely debated, once it had been declared righteous, and once the fighting had started, public support became almost universal.

Thus, the intensive media coverage of the Vietnam War helped to achieve something that countless bloody and destructive battles over many centuries had failed to do: It forced the American public into a reappraisal of its stereotypes about warriors and warfare.

SEX-ROLE STEREOTYPES AND MENTAL ILLNESS IN MEN

In spite of recent changes in public attitudes, the "macho man" or idealized warrior stereotype still persists, and in more or less subtle forms exerts a major influence on our lives. The self-esteem of many men depends greatly or even entirely on their capacity to sustain a sex-role stereotyped image of themselves (Hafner, 1984a). However, clinging to a sex-role stereotyped self-image may create major personal and interpersonal problems. For example, within marriage, it often inhibits or prevents the development of intimacy and role sharing: Unresolved conflicts in these areas may contribute directly to the development of psychological symptoms, as shown by the following case history.

The Invincible Man

James Cook was a 36-year-old married man who was referred by his family doctor with symptoms of depression. A tall, slim, handsome and heavily bearded man with a mild but direct manner, he described a progressive lowering of spirits, a general withdrawal of interest in life, and difficulty in concentrating on tasks over the previous 6 months. These symptoms had become severe enough to interfere substantially with his domestic life and his work as director of his own small manufacturing company.

James, who had an older sister to whom he was not close, had been raised in the outer suburbs of a large city. His father had been a merchant seaman and was away most of the time; even when on leave, he had spent little time with his family, preferring to drink and socialize outside the home. There were no relatives nearby, so that James grew up in the absence of any relationship with an adult male.

James's mother was a conscientious parent who did not work outside the home. She was unable to be affectionate to her children or to show any emotion toward them other than occasional anger or frustration. She was overprotective, preventing James from playing on the street, and discouraging him from bringing friends home. Thus, James became a very isolated child, spending most of his time in his room reading or daydreaming about heroic deeds of conquest in battle and in society at large. He developed a conviction that one day he would be a rich and famous businessman, and this often-rehearsed fantasy protected him from feelings of vulnerability, dependency, loneliness, and depression.

At 25, James married Jill, a 22-year-old woman from a similar background, who had been sustained by the fantasy that one day a strong, caring, and successful man would marry her and take care of her.

Once married, they both seemed to have fulfilled their fantasies. James took care of Jill financially, while she looked after their three children at home. Like his own father, James saw almost nothing of his children, generally working over 80 hours a week to develop his business. He insisted that all domestic and child-rearing tasks be carried out exclusively by his wife, and refused to be involved with the children even when at home.

Unfortunately, James was a poor administrator and organizer, unable to delegate tasks, and spending long hours attending to trivia rather than to more relevant aspects of his business. As a result, his business was barely viable, his income low and erratic, and financial crises common. He totally excluded his wife from the business, insisting that his role was to take care of her and protect her from financial and business worries and problems. However, Jill was constantly anxious about their chronic financial problems, with which she was intermittently and unpleasantly confronted when, for example, angry creditors called or telephoned demanding payment of outstanding bills. When Jill complained about these problems to James and suggested ways of avoiding them, he angrily accused her of undermining him and of unnecessary interference in his running of the business.

These pressures caused increasing conflict within their marriage, which had always lacked mutual affection. James felt isolated and unwanted at home, causing him to rely even more heavily on his conviction of ultimate success as a businessman, which in turn prevented him from accepting the reality of his business difficulties. All these problems contributed to James's depression and his referral to me for therapy.

During therapy it quickly became clear that James totally identified with the male sex-role stereotype: His whole sense of identity, value, and purpose was bound up in it. He believed that any display of weakness or emotion was unmanly and would not allow himself to shed tears. He admitted that at times he craved greater closeness and involvement with his children, but was confused and frightened by these feelings and felt awkward and clumsy in any attempt to be warm or affectionate with his offspring.

James's childhood reliance on a rich fantasy life had persisted and his daydreams still revolved around outstanding success in the business world or battles and conflicts in which he figured as a successful warrior. The idea of financially supporting his wife and protecting her from worldly problems was central to his self-esteem: His struggle to create wealth and success was sustained by a belief that achievement of these goals was fundamental to his family's well-being as well as his own.

Therapy focused on modifying James's stereotyped views of male attributes and functions. I encouraged him to shed tears, explaining why there was nothing "unmanly" about this, and pointing out the benefits of releasing emotion in this way. I suggested that his depression was in fact a good thing, since it would allow him to withdraw from the world for a while and reappraise the meaning and purpose of his life. He became more depressed, acknowledging for the first time that his business was on the brink of failure, and that he felt constricted and trapped by his stereotyped self-image. However, instead of battling against his depression and tearfulness, he accepted them as a necessary part of reassessing his life and letting go of unhelpful fantasies.

Gradually, James came to realize the huge extent to which he had clung to a male sex-role stereotype to guide him in the conduct of his life. As this realization emerged, he sought to change his attitudes, beliefs, and expectations so that they accorded more closely with reality. Slowly, his depression lifted.

Over a period of 8 months, during which I saw him on 14 occasions, James made the following changes. First, he shaved off his beard, looking so different that I barely recognized him when he subsequently entered my consulting room. He explained that he no longer needed the beard as an expression of his masculinity. Second, he restructured his business, employed a new manager, and concentrated on obtaining new retail outlets for his products. As a result, his weekly working hours were reduced to about 50, and his income began to increase. Third, he invited Jill to become an active partner in the business. She rapidly became a valuable asset and greatly enjoyed the work, which had come at just the right time—now that the children were all at school, she was becoming increasingly bored and dissatisfied with her exclusively domestic role. Fourth, he began to learn how to relate to his children, playing ball games with them in a local park, and sharing child-rearing tasks with Jill. Finally, he and Jill explicitly rearranged the overall division of labor, so that they more equally shared both domestic and business activities.

At the end of therapy, James's depression was no longer a major problem. However, he recognized that he still had a great deal of work to do on his stereotyping. Relinquishing lifelong assumptions and patterns of behavior was a formidable task, and old habits constantly threatened to reassert themselves. Nonetheless, he was committed to the task of shedding the influence upon him of sex-role stereotypes, and believed that his marriage would become more intimate and harmonious as a result. Although he still hoped for business success, he was able to contemplate life without it, and no longer required his fantasies of fame and fortune to sustain him.

Psychoanalytic Psychotherapy May Reinforce Sex-Role Stereotypes

Increasing awareness of the male orientation of psychoanalytic theory has led to the recent development of alternative, female-oriented therapies (Sturdivant, 1980). These have emphasized, *inter alia,* the need for women to free themselves from the harmful influence of sex-role stereotyping.

Hitherto, there has been comparatively little awareness of the harmful psychological effects on men of rigid adherence to a male sex-role stereotype (Mills & Bohannon, 1983). There is no established male equivalent to the feminist therapeutic approach. Thus, although many mental health workers are exposed to a feminist therapeutic perspective, and are beginning to incorporate related concepts and techniques into their clinical work, their therapy with men is likely to continue on traditional lines.

The psychotherapy training of most psychiatrists is still rooted primarily in psychoanalytic theory. Had James Cook been offered psychotherapy by a psychiatrist or psychotherapist with such a background and orientation, much attention would doubtless have been paid to James's failure to resolve the Oedipal phase of his development. Feelings of rivalry toward the therapist would have been interpreted as a displacement of suppressed hostility and envy originally experienced toward James's mainly absent father, whom James perceived as a threat to his desire for an exclusive relationship with his mother. James's constant struggle for outstanding business success would be interpreted as compensating for unconscious feelings of inferiority in relation to his father; and his failure to achieve success would be regarded as reflecting an unconscious fear of punishment ("castration anxiety" in psychoanalytic terms) for wishing to replace or outperform his father.

The aim of therapy would almost certainly have been to help James overcome his fear of failure and to facilitate his more effective pursuit of realistic occupational goals. Thus, the overall effects of a conventional psychoanalytic approach would probably have been to reinforce rather than weaken James's sex-role stereotypes, particularly in the area of work. A reciprocal effect of this would be increased pressure on his wife, Jill, to preserve her exclusively domestic role. Hence, in all likelihood, marital conflict would have increased rather than decreased, heightening the possibility of separation or divorce. Critics of individual psychotherapy for married people have forcibly drawn attention to increased marital conflict as a common, but largely unrecognized, side-effect of therapy (Hurvitz, 1967).

Had James been more seriously disturbed, intensive psychotherapy along psychoanalytic lines might possibly have been an appropriate treatment. For reasons to be elaborated in Chapter 3, some men cling with such tenacity to the male sex-role stereotype that only prolonged or intensive therapy allows them to modify their dependence on it. In such circumstances, the marital repercussions of therapy are determined primarily by their wives' flexibility. Where wives themselves cling rigidly to a stereotyped perspective on marriage, they are likely to resist the development of nonstereotyped attitudes and behavior in their husbands. This may make it extremely difficult for their husbands to initiate or maintain the kind of changes achieved by James.

Conversely, some husbands cling rigidly to a stereotyped view of marriage when their wives actively seek to relinquish such a perspective during individual psychotherapy.

In a more general sense, when one marriage partner clings to a stereotyped perspective while their spouse is consciously or unconsciously seeking to modify it, psychological symptoms may emerge within one or both partners. Precisely how this occurs is described in Chapters 4 and 5. The use of spouse-aided therapy in such circumstances is detailed in Chapter 9.

ORIGINS OF THE FEMALE SEX-ROLE STEREOTYPE

Protection against Man's Aggression

I have already argued that the presence of strong, aggressive males in hominid groups was essential for the territorial integrity of the group and thus its access to adequate food supplies, particularly during the northern winter or, in hotter climates, at times of drought. The more aggressive, strong, and agile were the adult males, the more likely was the group to survive. This observation leads to an important question: What prevented these aggressive males from fighting and injuring each other, or attacking females in their group, when they were not hunting or defending their territory against males from competing groups? The work of Lorenz (1966) is invaluable in answering this question.

Intraspecific aggression is paradoxical. On the one hand it is a constructive force, essential for the territorial integrity of pairs or small groups of animals; on the other, it is a destructive force, resulting in injury or death and reducing rather than increasing the likelihood of a species' survival.

As Lorenz has pointed out, territorial boundaries aggressively established and defended are essential for the optimum availability of food supplies and hence the survival of the species. Once a territory of appropriate size is established, the energies of the mating pair or small group can be devoted to food gathering and nurturing activities. In the absence of a defined territory, energy is constantly expended in general intraspecific competition for individual food items—a system so inefficient and potentially destructive as to virtually guarantee the disappearance of the species involved.

However, the successful maintenance of territorial boundaries requires the development of protective *rituals* and *submission gestures and postures:* Although territorial boundaries are established in most species by fighting between adult males, if such fighting regularly led to serious injury of the combatants, then the survival of the species would be threatened. A wide range of rituals and submission gestures and signals has evolved within different species to prevent serious injury to competing males. In brown rats, for example, familiar body odors appear to prevent a destructive escalation of conflict between males of the same species. In carnivores such as wolves, a fight between two males is immediately ended if the weaker animal turns its head aside and exposes the side of its neck, an area most vulnerable to attack; this submission gesture triggers an inhibiting mechanism in the stronger male, which therefore immediately stops fighting the submitting animal. Such submission gestures are as applicable to fights over mates and hierarchical status ("pecking order") as to territorial defense. Furthermore, their use not only stops the escalation of fighting, but often allows it to be avoided altogether. Thus, territorial integrity and status within small groups can be preserved by the use of appropriate submission signals.

Submission gestures and signals, and complementary inhibiting mechanisms, have evolved in humankind. Facial expressions such as smiling are clear signals of friendliness and generally elicit similar, nonaggressive responses in others. Male gestures such as bowing or kneeling are examples of submission signals: these postures expose the base of the neck, an area most vulnerable to a blow. Earlier in our social evolution, such signals inhibited aggression in dominant males. In today's society, they have become entirely ritualized and are used to formally acknowledge the presence of a social superior in countries that have preserved social hierarchies. The shaking of hands is a ritual that demonstrates the absence of weapons and mimics, in a displaced and harmless manner, a grasping and hitting movement. Thus, the hostile act of striking with a club has been transformed by ritualization into a gesture of friendliness and appeasement.

Mechanisms inhibiting the destructive escalation of combat have evolved primarily in males: They are absent or minimal in females. For example, when formally acknowledging the presence of a high-status person of either sex, women traditionally curtsy. Eye contact is preserved and the head is kept erect throughout this gesture, which is therefore fundamentally different from the male bow with its loss of eye contact and exposure of the vulnerable neck. If women have not evolved bio-behavioral submission gestures comparable to those found in men, how have they protected themselves against injury or death at the hands of stronger male aggressors?

In my view, this has been achieved primarily by the evolution of social mechanisms aimed at *avoiding* combat rather than inhibiting its destructive escalation. As we have seen, threatened physical confrontations or actual combat between male hominids were essential aspects of territorial defense and the establishment and maintenance of hierarchial structures within the group. In contrast, it was essential to *avoid* combat between male and female, since this would often lead to injury and incapacitation of the female and hence threaten the reproductive and survival capacity of the group. Thus, as our hominid ancestors evolved gender-related differences in size, strength, and behavior, group constraints developed in parallel to protect females from male aggression.

The most important of these constraints was social *distancing*, maintained by a system of totems and taboos. A general feature of social structure in tribal communities, presumably present in our more recent hominid ancestors, is the social separation of men and women. In marriage and family life, and in the larger tribal setting, relationships between men and women are determined by highly complex rules and regulations based upon totemic classifications (Levi-Strauss, 1966). Totemic structures are reinforced by taboos, the breaking of which incurs personal anxiety and predetermined punishments or counterrituals. In this way, social distance and conduct between the sexes is preserved, and opportunities or reasons for direct conflict between men and women are minimized.

In early Anglo-Saxon culture, traditions based on a sense of *historical continuity* largely replaced totemism as regulators of social structure and conduct. The removal of totemic constraints on conflict between men and women required the development of new social mechanisms to inhibit men's aggression towards women. There was only one universally applicable way of achieving this: *the development by women of a submissive posture in their direct dealings with men.* Only by habitually yielding to the wishes and demands of men in situations of potential conflict were women able to protect themselves from physical combat, with its danger of serious injury. Goldberg (1977) has shown that habitual female submissiveness to the male "dominance tendency" is *universal* in cultures that rely on historical tradition rather than on the more primitive totemism. The cultural background of all modern industrial societies is based on a strong sense of historical tradition, and the rapid growth of modern industrial society suggests that female submissiveness has been, until very recently, highly culturally adaptive.

Thus, the female sex-role stereotype enshrines the submissive posture that women originally embraced in order to protect themselves from male aggression. However, sex-role stereotyping has become a central theme of English-speaking societies only over the past century or so; I will now attempt to elucidate some reasons for this.

Stereotyping as a Response to Rapid Cultural Change

Allowing historical tradition to determine appropriate social conduct is workable only in relatively static cultures. If rapid social change occurs, traditions are of little value in determining appropriate social behavior under new conditions. As we saw in Chapter 1, the Industrial Revolution initiated sustained social change more rapid, radical, and widespread than had ever occurred in the history of the Anglo-Saxon culture. The essence of this change was the movement of a majority of the population from a predominantly rural to a predominantly urban environment.

In the cities of mid-19th-century England and North America, there was an almost complete absence of the rural social structure that previously had helped to sustain and reinforce traditional Anglo-Saxon culture. Large numbers of men and women lived in close proximity, with no established social conventions to determine their behavior toward each other. Although the size and composition of the basic nuclear family unit had not changed substantially, its social context had altered radically. No longer was family life conducted within the framework of small, tightly knit village communities. Instead, each nuclear family lived in relative isolation, with no opportunity to be guided or restrained by an effective local consensus about what constituted socially desirable behavior. The absence of local constraints and guidelines embodying cultural traditions created a social vacuum in the cities and large towns. This vacuum was filled by a variety of stereotypes that gradually replaced aspects of the more subtle and flexible locally reinforced social guidelines.

The female sex-role stereotype became widely and rapidly established because it was necessary for the protection of women's *self-esteem* as well as their physical well-being. In a traditional rural setting, constant and abundant opportunities existed for women to relate to and bond with each other in dyads and small groups. They were able to carry out virtually the full range of social behaviors, including self-assertion, without coming into direct contact (and possible conflict) with men. Women's self-esteem, collectively and individually, was sustained in important ways by their relationships with each other in a structured community setting.

The Industrial Revolution largely destroyed opportunities for traditional mutually supportive and protective relationships between women. In effect, it destroyed their only power base: their capacity for collective community influence. In the cities that flourished during and after the Industrial Revolution, women and their families generally occupied individual dwellings in streets and suburbs that had no local identity or focus. Instead of relating primarily to other women, married women were forced to relate mainly to their husbands and children.

Thus, to the powerlessness of married women was added a collective loss of self-esteem. The need to be submissive to their husbands to avoid conflict became more absolute, since welfare facilities in the cities were virtually nonexistent, and married women ejected by their husbands faced enormous problems of personal and social survival. The female sex-role stereotype evolved as an adaptation to the almost impossible position of women living in these cities: It made a virtue of necessity. Powerlessness, submissiveness, a self-sacrificing and exclusive devotion to the domestic, and total dependency on men, were turned into desirable attributes rather than questionable qualities arising primarily from unplanned, radical, and sudden social change. By totally identifying with men's idealized views of them, married women protected themselves from both intrapsychic and marital conflicts.

Once established, the female sex-role stereotype was perpetuated by, and became a part of, the process of industrialization. It still has enormous power to influence women's behavior and self-image, and may contribute directly to the development of psychological disorders, as illustrated by the following case.

A Case of Self-Starvation

Susan Y was a 25-year-old white married woman who was admitted to the hospital dangerously ill, in a state of advanced inanition. She had eaten and drunk almost nothing over the preceding 3 weeks; had this continued, she would have died within 5–10 days. For about 6 months before ceasing to eat she had dieted very strictly, losing some 58 pounds. On admission to the hospital she weighed 68 pounds. Her height was 5 feet 3 inches; the average weight of a woman of this height is about 120 pounds.

Susan's family of origin was characterized by a sense of duty and obligation. Susan's mother, Cynthia, had lost her father when aged 12. He had died suddenly and unexpectedly of a heart attack. Although Cynthia was very close to her father, and idealized him as a strong and charismatic figure, she had been unable to mourn his death, and instead buried her feelings of sadness, loss, and anger deep within her.

In adulthood a beautiful woman, Cynthia chose her husband Edward because he strikingly resembled her father in several ways. However, she was not consciously aware that Edward represented an attempt to replace her father. Edward, a rather dull, mousy-looking man, was flattered by Cynthia's attention, and the couple married after a brief courtship when Cynthia was 23 and Edward 25.

Cynthia idealized Edward, and was determined to be a perfect wife and mother. She had attended a good university, gained an arts degree, and had begun a media career, the pursuit of which she greatly enjoyed. However, she abandoned her career aspirations when her son was born a year after her marriage, believing that to be a perfect mother and wife required a full-time commitment. Susan was born 18 months later.

In order to provide for his family, Edward worked long hours at a rather mundane and poorly paid job. At weekends he either worked, rested, or played golf, his only interest outside work and family. Hence, Cynthia raised her children virtually single-handed. In her anxiety to be a perfect wife and mother, she focused all her energy and attention upon her two children and husband. At times she craved a return to her career, but continued to believe that even part-time work was incompatible with her domestic ideals. She buried feelings of sadness and anger about the loss of her career almost as deeply as she had earlier buried such feelings in relation to her father's death. Cynthia was sustained by her enduring idealization of Edward, and by the idea of being a perfect wife and mother.

Susan received very little affection from Cynthia, and as an adult could recall no childhood embraces from her. However, Cynthia was constantly correcting Susan's speech, dress, manners, and deportment, and constantly urging her to do better. At the same time, she was grossly overprotective of Susan, insisting that she stay at home after school rather than play "dangerous" games with the neighborhood children. However, she permitted Susan's brother this social outlet. Any attempts by Susan to question Cynthia's treatment of her was met by anger, harsh criticism, or silence.

Edward idealized Susan almost as much as he did Cynthia, and called her his "Little Queen." However, he spent very little time with her, and their contacts were characterized by his emphasizing what a "pretty little girl" she was. He thoroughly spoiled and indulged her, to the unspoken frustration of Cynthia, whose harsh treatment of Susan was in part a response to Edward's excessive indulgence of her.

Susan was a poor student, with no friends at school. As a teenager, although slightly plump, she was quite attractive, but less so than her mother. She fantasized during her teens about marriage to a strong, caring man who would idealize, support, and protect her. Quite unconsciously, Susan had come to identify totally with the female sex-role stereotype. She believed, for example, that she could attract her ideal husband only by being dependent, timid, unassertive, deferential, and generally solicitous to him. She had, in fact, been conditioned to this stereotyped view of male–female relationships since early childhood. Cynthia, with whom Susan strongly identified, had constantly emphasized the sacrifices and efforts she had made to be a good wife and mother. Susan saw Cynthia as living entirely for and through her children and husband, with no life or interests beyond the family. Susan herself identified with these attributes, which were reinforced by her father, who acknowledged only her dependent, "feminine" aspects. Since her parents never argued, Susan came to believe that an ideal marriage was based on rigid, stereotyped sex-roles with little or no overlap between them. This belief was reinforced by the media and by popular romantic literature.

Cynthia's overprotection and criticism had left Susan very lacking in self-confidence, and she had avoided dating prior to meeting Wilbur, her husband-to-be. Wilbur's family of origin was similar to Susan's, and he shared her view, albeit largely unconsciously, that a happy marriage was based on rigid adherence to sex-role stereotyped attitudes and behavior. A shy, insecure man with poorly defined personal goals, his self-esteem was greatly elevated by Susan's deferential and dependent behavior toward him. Marriage to Susan seemed an ideal solution to his personal doubts and inadequacies.

Wilbur and Susan married when he was 23 and she 20. For Susan, marriage was a welcome opportunity to stop her boring clerical work in a small office. A son, Jeremy, was born 13 months after their marriage. Susan, like her mother Cynthia, was determined to be a perfect wife and mother, and devoted herself exclusively to the welfare of her husband and son.

However, Susan's relationship with her husband Wilbur was in reality very different from the relationship between Cynthia and Edward, which, in spite of its stereotyped nature and lack of genuine intimacy, contained much affection, humor, and mutual respect. For example, Wilbur proved to be unwilling to reveal his feelings about matters of mutual interest or concern; when the need for shared problem-solving activities between Wilbur and Susan arose, Wilbur rapidly became angry and short-tempered, often shouting or leaving the room before the discussion was completed. Although he claimed to respect Susan, he often made decisions unilaterally that affected both of them, becoming angry when Susan complained about this. There was a complete division of labor within the marriage: Susan did all the child care and domestic work and waited upon Wilbur hand and foot. This arrangement was agreeable to both; Wilbur believed that his role as breadwinner required a complementary role of domestic servitude in Susan, and Susan concurred with this.

Most frustrating of all for Susan was Wilbur's tendency to do or say things that caused difficulties between them and then to deny that he had said or done them. Initially, when Susan had a particularly clear recollection of such an event or some way of corroborating it, she would gently but firmly confront Wilbur. Almost always he reacted angrily, insisting that she was wrong and that she was either crazy or deliberately inventing lies to aggravate him. Thus, she rapidly learned not to pursue such matters, often half convinced that her own memory was distorted or that she was mentally unstable as Wilbur suggested.

Against a background of such interactions and mounting marital tension, Susan became depressed. She blamed herself for all the marital difficulties, accepting Wilbur's view of her as incompetent, irrational, and emotionally unstable. She remained desperate to please Wilbur and focused on the one area that seemed to be left under her control: her weight. As noted earlier, she had tended to plumpness in adolescence and had attributed much of her self-dissatisfaction to her weight.

In a last, desperate attempt to please Wilbur, she began to diet. At the same time, she put even more than her usual time and energy into maintaining an immaculate household, cleaning, washing and dusting daily. She spent several hours each day preparing Wilbur's "favorite meals." By this stage, her son was 3 years old, and seeking a degree of autonomy. Susan did not trust others to take adequate care of him, believing that only she could preserve the necessary standards of maternal supervision. Since she had no social life beyond her immediate family, and did not often leave the house except for shopping, mother and child were confined together most of the day. This was frustrating for both, and Susan often shouted at her son without justification, and not infrequently hit him. Her profound guilt about this abuse (which she did not at the time reveal to anyone) added to her general sense of inadequacy, despondency, and self-blame.

As Susan lost weight, the feeling that she was succeeding at *something*, combined with the euphoriant effect of fasting, elevated her mood. Wilbur, who preferred her to be slim, initially complemented her, although he became critical of her when she became gaunt and thin. Relatives expressed concern, but by this time Susan found it very difficult to eat, and continued to starve herself until admitted to the hospital.

STABILIZING THE MARRIAGE BY MAINTAINING WEIGHT LOSS

While in the hospital, Susan explained her weight loss by saying simply that she had been unable to eat. However, she became able to eat and drink normally after some initial persuasion, and had achieved a weight of 108 pounds after 3 months in the hospital. She was very reluctant to become heavier. In spite of considerable discussion, Susan saw no reason to relinquish her stereotyped views of marriage and motherhood, and she insisted that her marriage was ideal. She was anxious to resume her attempts to be a perfect wife and mother as soon as her health permitted. Her doctors thought it unwise to try and persuade her to change her views about her marriage, particularly as there was disagreement between them about its contribution to her weight loss. Thus, she was discharged at a weight of 108 pounds, although she felt it likely that she would lose weight again. This she did, but stabilized at about 100 pounds, refusing to increase her weight above this, and claiming to be in excellent health and spirits.

While Susan was in the hospital, Wilbur had cared for his son and had managed the household with the help of his mother. After Susan's discharge, he remained usefully involved in child care and household management, which contrasted sharply with his earlier refusal to do so. He was notably more sympathetic and understanding in his treatment of Susan. By preserving her weight around 100 pounds, Susan maintained a marital relationship that was viable. Wilbur was concerned that she would lose more weight and be readmitted to the hospital unless he continued to treat her with sufficient respect, sympathy, and understanding. As a result, both he and Susan were able to modify their previously rigid stereotypes of marriage slightly, and came to regard as legitimate the modest amount of role sharing that had initially been thrust upon them by Susan's illness. In this way, their marriage became a realistic proposition, rather than an impossible undertaking based on fantasies and stereotypes.

THE MUTUAL DEPENDENCE OF MALE AND FEMALE STEREOTYPES

Male and female sex-role stereotypes are mutually dependent. Each exists only by virtue of its opposite. The male sex-role stereotype has no meaning unless contrasted with the female sex-role stereotype, and vice versa. The reciprocal nature of sex-role stereotypes is evident in whatever context they are examined. For example, the stereotyped practice of fatherhood can be sustained only by the reciprocal stereotype of motherhood. In contrast, nonstereotyped motherhood invites flexibility in the paternal role, and vice versa. This theme is demonstrated by the following case.

The Territorial Couple

Paul, 34, and Wilma, 30, were referred to me by their family doctor because of severe marital problems over the preceding 12 months. Both had developed psychological symptoms in relation to their marital difficulties: Paul was moderately depressed, and complained of severe migraines; Wilma was experiencing anxiety symptoms such as dizziness, breathlessness, palpitations, and sudden, unexpected episodes of acute panic that frightened and upset her very much.

Paul's parents had separated 4 years previously, ostensibly because of chronic marital arguments. Paul's father was a moderately successful businessman who had not been significantly involved in Paul's upbringing, and with whom Paul maintained a rather distant, ambivalent relationship. Paul's mother had not worked since marrying Paul's father. Paul was strongly attached to his mother, but recognized that most people found it extremely difficult to get along with her because of her overcritical and suspicious attitudes.

On leaving school, Paul had joined a large insurance company, where for 10 years he worked quite successfully, achieving junior executive status with good prospects for further promotion. However, he was constantly dissatisfied with his work, feeling the need to "prove himself" in ways that were difficult or impossible in a corporate setting.

At 28 Paul resigned and set up his own insurance agency. Although the business proved viable, it did not flourish as he had hoped. He sold out after 3 years, using the capital to buy a large general store that employed 11 people and that was open for 12 hours 7 days a week. He threw himself wholeheartedly into this undertaking, determined to increase profits and expand the business.

Wilma's family background was quite different from Paul's. Wilma regarded her parents' marriage as ideal, recalling that her father and mother had never argued, and that her mother had seemed happy and content with an exclusively domestic role.

Wilma had been a gifted student at school, and had hoped to become an optometrist. However, she had left school prematurely at the request of her mother, who needed Wilma's help in coping with a father dying of lung cancer and a mother severely disabled by arthritis. At 18 Wilma started as a stenographer in an employment agency. Although not her original choice, she enjoyed her work and was rapidly promoted to supervize a section of five employees.

Wilma married Paul at 23, and conceived 4 months later, stopping work when 7 months pregnant with her first child, a daughter. A son was born 16 months later. Wilma's view of marriage and motherhood was strikingly stereotyped. She strongly identified with her mother, who had preserved marital harmony by invariably acceding to her husband's wishes. Wilma avoided conflict or arguments with Paul in the same way. Paul welcomed her submissiveness, because it made him feel capable, confident, and in control, and because it protected him from disputes like those that had characterized his parents' marital relationship—disputes that had left Paul with an intense fear of overt conflict within his own marriage.

Wilma was intensely possessive and overprotective of her children, and trusted no one other than her own mother to look after them. This mistrust extended to Paul and had been reinforced by Paul's own ambivalence to his child-rearing role. He felt uncomfortable when alone with his children, and became easily irritated by them. His extreme reluctance to change diapers when they were infants, episodes of apparent neglect and lack of supervision, and his tendency to shout at and smack the children in Wilma's presence, engendered in Wilma a firm belief that Paul was not to be trusted with them. As a result, she had generally refused to leave them alone with him, even though he proclaimed a genuine desire to spend more time with them. Wilma regarded Paul's lack of nurturing skills as entirely compatible with her stereotyped view of men and fatherhood.

Wilma's "territorial" views on child rearing extended to other aspects of domestic life. She regarded domestic activities as being exclusively her own domain, and saw any attempts by Paul to help with her routine chores as slighting her competence. This belief was based on Paul's suggestions, early in their marriage, about how Wilma's domestic routine could become more efficient: When Wilma had politely suggested that a household with two young children could not be run along the lines of a military camp, Paul regarded this statement as further evidence of her ignorance of organization principles and increased his efforts to "help" her. However, such efforts to help in the kitchen and elsewhere proved in practice to be more trouble than they were worth, which was partly a reflection of Paul's ambivalence to role sharing.

In his own way, Paul was as "territorial" as Wilma. He had strong, stereotyped views about marital roles and believed that his family's well-being depended on Wilma's full-time commitment to home duties. He refused to allow Wilma to be systematically involved in managing the general store, stating that this would interfere with her domestic commitments, and that she lacked the necessary business skills. In suggesting the latter, he relied on his stereotyped view of women, completely overlooking Wilma's previous successful administrative and business experience.

Their marital disputes began when Paul developed severe, incapacitating migraine headaches about 18 months before I first saw the couple. So severe and frequent were these headaches and the associated nausea and vomiting, that Paul spent a lot of time away from work. Because of his autocratic management style, this often created major problems in the store, which Wilma was required to resolve. When Wilma was in the store, she reluctantly left the children at home with Paul. Usually, she returned to weepy, upset children and an angry, frustrated husband. Arguments often followed, during which Wilma abused Paul for his domestic and paternal incompetence, and Paul abused Wilma for her incompetence as a business manager. These disputes escalated progressively, and the couple were on the brink of separation when I saw them.

THERAPY

Therapy focused on educating Paul and Wilma about the inappropriate nature of their sex-role conditioning and beliefs. In the course of this, it emerged that Paul craved to give affection and love to his children, but felt completely unable to do so. In the second therapy session, he wept copiously (to Wilma's amazement), explaining that at night he would sometimes look in upon the sleeping children, and find that tears were streaming down his cheeks: These tears, he thought, were an expression of his conflicts about nurturing his children. Wilma was fascinated and astonished by Paul's revelations, for she had come to believe that he had no wish to be a more loving and caring parent, and that he thoroughly resented spending time with the children.

At first, Wilma denied any frustrations in the conduct of her domestic role, totally disclaiming any feelings of sadness or disappointment about her failed professional aspirations or the loss of her career. When it was established that she was in fact extremely competent at managing the general store during Paul's absences, she admitted for the first time some ambivalence towards her domestic commitments and expressed a wish to be more systematically involved in managing the store.

After a total of 6 therapy sessions over a 2-month period, the couple's marriage relationship had improved dramatically. Both Paul and Wilma had largely relinquished their stereotyped attitudes about sex roles. Instead of abusing each other about their incompetence in managing each other's "territory," they were actively teaching each other the necessary skills and attitudes to cope more effectively. At a practical level they were sharing domestic and business tasks more equally. This improvement was maintained throughout a 6-month follow-up, in the course of which Paul's migraines stopped and his depression lifted. Wilma's anxiety symptoms resolved. Both agreed that although their more open, intimate, and equal relationship required a lot of work to maintain, they could never go back to their previous, stereotyped marriage.

COMMENT

Before therapy, Paul and Wilma were trapped within their sex-role stereotypes, which created artificial territorial boundaries between them. As long as they remained within these boundaries, overt conflict between them was minimal. They regarded any role sharing or blurring of territorial boundaries as unacceptable, and their attempts to maintain this rigid posture contributed to the development of their psychological symptoms. Paul's migraines, precipitated by the difficulty of maintaining a rigidly stereotyped marriage relationship, led to an enforced breaching of the traditional territorial boundaries within the marriage. As a result of his migraines, Paul was forced to stay at home in Wilma's "territory," and Wilma was forced reluctantly into Paul's "territory" at work.

Because this role sharing was thrust upon them, they resented it and were unable to feel comfortable or competent in each other's traditional territories. Instead of helping and supporting each other in role sharing, they undermined each other, adding to their difficulties, which were compounded by the development of psychological symptoms.

During therapy, Paul and Wilma were able to relinquish their sex-role stereotypes, and came to welcome role sharing as a chance to enrich their lives and develop new skills and interests. As a result of these changes, their marriage became more harmonious and equitable, and their personal well-being was greatly enhanced.

As Broverman *et al.* (1972) have shown, therapists are not immune from sex-role stereotypes. A therapist with a sex-role stereotyped perspective would not have regarded the rigid division of labor within the marriage as a central problem. Therapy would probably have focused on ways of enhancing the couple's performance within their respective roles, rather than on facilitating role sharing or role reversal. Thus, the couple's marital problems and psychological symptoms might have been perpetuated rather than resolved by therapy.

Had Paul or Wilma chosen different marriage partners, they might well have avoided major marital problems or personal psychological symptoms: It was the complementary, interlocking nature of their marriage attitudes that led to their difficulties. If, for example, Wilma had married a man with a nonstereotyped view of marriage, her own stereotypes might have weakened rather than consolidated.

SEX-ROLE CONFLICT

Social psychologists have theorized extensively about the nature of social roles. Out of this has emerged concepts such as "role strain" and "role conflict." Conflict over roles is particularly common when role expectations in a social system are unclear. Central to what follows is the idea that sex-role expectations in English-speaking countries have changed so rapidly over the past generation that social expectations of them are now inconsistent and confusing. This has caused sex-role strain and conflict to become endemic.

Interpersonal conflict over roles or conflict between role expectations and personal values can be potent contributors to the development of psychological symptoms (Wallace, 1970). It is my contention that sex-role conflict is currently a major cause of psychological symptoms in married people. However, because widespread sex-role conflict has emerged only over the past 25 years or so, models of psychotherapy have not yet adapted to this trend. Thus, although there is increasing awareness of the harmful psychological effects of sex-role stereotyping, there is as yet comparatively little understanding among psychiatrists, clinical psychologists, and other mental health workers of the central contribution of sex-role conflict to the development and maintenance of psychological symptoms.

Evidence and Effects of Changing Sex-Role Expectations

Slevin and Wingrove (1983) surveyed 103 college women, 88 of their mothers, and 30 of their maternal grandmothers, using a questionnaire comprising six subscales measuring different aspects of the female role. Daughters scored significantly lower than their mothers on all six subscales, indicating a substantially more liberal attitude to sex roles. Differences between mothers and grandmothers were significant on only four of the subscales. This suggested that the "generation gap" between mothers and daughters was greater in some key respects than that between mothers and grandmothers. These data provide empirical support for the observation that sex-role expectations have changed particularly rapidly over the past 25 years.

There were wide variations in the scores within all three groups of women. However, scores of mothers and daughters correlated significantly on the subscales measuring attitudes to marital roles and dating/courtship etiquette, suggesting that mothers still had a substantial influence on their daughters in these areas.

Interestingly, mothers who had liberal attitudes to the female role reported significant conflict with their husbands over issues of personal freedom and autonomy. This was not a problem with the grandmothers, presumably because their attitudes to such matters were less liberal. Others have found that contemporary men of all ages report more restrictive attitudes than women toward the female role (Hare-Mustin, Bennett, & Broderick, 1983; Merriam & Hyer, 1984).

Findings comparable to those of Slevin and Wingrove (1983) were reported by Merriam and Hyer (1984) who asked 270 women to evaluate the importance of five family-related developmental tasks. When divided into three age groups, the older women viewed all five tasks as significantly more important than did the younger women.

Hare-Mustin et al. (1983) focused specifically on attitudes to motherhood in a population of 274 undergraduate and graduate students. They found that a highly stereotyped, idealized image of motherhood was reported by many respondents, particularly by older women and younger men. They suggested that "for a minority of women in this sample, the motherhood myth persists in conventionalized beliefs that shadow those of older women. This persistence becomes a social concern to the extent that unrealistic ideas of the status and happiness of motherhood may be powerful, albeit unconscious, incentives for young women to become pregnant. . . . It appears that those who are least involved, men, subscribe most to the myth."

These research findings support the clinical impression that sex-role conflict often emerges within young women because their views on sex roles differ from those of their parents. The research data suggest also that when a young woman marries, her husband is likely to have a more traditional view of sex roles than she does—a view that will probably be endorsed by his parents.

Thus, a young married woman is likely to be exposed to no less than three different sources of sex-role conflict or strain: her parents; her husband; and her husband's parents. If she herself has a confused, uncertain, or inconsistent perspective on sex roles, then she is likely to develop psychological symptoms in the early years of her marriage, particularly if she has young children and does not work outside the home (Tennant, Bebbington, & Hurry, 1982).

A relationship between sex-role conflict and psychological symptoms in married women was confirmed empirically in a study by Krause (1983) of 134 full-time housewives. The measurement of sex-role conflict was based on the extent to which wives' perceived their husbands' views as differing from their own. Wives who endorsed nontraditional views, but felt that their husbands had traditional expectations, had a significantly increased chance of being depressed. Although depression was significantly correlated with dissatisfaction over the housewife role, sex-role conflict was by far the most powerful predictor of depression. This suggests that sex-role conflict leads both to dissatisfaction with a traditional domestic role and to depression, although the possibility cannot be excluded that depression contributes to sex-role conflict.

There are very few systematic empirical studies of the relationship between sex-role conflict and psychological symptoms, and the methodology is poorly developed. At this stage, we must rely primarily on clinical studies for an understanding of the mechanisms and processes involved. Once these are identified at a clinical level, they can be systematically investigated using scientific methodology. The following case describes sex-role conflict and the emergence of psychological symptoms in a young married woman.

The Ambivalent Student

Zelda, a 24-year-old married woman with a 7-month-old daughter, was referred to me by her family physician. She described her main problem as follows: "The attacks start with a tingling feeling going up my spine which enters my head and causes a sensation of faintness and nausea. I feel I'm going to lose control or lose consciousness; it's very frightening. With the first few attacks I thought perhaps I was going to die, and I started to panic. Palpitations, a choking feeling, trembling, feelings of numbness all seem to come together. It's like a nightmare. It feels like an eternity, although the attacks only last a few minutes or so. Although I realize now that I won't die, I can't control the panics. After the worst ones, I don't feel right for several days. I never know when to expect the attacks, and I dread them."

These panic attacks had started about 2 years previously, and an attack she had about 6 months after their onset was of particular significance. Zelda's husband Rico was working a night shift at the time, and he had asked Zelda to prepare him a good meal and to wake him up for it in time for work. Zelda fell asleep and woke up about 30 minutes later than she had planned. A few minutes after hurrying to the kitchen to prepare Rico's meal, she had a panic attack of such severity that she had to lie down on her bed. Unable to explain the way she felt, Zelda became so distraught that Rico called an ambulance. Since the slightest movement of her head caused acute dizziness, Zelda had to be carried out to the ambulance on a stretcher.

No physical abnormalities were revealed on examination at the local hospital, and she was referred to a psychiatrist who admitted her for observation to a private psychiatric hospital, where she stayed for 10 days before discharging herself, totally disillusioned with psychiatric treatment. Subsequently her family physician prescribed oxazepam, and she experienced some improvement, although the panic attacks continued to be troublesome, particularly when she tried to reduce the dosage. About 6 months before she came to see me, she had started taking imipramine instead of oxazepam, and she found that 75 mg at night prevented the panic attacks. Nonetheless, she felt restless, uneasy, and in a state of uncertainty about her health, an uncertainty that was reinforced by the fact that her panic attacks returned whenever she reduced the dosage of imipramine. She was fearful that the symptoms might continue indefinitely, and that she would become dependent on drugs.

Although Zelda was not aware of it, her panic attacks had been initiated and maintained primarily by sex-role conflict. Zelda's mother had never worked outside the house after getting married, and had a very traditional view of marriage and motherhood. Sexual matters were never discussed in the household, and Zelda went to a convent school, remaining ignorant of boys (a younger sister was her only sibling) until she started her studies at a university.

In her third year at college, she had fallen in love with Rico, of whom her mother strongly disapproved because of his Mexican origins and poor socioeconomic status. As the relationship developed sexually and emotionally,

Zelda felt increasingly torn between her mother's view that she was behaving with moral and social impropriety, and her wish to make her own choices in life. Although her relationship with her mother was tense and ambivalent, Zelda was nonetheless strongly influenced by her views.

Zelda's first panic attack occurred shortly after a fierce argument with her parents over her decision to marry Rico. In spite of parental opposition, Zelda married Rico soon after obtaining her degree. She then enrolled to study for a postgraduate diploma in social administration, with the aim of becoming a social worker.

Rico had problems with his own course and was repeating some second-year subjects. He expected Zelda to help him with these, and she ended up writing his essays for him, even though this required extensive study of subjects quite different from her own. In spite of Zelda's efforts, Rico dropped out halfway through the year. Zelda did badly in her own course and was discouraged from continuing into the second year. She attributed her academic failure to the time and effort she spent helping Rico and the disruption caused by her panic attacks and related health fears.

Zelda discovered that she was pregnant shortly before the end of the first year of study for her postgraduate diploma, and as a result, she felt unwilling to dispute the university's view that she should not proceed to the second year of her course. Nonetheless, she was bitterly disappointed at her failure and became mildly depressed. Although her panic attacks lessened somewhat during her pregnancy, they worsened again after the birth of her daughter and remained troublesome until she started taking imipramine.

THERAPY

Although Zelda was aware of sex-role stereotyping and conflict as an area of academic study, she had entirely failed to apply her knowledge to her own situation. However, when I brought this to her attention, she gradually became aware of the central importance of sex-role conflict in the genesis and continuation of her panic attacks.

She was able, for example, to acknowledge her rage at Rico for dropping out of his degree course after she had made so many sacrifices to help him succeed—sacrifices she had felt compelled to make because of her sex-role conditioning. She came to realize that the panic attack that had precipitated her ambulance ride to the hospital was a product of overwhelming sex-role conflict and rage: Rico, who had just dropped out of college and started low-status night work, expected her, a budding professional, to cook all his meals, wait upon him, and do all the housework. Her sex-role conditioning and the example of her mother's exclusive devotion to husband and children had prevented her from seriously questioning these aspects of her relationship with Rico. Her love for Rico had inhibited any expression of anger towards him. Feelings of overwhelming panic, numbness, and "paralysis" were her only means of experiencing and expressing her profound dilemma.

Once the panic attacks became established, they provided an excuse for her failure to study effectively, though the real origins of her study problems lay in sex-role conflict. By example and repeated exhortation, Zelda's mother had conditioned her to believe that a woman's role in life should be to marry as well as possible, and then devote herself exclusively to her husband and family. Zelda's father, with whom she identified unusually strongly, had a different view. Recognizing that she was highly intelligent, he urged her to study hard and to aim for a career. Identifying *primarily* with her mother, Zelda was intensely ambivalent about her professional aspirations, an ambivalence that was reduced when her panic attacks and related anxieties prevented her from studying. However, academic failure greatly lowered her self-esteem and created new anxieties, establishing a vicious cycle in which anxiety symptoms and study problems reinforced each other.

Once her daughter was born, Zelda gave up the idea of further study altogether, and planned a second child primarily out of duty to the first, whom she did not wish to be an only child. She was convinced that marriage and motherhood were incompatible with work or study and believed that she had to devote her full attention to her children and husband. Nonetheless, the prospects of full-time, conventional motherhood stretching endlessly ahead filled her with despair. She felt panicky and unsettled whenever she thought of the university and the life she might have hoped for had she continued her studies.

Although imipramine prevented major panic attacks and improved her mood, while on the drug she felt in a state of limbo and helplessness, unable to make any decisions, and concerned about her health and her capacity to cope with anything other than routine commitments.

As Zelda came to understand the full extent of her hitherto unconscious conflict about sex roles, she began to realize that her ideas of motherhood were based on a stereotype rather than on reality. Concurrently, she was able to start making decisions again. She negotiated with the university a basis for resuming her postgraduate studies, and, when she started, made appropriate child-care arrangements. Her guilt about leaving her daughter with others gradually resolved when she saw that the child was happy with the arrangement. Once settled back into a study routine, she stopped her imipramine and experienced no more panic attacks.

At the same time as she was making these changes, Zelda was attempting to negotiate a more appropriate domestic division of labor with Rico. This proved extremely difficult because of Rico's highly stereotyped view of marriage and motherhood. Four conjoint marital sessions were required to facilitate a readjustment of the marital system.

I followed Zelda up informally for 18 months, during which time she remained free of panic attacks and obtained her postgraduate diploma without major difficulty. Therapy had occupied a total of 12 sessions (including the 4 conjoint interviews) over a period of 14 weeks.

COMMENT

Diagnostically, Zelda matched the *DSM-III* panic disorder category. Recent research has emphasized the effectiveness of imipramine in treating this condition (Garanki, Zitrin, & Klein, 1984), and the drug certainly reduced Zelda's panic attacks. However, it did not help her to examine or resolve her underlying sex-role conflict. Indeed, drug treatment, by ameliorating her symptoms, allowed her to postpone an inquiry into their real origins. Although the prospect of full-time motherhood filled Zelda with despair, she had nonetheless settled for it because alternatives, such as a return to the university, appeared too challenging. Being on drugs reinforced the poor self-esteem and low self-confidence that had been the result of her academic failure. Furthermore, drug treatment had consolidated the idea that the problem lay entirely *within* her: This reduced any incentive to look for environmental contributors to her symptoms. This contributed, for example, to her failure to confront Rico about his assumption that she would always sacrifice her own interests for his, an assumption that was a major contributor to Zelda's sex-role conflict, and hence central in precipitating and perpetuating her symptoms.

Although there is scientific evidence for a genetic contribution to panic disorder (interestingly, Zelda's father also suffered from anxiety symptoms), this contribution represents primarily a tendency to react to stress and conflict with panic attacks rather than, say, depression. Emphasizing genetic factors reinforces the idea that patients are suffering from an illness that is beyond their control or responsibility.

Psychotherapy was helpful to Zelda primarily because it allowed unconscious conflicts about sex roles to become conscious: She was then able to resume making decisions about her life. Zelda might, of course, have made a deliberate decision to relinquish her professional aspirations, rather than continuing to feel that she had been forced by circumstances to cease studying. Instead, she chose to relinquish the stereotype of full-time motherhood with which she had been imbued since early childhood. After a year back at College, she had no doubt that her decision was a correct one.

Psychotherapy that did not focus on Zelda's sex-role conflict would probably have been unhelpful. A psychoanalytic approach would doubtless have dwelt on her ambivalence to her mother and her unusually strong identification with father. This would probably have had the effect of reinforcing a conventional perspective on sex roles, particularly if that reflected the therapist's views. Such an approach may have lessened Zelda's ambivalence to full-time motherhood in the short term, but at the price of invalidating her professional aspirations.

Detailed attention to personal historical issues would have been unlikely to reduce the panic attacks, particularly if it obscured the relevance of current marital interaction. Indeed, psychoanalytic psychotherapy is generally acknowledged to be an unsatisfactory treatment for panic disorder and related syndromes such as agoraphobia. The ineffectiveness of psychotherapy has encouraged the use of drugs and behavior therapy as alternatives. However, systematic clinical research into such unimodal therapies has led to an overestimation of their effectiveness; some reasons for this are discussed in Chapter 5.

THE IMPACT OF SEX-ROLE RESEARCH ON CLINICAL THEORY AND PRACTICE

Psychiatry and Sex-Role Research

There is a growing body of research into the effects of sex-role stereotyping on women's mental health, and this has recently been reviewed by Franks and Rothblum (1983). This research has been largely overlooked by psychiatrists in their clinical practice and theorizing, for the following reasons.

First, the prevailing illness model of psychiatric disorder favors the idea of an underlying biochemical or genetic abnormality and discourages a social–interpersonal perspective. Thus, most clinicians focus primarily on the patient's *individual* characteristics. This approach is enshrined in the *DSM-III*, which has been strongly criticized, *inter alia*, for its lack of an interpersonal diagnostic framework (McLemore & Benjamin, 1979). The main thrust of psychiatric research parallels this focus on the individual.

Second, outstanding and influential clinicians, teachers, and researchers in psychiatry are almost all men, although women are slowly but steadily infiltrating the corridors of power. Outstanding success, recognition, and influence in psychiatry, as in any other profession, requires a large amount of sustained personal commitment and very hard work. It is virtually impossible to build an outstanding career in psychiatry without working during many evenings and weekends: This is generally incompatible with an extensive practical involvement in family and domestic matters, which must therefore be taken care of by others.

In common with successful men in other professions, many outstanding psychiatrists are married to wives who have selflessly supported them in their professional endeavors, identifying with their husbands' successes and willingly sacrificing or postponing many of their own personal aspirations for the sake of their husbands and children. In preserving a mainly domestic focus to their lives, these women have gone along with a sex-role stereotyped perspective on marriage. Psychiatrists with such wives are unlikely to question the desirability of sex-role stereotyped marriage relationships, and, therefore, tend to perceive research into sex-role issues as irrelevant.

Third, female psychiatrists have tended to overlook sex-role stereotyping in their work with women. This is perhaps most obvious in the psychoanalytic literature, in which a majority of female therapists appear to have identified with a Freudian perspective without acknowledging its intrinsic bias against women. It may be that in choosing medicine as a career, women have avoided or transcended sex-role stereotyping. If so, they do not appear to have identified this achievement as a central task for their female patients.

It is perhaps easier to understand why female psychiatrists have hitherto failed to emphasize the central role of sex-role conflict in generating and perpetuating psychiatric disorder in married women. In common with other relatively affluent professional people, they can afford to pay for housekeepers and skilled, safe child care in their own homes or elsewhere. In such circumstances, both they and their husbands can pursue full-time careers relatively free of guilt and conflict over sex-role issues. Unfortunately, the ability to purchase a measure of freedom from sex-role conflict is beyond the financial means of most young couples.

Marital Therapy and Sex-Role Research

As part of my preparation for this chapter, I systematically surveyed recent volumes of the major journals dealing with marital and family therapy. I was struck by the small number of articles that referred specifically to sex-role stereotyping in a therapeutic context.

One reason for this may be related to the preponderance of male authors (Cross, 1984). In *Family Process*, during the 4 years from 1979 to 1982, 60% of the articles were written by men alone and 18% by women alone. In the 20% of articles written by both male and female authors, the senior author was a man in 13 percent and a woman in 7%. For the *Journal of Marital and Family Therapy*, the figures were virtually identical. This pattern of authorship suggests that a male perspective still predominates in the professional literature on marital and family therapy.

A second reason relates to prevailing theoretical models in marital and family therapy. Systems and communications theorists rely on models derived essentially from mathematical rather than social theories. While such an approach facilitates the creation of the complex models necessary for a comprehensive formulation of relationships within family systems, it cannot easily incorporate sociological concepts such as sex-role stereotyping. For example, James and McIntyre (1983) have argued that systems theory has been a major contributor to the failure of family therapy to respond to recent critical analyses of the contemporary family, particularly with regard to traditional sex roles. As a result, family therapy "cannot investigate the possibility that 'dysfunction' in families is socially created and maintained. Family therapy's failure to consider the broader contexts of family functioning, a failure that is facilitated by the use of systems theory . . . results in an uncritical acceptance of the contemporary family form" (p. 119).

However, as Chapman and Park (1984) point out, techniques derived from systems theory lend themselves particularly well to dealing with sex-role issues, and there are clear signs that systems theorists are becoming more aware of the importance of this area.

Under the influence of learning theory, behavioral therapists have tended to focus on behavior per se, rather than on its social matrix. Nonetheless, as Margolin, Talovic, Fernandez, and Onorato (1983) point out, behavioral marital therapists have made preliminary attempts to grapple with sex role issues: "Behavioral marital therapists' attempts to avoid succumbing to sex role stereotypes are commendable. Unfortunately, however, these attempts have been accompanied by an indifference to male–female differences . . . overlooking sex role issues, whether it takes the form of reinforcing traditional values or automatically assuming that an egalitarian relationship exists, communicates a lack of respect and appreciation for clients' life-style choices. Either stance narrows our understanding of a couple's problems and limits our ability to help couples achieve what they view as satisfactory outcomes" (p. 143).

Therapists with a psychoanalytic perspective have tended to perpetuate the male bias inherent in a Freudian approach (Hare-Mustin, 1982).

Thus, up to the present, there has been little theoretical impetus for family and marital therapists to address sex-role issues as central themes in their clinical work.

A third reason that so little attention is given to sex-role stereotyping by family and marital therapists relates to the clinical material. A couples approach is now almost universal among marital therapists. For a couple to accept conjoint marital therapy as a valid undertaking, both partners must presumably acknowledge that marital conflict is the main problem. There is evidence that rigid adherence to sex-role stereotypes protects against overt marital conflict, although it contributes to the development of psychological symptoms, particularly in the female partner (Hafner, 1984a; Tinsley, Sullivan-Guest, & McGuire, 1984). These symptoms are usually presented for *individual* treatment, serving as a displaced focus of marital conflict and dissatisfaction. Thus, couples who adhere rigidly to sex-role stereotypes are unlikely to seek marital therapy and are therefore presumably underrepresented in related clinical practice and research.

The likelihood of a couple seeking marital therapy is also reduced if either or both partners rely heavily on projection or denial as psychological defense mechanisms. In such circumstances, the interaction of personality abnormalities and sex-role conflict is likely to precipitate psychological symptoms in one partner (Hafner, 1983a). Once again, the symptoms may become a displaced focus of marital conflict, in which case the symptom-bearer will generally seek individual rather than marital therapy. As a result, couples in whom major personality abnormalities and sex-role conflict coexist are probably underrepresented in the caseloads of marital therapists.

Treating patients who present with psychological symptoms as a displaced focus of marital conflict is a major challenge. This challenge provided the impetus for the development of spouse-aided therapy, the principles and practice of which are detailed in Chapter 9.

Feminist Therapy and Sex-Role Research

The development of feminist therapy has been helped greatly by research demonstrating the adverse effects on women's mental health of sex-role stereotyping and conflict (Sturdivant, 1980). Reciprocally, the recent impetus toward research into sex roles and mental health owes much to feminist philosophy. As a result, the contribution of sex-role stereotyping and conflict to the development of psychological symptoms in *men* has received comparatively little attention. One of the aims of this book is to redress this imbalance.

CHAPTER THREE

Choice of Marriage Partner

In Chapter 1 we established that before the present century, formal marriage in English-speaking countries was restricted to the comparatively wealthy. The primary function of marriage was the preservation or enhancement of the socioeconomic status of the marriage partners and their respective families of origin.

During the present century, not only has the basis of marriage changed from an economic to a personal psychological one, but the proportion of people who marry has increased substantially. These radical changes have been accepted almost without question, perhaps because freedom of choice and equality of opportunity are principles long enshrined in English-speaking cultures. However, there is no empirical evidence that these changes represent an improved basis for marriage. The opposite may be true. Universal access to marriage based on free personal choice of mate may in reality be a system less desirable or workable than the long-established system, based on economics, that it has replaced.

Whether or not this is true in a general sense, it is my contention that many people today choose their marriage partner on a basis that is poorly informed or ill-advised and that leads directly or indirectly to the development or maintenance of psychological symptoms. Stated bluntly, modern marriage is a major contributor to the relatively high level of persisting psychiatric disorder that is a feature of contemporary English-speaking countries.

Such a viewpoint is not unusual among psychiatrists with an interest in marital dynamics (Ackerman, 1958; Eisenstein, 1956). However, there is a need for theoretical and practical formulations in the area that would take into account research findings of the past decade. This is one aim of the present chapter.

PERSONAL AND GENDER IDENTITY

Central to an understanding of pathogenic mate selection are the concepts of "personal identity" and "gender identity." The latter term refers to the personal sense of being male or female. For many, marriage represents an abandonment or postponement of the search for personal identity. Within such marriages, changes in marital dynamics are regarded as a threat to the sense of identity of one or both partners. Those threatened in this way will naturally struggle to preserve the marital status quo. Psychological symptoms often emerge in relation to this struggle.

The work of Erikson (1968) is still widely regarded as definitive in the area of identity formation. However, as Hare-Mustin (1982) has pointed out, Erikson's work is rooted in a psychoanalytic perspective and is therefore based primarily on the normative male experience. Recent awareness of the limitations of psychoanalytically based ideas about personal and gender identity has led to the creation of new hypotheses and theories. Although some of these are strikingly original and thought provoking, none have yet achieved the status, substance, or coherence of the male-oriented theories that they seek to modify or replace. What follows is in part an attempt to synthesize some of the more recent ideas about identity formation with older, psychoanalytically oriented notions.

Individuation

Fundamental to psychoanalytic thinking about identity formation is the concept of "individuation," which is basically the process of gradual separation from parental control and influence. As Parker (1983) has established, parental overprotection is a potent obstacle to individuation, particularly if combined with affectionless control, neglect, or rejection. Overprotection per se appears to be rare: It is nearly always associated with parental behavior and attitudes that damage or impede the development of a healthy self-image. Thus, in understanding problems of individuation, it is essential to comprehend the normal and abnormal development of intrapsychic structures.

Individuation is particularly relevant to mate selection. Failure to individuate is often associated with the unconscious fantasy that the challenging task of individuation can be avoided by selecting a spouse who functions as a replacement for one or the other parent. If such an expectation is held by both partners, it is rarely compatible with a satisfactory marriage relationship.

The Development of Intrapsychic Structures

"Internalization" is a general term for the highly complex process by which the outer world comes to be internally represented, thus forming a basis for the sense of inner self. If there are deficiencies or abnormalities of the internal mental world, then these impede the process of identity formation, not only directly, but also indirectly by interfering with individuation.

A theoretical framework for conceptualizing intrapsychic development

CHOICE OF MARRIAGE PARTNER

and structure is essential for understanding interpersonal dynamics. There are several such frameworks and all share the same fundamental limitation: They are based on the mental life of infants who are at a preverbal stage of development. Thus, theories of early mental life must rely on inference and speculation rather than on direct observation.

In spite of such constraints, coherent and logical theories about early mental life have been developed. Of these, the most relevant to the present discussion is "object relations theory," which has been described as "the psychoanalytic approach to the internalization of interpersonal relations" (Masterson, 1976).

Notwithstanding heroic attempts to clarify and systematize object-relations theory (Guntrip, 1969), it remains extraordinarily difficult to understand and describe the concepts involved. I was privileged to attend over a period of 3 years, weekly meetings to which a specialist in object relations theory was a regular contributor. My initial reaction to his formulations, and that of most of my colleagues, was one of disbelief, amusement, and even ridicule. Such reactions can be understood in the light of some typical formulations by an extremely articulate and highly regarded object relations theorist: "As she had previously spilt a glass of water on the couch when she put me to bed on it, I interpreted that one watch was mummy's breast full of milk, while the other was mummy's breast when she felt that she had angrily filled it with wee-wee. I also said that she did not want a string on the yellow one because she did not want to take the bad 'wee-wee' breast inside her. . . . So now there were three breasts, a good one full of milk, a bad one full of wee-wee, and an intermediate one which had been good the day before, but which she showed me she herself had cut, and therefore spoiled" (Segal, 1973, p. 79).

And: "For the little girl, the first oral turning to the penis is a heterosexual move paving the way to the genital situation and the wish to incorporate the penis in her vagina. But at the same time it contributes to her homosexual trends in that, in that stage of development, the oral desire is linked with incorporation and identification, and the wish to be fed by the penis is accompanied by a wish to possess a penis of her own" (p. 110).

While several of my colleagues were alienated by such formulations, I persevered. It gradually became clear to me that only by accepting the irrational, primitive, and symbolic aspects of intrapsychic development and structure could I begin to understand the marital difficulties and intrapsychic conflicts of severely disturbed psychiatric patients. Behavioral or systemic formulations of marital interaction that ignored the primitive, "primary process" aspects of intrapsychic life seemed inadequate when it came to understanding the marital and personal difficulties of those with major problems of psychosocial development and adjustment. Unfortunately, the opportunity to witness at first hand the power of primitive unconscious events and processes to influence human behavior is restricted primarily to those trained in psychodynamic psychotherapies. These unconscious phenomena are almost totally disregarded in sociological, behavioral, and systems perspectives on marriage.

In spite of the enormous difficulties in generalizing object relations theory to everyday clinical practice, a number of authors have written comprehensive and readable accounts of its relevance to marital pathology (Dicks, 1963; Meissner, 1978). Although this is not always sufficiently acknowledged, contemporary object relations theory is based on the fundamental contributions of Melanie Klein (Segal, 1973). So logical and coherent are Klein's hypotheses that, once translated into nontechnical language, they still provide the most comprehensive basis for an understanding of object relations theory and its relevance to the marital interactions of people with major psychological abnormalities or psychiatric disorders.

The Theories of Melanie Klein

In the first few months of life, the infant cannot distinguish between itself and its environment. Hence, its feelings are projected onto the outside world and become part of it. When the infant is in a state of fear or hunger, unpleasant feelings are projected outward (primarily onto the mother), where they form the "bad object." Pleasant feelings, such as those experienced during and after breast feeding, are projected outward in the same way to form the "good object."

In normal development, the infant struggles to keep the good and bad objects as separate as possible, primarily to keep the good object from harm. This separation of good and bad objects is the origin of the important clinical concept of "splitting" (Akhtar & Byrne, 1983).

As the infant becomes aware of the separate existence of the outside world, the bad object becomes increasingly persecutory and frightening. The threat of the bad object can be ameliorated in a number of ways, the most common of which is through "introjection," a mental mechanism by which the external object is absorbed within the self. Once introjected, the bad object can be projected outward again, in whole or part. This mechanism of reprojection leads to the fundamental clinical concept of "projective identification": When parts of the self and related internal objects are projected into external objects, these become "possessed by, controlled and identified with the projected parts" (Segal, 1973). In the case of projection of the bad object, in whole or in part, this leads to a fear of retaliation by the attacked external object through counterprojection. There is also often a fear of having parts of the self controlled by the object onto which they have been projected.

Less common ways of dealing with the external bad object include "denial" of its existence, usually through the fantasy of its total annihilation; and "idealization," in which the bad object becomes a "pseudoideal" object. The final recourse of an overwhelmingly threatened sense of self (or ego) is "disintegration." When this unconscious defense mechanism is used in adulthood, it often evokes overwhelming fear and panic. Indeed, so frightening is the associated feeling of impending psychic disintegration or loss of the sense of self that those afflicted (often severely disturbed psychiatric patients) may cut, burn or otherwise injure their skin in order to experience a physical sensation or witness the flow of blood: This confirms their bodily integrity. Sometimes, such people say that they would prefer death itself to a continuation of such feelings of overwhelming terror or imminent doom. I recall two patients—both men—who experienced these feelings when alone in crowded public places. They refused to leave their wives, or the safety of the hospital environment, unless accompanied by someone able to give them an immediate intravenous injection of tranquilizing medication should they sense the threat of psychic disintegration.

The likelihood of invoking such primitive defense mechanisms in adulthood is reduced by positive nurturing experiences in early childhood, which allow the good object to become stronger and more substantial. This lessens the need for splitting, and ushers in what Klein termed the "depressive position," the negotiation of which is a vital developmental task normally achieved in the second year of life. Failure to negotiate the depressive position means that the primitive psychological structures and mechanisms outlined above will be preserved indefinitely.

The Depressive Position

When, toward the end of the first year of life, the infant begins to recognize its mother as a *whole* object, rather than as separate good and bad objects, this creates a sense of helplessness. Concurrently, the infant is forced to realize that it loves and hates the same object. This leads the infant to fear that its destructive, aggressive impulses will destroy the loved object (usually the mother). Even more frightening is the idea that these aggressive impulses have actually destroyed the loved object when it is not present. Similar fears exist in relation to internalized representations of the loved object. Introjection of the loved object is a particularly active defense at this time.

If the feelings evoked by the early phases of the depressive position are too frightening, the infant may regress to an earlier phase of development characterized by splitting and can remain fixated indefinitely at that level. The maintenance of such a defensive positive requires a concurrent reliance on "repression." Fixation at the early stages of the depressive position leads, *inter alia*, to profound "separation anxiety" in later childhood and adulthood. This is because of the constant fear that the good or loved object will be (or has been) destroyed in its absence.

Failure to negotiate the depressive position is a major cause of subsequent disturbances in personal relationships. However, *earlier* failure to achieve the protective separation of good and bad objects can also create problems in adult life. Klein suggested that when there is excessive *envy* of the emerging good object, it may be attacked and spoiled, so that the bad object contaminates or becomes part of the good object. The absence of an unspoiled good object in infancy is associated with extreme ambivalence in subsequent interpersonal relationships, a problem that often persists into adulthood.

The Oedipus Complex

From a Kleinian perspective, the Oedipus complex is an integral part of the development of the depressive position. The infant's awareness of the parental dyad, and of his exclusion from the sexual aspects of it, leads to intense feelings of deprivation, envy, and jealousy. Failure to resolve the depressive position leaves a reliance on denial, splitting, and idealization that may take various forms. For example, there may be a splitting between "good" asexual parents and "bad" sexual ones. Or one parent may be perceived as ideal, while the other is regarded as a persecutor. When splitting is extreme, positive and negative feelings toward the idealized or hated parent may be very intense indeed. Failure to resolve the Oedipus complex consolidates denial, splitting, and idealization as a basis for dealing with interpersonal relationships in adult life.

Object Relations Theory and Identity Problems

When the family environment is satisfactory, the gradual separation of the child from its parents is associated with the development of a coherent and cohesive sense of self. The child's experience of its inner psychic structures is characterized by a sense of sameness and continuity. This sense of self-cohesion is the basis of the child's capacity to differentiate between self and other in the context of emotionally involved relationships. The capacity to tolerate the separateness and differentness of emotionally significant others is a central feature of a well-developed sense of personal identity.

Failure to resolve the depressive position and any related oedipal difficulties prevents the formation of a coherent or differentiated sense of self. In adolescence, this inhibits the achievement of a sense of personal identity, and is often associated with excessive, ambivalent dependency on the parents.

Meissner (1978) has pointed out the cognitive–perceptual consequences of failure to achieve a sense of personal identity during adolescence: "Such individuals who have an impoverished or deficient identity never really develop values or beliefs that are clearly their own. They either adopt the values derived from their immediate family or adapt themselves to the strengths they find in other people and thus come to operate with a borrowed identity" (p. 33). This borrowed identity is also termed the *false self*.

When a person's sense of personal identity is deficient or absent, marriage usually represents a transfer of dependency from the family of origin onto the marriage partner. If this is true of both partners, they unconsciously seek to obtain from each other a stable, coherent sense of identity. However, neither partner is perceived accurately by the other, but is idealized or denigrated according to the level and nature of each partner's intrapsychic development.

Object relations theorists have created theoretical frameworks of enormous complexity in an attempt to systematize and understand the mutual projections and introjections of such couples. However, male–female differences have been insufficiently considered in these formulations, which also pay inadequate attention to recent theories of gender identity development. Some of these theories will now be outlined and integrated.

Gender Identity

Gender identity usually coincides with biological sex, but may transcend it, giving rise, for example, to gender identity disorders. Gender identity normally blends with the overall sense of personal identity that consolidates during late adolescence. However, it originates in an earlier phase of development, and its formation differs substantially between males and females.

Under the impetus of feminism, the idea of "androgyny" has challenged traditional assumptions about gender identity (Bem, 1974). Hitherto, it has been a fundamental assumption that normal male and female gender identities are essentially and necessarily different in nature, and that their developmental paths must inevitably diverge early in childhood.

These assumptions were made in the context of a society that accepted as natural different roles for men and women. These role differences were validated by marked gender differences in attitudes and behavior, which in turn reinforced sex-role dimorphism. Such basic assumptions are still fundamental to psychoanalytic and social learning theories of gender identity, which to date have failed to incorporate the concept of androgyny.

Androgynous individuals report high levels of both "masculine" and "feminine" attributes, whereas sex-role-stereotyped individuals emphasize personal attributes traditionally associated with their own sex. Those who score *low* on both masculine and feminine attributes are termed "undifferentiated" with regard to gender identity.

THE DEVELOPMENT OF A MASCULINE GENDER IDENTITY

From a traditional sex-roles perspective, events are as follows. The infant boy identifies first with his primary care giver, nearly always his mother or a female substitute. He internalizes mainly female attributes in the first 3 to 4 years of his life, because most of his time is spent with his mother and other females. The more strongly he identifies with his mother, the more powerful and coherent will be his female internalizations.

When, at the age of 3 or 4 he starts preschool or kindergarten, he finds that he is expected to relate to peers as a little boy. Because little boys behave in public in ways that are quite different from little girls, he must rapidly learn to relinquish his primary identification with mother, and behave in a more aggressive, assertive, unemotional, and independent manner. He must learn to conform with the childhood equivalent of the male sex-role stereotype.

If the parents have a reasonably harmonious and intimate relationship, and relate fairly well to their son, the task of relinquishing a basic identification with mother is not insurmountable. Gradually, the boy comes to identify with his father or the equivalent man in his life, and the consequent male internalizations slowly and systematically combine with the female ones. He will enter adolescence with a secure sense of gender identity based on extensive and intimate contact with a caring male figure or figures. This will not exclude "feminine" attributes of tenderness, emotionality, and nonassertiveness when appropriate. Thus, a secure and flexible sense of gender identity will blend harmoniously into a robust, positive sense of personal identity during adolescence.

This sequence of events is held to be quite different in boys who have little or no intimate or satisfactory contact with their fathers or equivalent male figures. When they seek to reduce their identification with their mothers, they have no adequate male figure with whom to identify. Thus, they cannot blend male internalizations with their preexisting female ones. In such circumstances, it is argued, their sense of gender identity in adulthood will be inadequate or poorly defined. This will create difficulties in adjusting to the normal male sex role, difficulties that are likely to lead to a range of psychological and interpersonal problems.

This traditional view of gender identity formation has been challenged by Pleck (1981), who demonstrated that the effect of the father on gender identity formation in male children is much less than generally assumed. Instead, Pleck argues, social and peer pressures to conform with sex-role stereotypes and norms are the major determinants of a masculine gender identity. He points out that sex-role stereotypes are a widely shared belief about what the sexes are actually like, whereas sex-role norms are widely held beliefs about what the sexes should be like. Although stereotypes and norms may often coincide, little research has been done on sex-role norms and their relationship to stereotypes.

A central feature of Pleck's theory is the fact that sex-role stereotypes and norms are in reality unattainable. Thus, striving toward them creates "sex-role strain." It is primarily sex-role strain that creates psychological problems in adulthood, and not, as generally assumed, the absence in childhood of adequate masculine sex-role models.

Pleck's theories, which he termed the "sex-role strain paradigm," complemented my own observations. I had come to speculate about why so many of the men I met, whether in a clinical or a social setting, adhered rather rigidly or unquestioningly to male sex-role norms and stereotypes. Within broad limits, the level of adherence appeared to be largely independent of the precise quality of the father-son relationship.

However, a significant proportion of men whom I interviewed in a clinical setting revealed a total identification with the male sex-role stereotype. It was a fundamental, unquestioned and seemingly inflexible aspect of their sense of personal identity. Indeed, these men appeared to base both their gender and their personal identity on a rigid, literal, adherence to the male sex-role stereotype.

Almost without exception, these men described highly unsatisfactory childhood relationships with their fathers, or had lost their fathers in childhood through separation, divorce, or death. It seemed that they had *compensated for the absence of good fathering by identifying with and internalizing the male sex-role stereotype.*

However, there is nothing genuine or real about this internalization, based as it is on images of manhood derived from the media, popular fiction and entertainment, male sporting heroes, and romantic fantasies. As a result, the internalized stereotype cannot blend or harmonize with the previously established feminine internalizations based on a primary identification with the mother. These feminine internalizations are therefore ruthlessly suppressed as incompatible with the internalized male sex-role stereotype. From this emerges a rigid adherence to sex-role stereotyped attitudes and behavior and fierce rejection or suppression of supposedly feminine traits such as warmth, tenderness, emotionality, dependency, and the expression of loving, · caring feelings.

The marital and clinical repercussions of this constellation of events will be discussed in Chapter 4.

THE DEVELOPMENT OF A FEMININE GENDER IDENTITY

In females, the development of gender identity is relatively uncomplicated, because they are not required to relinquish a primary identification with their mothers. If they have access in childhood to a father or equivalent male figure with whom they develop a reasonably intimate, open, caring relationship, they will internalize realistic male attributes that will harmonize with established female internalizations. Thus, in adolescence and adulthood they are as capable of behaving assertively, unemotionally, and competitively in some situations as they are of behaving in a warm, tender, or submissive manner in others. However, social pressures to conform with sex-role stereotypes and norms will inhibit to a greater or lesser extent their willingness to diverge from traditional sex-role behaviors.

In the context of a highly sex-role-stereotyped parental relationship, or where for other reasons it is difficult or impossible for daughters to identify with their fathers, girls may enter adolescence without internalizing any of the supposedly masculine attributes such as independence, competitiveness, and assertiveness. Thus, they will themselves seek stereotyped relationships based on the idea of being cared for and protected by a strong or "macho" man. If they have identified with the female sex-role stereotype as an alternative to a valid personal identity, then they are unlikely to challenge a sex-role-stereotyped basis for their own marriage.

The increasing proportion of single parents, still overwhelmingly female, has important implications for the development of feminine gender identity. Single women standing alone as parents are the antithesis of the female sex-role stereotype. Daughters who identify with their independent, capable, and competent mothers develop a sense of gender identity that is incompatible with traditional sex-role expectations. In adulthood, this creates a high level of role strain, particularly in their relationships with men who have a traditional view of sex roles.

Integration of Object Relations and Sex-Role Strain Paradigms

As Erikson (1968) has pointed out, a major task of adolescence is the consolidation of a sense of identity. This requires the blending and coalescence of internalized objects and self-representations that have been previously accumulated. When internalizations are reasonably consistent and harmonious, their integration during adolescence occurs without difficulty, and the young adult will emerge with a fairly clear and consistent sense of personal identity. This will facilitate the development of balanced, harmonious, and intimate relationships in adult life. Those with a robust personal identity are able to develop ideas and beliefs of their own and can, for example, withstand pressures toward conformity and stereotyping that might overcome those whose identity formation is distorted, impaired, or incomplete.

When, through inadeqate parenting, object relations are impaired, the task of identity formation during adolescence is extremely difficult. This leads to an excessive reliance on the "false self" that is a feature of those with poor object relations (Akhter & Byrne, 1983). The true self withdraws inward, usually to be totally repressed and denied. Concurrently, cognitive processes remain immature, and this leads to oversimple, concretized representations of the outside world. External objects are divided into rigid, mutually exclusive categories that are regarded as "all good" or "all bad." This is a reflection of the continued reliance on splitting as a basic psychological defense mechanism.

In these circumstances, the false self comes to be equated with the sex-role stereotype that coincides with the gender of the individual concerned.

Thus, the task of identity formation is sidestepped by the emergence of a spurious sense of identity based on a total identification with the sex-role stereotype.

Rotter and O'Connell (1982) have provided substantial empirical evidence suggesting a relationship between sex-role stereotyping and impaired object relations and personal identity. They found that men and women who adhered to sex-role stereotypes "reflect a tendency to compartmentalize, to overgeneralize, to minimize conflict, and to be intolerant of differences from the self. They are more likely to see others as invariably masculine or feminine, good or bad, right or wrong" (p. 1218).

Once this central hypothesis is accepted, it becomes impossible to comprehend impaired object relations and their impact on mate selection without acknowledging the central role of sex-role stereotyping. Here it is of interest that Dicks (1963) has implied a crucial place for sex-role stereotyping in his seminal paper on marriage and object relations theory. Although he does not mention sex-role stereotyping as such, he suggested that "people who came to one's clinical notice for their marriage troubles had strongly 'built-in' role models for their own and their spouses behaviour *which they were unconsciously testing in marriage and found wanting in intimate daily interaction* [italics added]. . . . The 'built-in' role models were based on ambivalent relations to earlier love-objects, most often the person's parents—not necessarily of the opposite sex" (p. 125).

The italicized part of Dicks's comments is an implicit reference to sex-role strain, although Dicks clearly arrived at this insight through clinical observations rather than by theorizing about sex-role stereotypes and norms.

Gender Identity, the False Self, and Sex-Role Strain

Basing a sense of *personal* identity on a sex-role stereotype to create a viable, relatively stable false self requires the suppression of *gender* identity if it is incompatible with the sex-role stereotype. This creates sex-role strain. *The more that gender identity differs from the sex-role stereotype, the greater will be sex-role strain.*

The implications of this differ substantially between the sexes; women will be considered first.

SEX-ROLE STRAIN IN WOMEN

Where inadequate parenting and a rigidly sex-role-stereotyped parental relationship coincide, both gender and personal identity in the daughter will be equally determined by sex-role stereotyping. Thus, in adolescence, the daughter will experience minimal sex-role strain. If she herself contracts a rigidly sex-role-stereotyped marriage, then she is likely to remain free of sex-role strain as long as a stereotyped relationship remains satisfactory to both partners. However, the absence of sex-role strain does not protect against the development of psychological symptoms, as was demonstrated in "A Case of Self-Starvation" in Chapter 2.

Where parenting is both inadequate and *divergent* from the sex-role stereotype, the daughter's gender identity will differ from the sex-role stereotype. Such parenting is reported very commonly by married women with severe, persisting psychiatric disorders.

Classically, the father is largely uninvolved in parenting, and has major psychological problems of his own. In most cases, the father's difficulties and aberrations are attributed to alcoholism. The parental dyad is disrupted by the father's disturbed behavior, and the mother is regarded as the "backbone" of the family. She is seen as struggling not only to care for her children, but to cope with and support an alcoholic, disruptive, and intermittently absent father.

The daughter identifies with her mother, but their relationship is strained and ambivalent because of the constant stresses that the mother experiences in her attempts to cope with an almost impossible domestic situation. The daughter can internalize few of her father's attributes. She has no model of a constructive, cooperative, relatively harmonious parental relationship.

Concurrently, she is exposed through the media, popular literature, and peer pressure to stereotyped and romanticized images of men and male–female relationships. She internalizes these images to fill the vacuum left by the absence of a satisfactory relationship with her father, or to counter the destructive effects of her father's behavior. By the time she enters adolescence, her notions of the ideal man, and the ideal man–woman relationship, are based almost entirely on sex-role-stereotyped, romanticized images and fantasies.

However, her gender identity is based on identification with a mother whose behavior was in many ways antithetical to the female sex-role stereotype: a mother who coped virtually single-handed to bring up her children against enormous difficulties.

Daughters with such a family background are occasionally alienated from men in general, or from men who appear stereotyped, but far more commonly they are attracted to men whose behavior and attitudes are based on a rigid adherence to the male sex-role stereotype (Orlofsky, 1982). If, as commonly occurs, they marry such a man, profound sex-role strain and conflict soon develop. The husband expects his wife to conform strictly to a female sex-role stereotype. However, her gender identity is antithetical to this. But because of her impaired object relations and personal identity, she will be unable to resist his demands and expectations. To cope with the profound sex-role strain and conflict that results, she suppresses her own gender identity and comes to identify with her husband's stereotyped view of her. In terms of object relations theory, gender identity equates with her true self, and the stereotype equates with her false self.

Because she is experiencing a high level of interpersonal and intrapsychic stress, she copes by utilizing primitive psychological defense mechanisms such as splitting and projective identification. The emergence of psychological symptoms often reduces sex-role strain and conflict, stabilizing the marriage. Precisely how this occurs will be elaborated in Chapter 4.

SEX-ROLE STRAIN IN MEN

As outlined earlier in this chapter, boys who lack adequate fathering often identify with the male sex-role stereotype as an alternative to a genuine sense of personal identity. When the overall quality of parenting is poor, and object relations are impaired, the stereotype becomes consolidated as the false self. The primary identification with the mother, which represents the true self, is rigidly suppressed because it is totally incompatible with the male sex-role stereotype.

In adolescence, this pattern of events is associated with profound sex-role strain. This is commonly dealt with by seeking constant reinforcement of the male sex-role stereotype. Such behavior includes excessive involvement in "macho" sports such as football, boxing, and wrestling, or in solo activities such as bodybuilding and weight lifting. The extreme example is the gang warfare that is endemic in many large American cities and that also occurs in Canada, Australia, and England.

For a man who relies on constant external reinforcement to preserve his sex-role-stereotyped image of himself, marriage often appears to be an ideal way of achieving this.

If he marries a woman in whom both gender identity and personal identity coincide with the female sex-role stereotype, the marriage relationship may adequately reinforce his stereotyped self-image for many years. Sometimes, as the couple mature together, they are able to gradually relinquish their stereotyped relationship in favor of one based on genuine intimacy and understanding.

If, however, such a man marries a woman whose gender identity diverges markedly from the stereotype, he will experience increasing sex-role strain. Primitive defensive maneuvers based on splitting and projective identification will soon emerge. If his wife's overall psychological adjustment is superior to his own, and she remains in the marriage, then he is likely to develop psychological symptoms. If her adjustment is equal to his, or inferior, then she is likely to become the symptom bearer. Once again, the emergence of psychological symptoms reduces sex-role strain and conflict, and the marriage is stabilized. Precisely how this occurs will be illustrated and discussed in Chapters 4 and 5.

MATE SELECTION

The model outlined above applies mainly to people with substantial problems of psychological adjustment and identity formation. It assumes an assortative mating process based primarily on the marriage partners' mutual overdetermination of sex-role stereotypes. I will now outline a model of mate selection that, while directly relevant to the emergence of psychological symptoms from marital interaction, is of a more general nature. It acknowledges existing psychodynamic and sociopsychological models of marital choice, and integrates them in the context of recent research into sex roles and stereotypes.

Sex-Role Stereotyping and Mate Selection

Hitherto, theories of mate selection have been primarily clinical–psychodynamic (Ackerman, 1958; Eisenstein, 1956; Sager, 1976) or socio-psychological (Adams, 1979; Murstein, 1970). Although there is implicit reference to sex-role stereotyping in all of these theories, none have explicitly or systematically considered it as a central theme.

In Chapter 2, I offered some explanations for the apparent neglect of sex-role stereotyping by contemporary marriage therapists. In discussions with colleagues in North America, Britain, and Australia who share my interest in couples therapy, I have formed the impression that some regard the issue of sex-role stereotyping as of historical interest only. I assume that this reflects the fact that they themselves, most of their friends and colleagues, and many of their clients, have transcended sex-role stereotypes in their personal lives. They therefore tend to believe that this is true of society in general.

Contemporary research reveals that such a belief is false. I shall review shortly a number of papers that suggest that although over the past 10 years or so there has developed a more general awareness of sex-role stereotyping, this has yet to be translated into a substantial, overall change in attitudes and behavior. What has been achieved is primarily a marked increase in sex-role strain and conflict in society at large.

In writing this book, I have emphasized a historical perspective, and nowhere is this more important than in a consideration of sex roles and stereotypes. In her incisive and readable book, Oakley (1972) has shown clearly that attention to sex-role issues in English-speaking societies has occurred in cycles: "It seems to be revived at times when the existing roles and statuses of male and female are changing, and three periods in particular stand out: the century from about 1540 to 1640, the Victorian era, and the present time. In the last two, distinct 'women's movements' have arisen, and their existence suggests that, since the seventeenth century and the growth of industrialization, basic issues to do with the role of women have never been solved" (p. 9).

This historical perspective is a warning to those who believe that the battle against sex-role stereotyping and its destructive effects has been won. In truth, it is still in a very early stage. What gains have been achieved so far might yet be reversed.

On the basis of an exhaustive study that included the latest research then available, Prochaska and Prochaska (1978) discussed the *companionship* form of marriage as an alternative to a sex-role stereotyped basis for mate selection. They conclude: "If dating and mating selection is still restricted by such traditional variables, including such a non-functional variable as height, it can be expected that the transition to a companionship form of marriage in our society will continue to be only a slowly evolving phenomenon. In fact . . . there are little if any data to support the claim that a significant proportion of American marriages have progressed into egalitarian relationships. At this stage in our history, the companionship marriage is more an ideal than a reality" (p. 9).

If there has been a significant move away from sex-role-stereotyped attitudes to marriage in the 7 years since these views were espoused, it would be most visible in college students, since they represent a highly educated population that is actively involved in dating and courtship activities.

Robson (1983) asked 140 college students aged 18 or 19 to complete the Tamashiro Marriage Concepts Questionnaire. This categorizes subjects as falling into one of four developmental stages: magical, idealized conventional, individualistic, and affirmational. In the least mature magical stage, "the individual has a fairy-tale view of marriage. Married persons are seen as living together happily and sharing their love, with neither spouse having any flaws or faults" (p. 647). At the idealized conventional stage, marriage is thought of in terms of strict, conventional rules.

An astonishing 67% of the college students were still in the magical stage, with 29% in the idealized conventional stage. Only 4% were in stage 3, and none in the mature stage 4. Ninety percent planned to marry and have children.

These findings suggest that the power of idealized and stereotyped attitudes to influence choice of marriage partner is still overwhelmingly strong in late adolescence. This interpretation is supported by the fact that those students whose parents had divorced reported marriage attitudes that were just as idealized and stereotyped as those reported by students whose parents were still together. Presumably, therefore, the reality of the parents' marriage has less influence on the children's attitudes than stereotypes determined by the media and peer pressure.

That these findings are not atypical is suggested by Goldman and Goldman's (1983) study of 838 children aged 5 to 15 in North America, Australia, England, and Sweden. They concluded: "Overall, children view adults in terms of traditional sex roles. . . . The fact that this study was cross-national and included children from Sweden, which has had compulsory sex and human education in schools for some three decades, the similarity of responses in the four countries (including three without compulsory sex education) does not auger well for enlightened approaches to sex roles and human relationships in their various forms. Present societal sex roles appear to be of stronger import than the content of educational courses aimed at lessening such distinctions" (p. 811).

Further evidence for the pervasive and powerful effects of sex-role stereotyping on the attitudes of adolescents toward marriage and family life comes from a major study by McDermott *et al.* (1983). They examined attitudes toward family values in 158 Caucasian and Japanese-American families, finding that "differences were striking between adolescent boys and girls, regardless of ethnicity: girls valued family affiliation, closeness, and emotional expression significantly more highly than did boys" (p. 1318).

McDermott *et al.* suggested that the concept of separation–individuation as the major goal of adolescence needed to be reexamined. Too much emphasis on individual achievement and separation from the family may cause an insensitivity to the feelings of others, with subsequent problems of personal adjustment. In contrast, "individuals who retain strong ties and an orientation to relationships may be more, rather than less, mature than those who separate completely from the family" (p. 1321).

Sex-Role Stereotyping, Marital Intimacy, and Psychological Symptoms

There is evidence that sex-role-stereotyped attitudes in husbands militate strongly against emotional intimacy within marriage (Parelman, 1983). In contrast, the likelihood of emotional intimacy is greatest if both marriage partners are androgynous.

It is well established that men who adhere to a male sex-role stereotype generally find difficulty in talking about feelings of vulnerability and dependency and other intimate aspects of themselves (Lombardo & Lavine, 1981). This makes honest, open communication within marriage very difficult. Since a rigid adherence to a male sex-role stereotype also increases the likelihood of sex-role strain and conflict, men with strongly stereotyped attitudes bring a double problem into their marriage: They maximize the likelihood of sex-role problems and minimize the likelihood of their resolution through mutual discussion between husband and wife.

The male and female sex-role stereotypes reflect fundamentally different attitudes and approaches to solving interpersonal problems (Ickes & Barnes, 1978). Thus, where both marriage partners adhere rigidly to sex-role stereo-types, the likelihood of shared, constructive problem-solving activity is minimized. A persisting failure to discuss or resolve problems, particularly in a domestic context, will inevitably reduce or inhibit emotional intimacy.

Thus, rigid sex-role stereotyping is a powerful inhibitor of emotional intimacy within marriage, both directly because it impedes communication and shared problem solving, and indirectly because it maximizes sex-role strain and conflict.

In a landmark study, Henderson, Byrne, and Duncan-Jones (1981) examined the influence of social relationships on the development of psychological symptoms. They studied an initial community sample of nearly 800 people and examined the personal and interpersonal factors associated with the development of significant psychological symptoms over the subsequent 12 months. Their study is exceptional for its methodological rigor.

The authors found that the perceived adequacy of social relationships was a powerful predictor of the emergence of psychological symptoms, but only when combined with adversity. An individual was likely to develop major psychological symptoms if he or she experienced significant problems and lacked a relationship that was perceived as adequately supportive or intimate.

It is noteworthy that the *extent* of the individual's social network was unimportant: It was the perceived quality of relationships that predicted the likelihood of psychological symptoms. The measure of adversity used in the study was particularly sensitive to domestic problems. Of the 73 items (excluding financial problems, which were dealt with in 5 separate items), 36 referred to marital and family matters. Thus, in the case of married people not working outside the home, the measure of adversity largely reflected the presence or absence of marital and family problems.

The findings of Henderson *et al.* are strikingly consistent with those of an earlier landmark study by Brown and Harris (1978). These authors studied the social origins of depression in a large population of women. They found that women who had an intimate, supportive relationship with their husbands or boyfriends were protected from depression even if they had been subjected to major stressors. Subsequent research has yielded a striking consensus that the level of intimacy within the marital relationship is a central factor in determining whether or not the wife develops symptoms (Bebbington, Sturt, Tennant, & Hurry, 1984; D'Arcy, 1982).

Thus, there is now considerable evidence that the lack of an intimate, supportive marital relationship is a major contributor to the development of psychological symptoms. If we accept that sex-role stereotyping is a potent obstacle to emotional intimacy within marriage, then the following hypothesis can be generated: *The likelihood of psychological symptoms emerging in a married person is directly related to the extent and rigidity of sex-role stereotyping within the marriage.*

Although systematic, methodologically sound research in this area is embryonic, there is already some empirical support for this hypothesis (Elpern & Karp, 1984; Tinsley *et al.* 1984). Sex-role stereotypes and related role strain appear to be particularly potent contributors to psychological symptoms when associated with powerlessness (Horwitz, 1982). In contrast, androgyny may protect against the development of psychological symptoms in married women "as a foundation for or facilitator of positive coping behaviours, which in turn minimize the degree of distress experienced" (Patterson & McCubbin, 1984, p. 102).

However, a rigid adherence to sex-role stereotypes is not the only obstacle to marital intimacy. Personality factors are equally important, and will be considered in later chapters.

Dating and Courtship as Preparation for Marriage

Once it is accepted that attempted adherence to rigid sex-role stereotypes within marriage is a potent contributor to sex-role strain and conflict, and hence to the development of psychological symptoms in one or both partners, it becomes clear that a nonstereotyped marriage relationship is likely to protect against psychological symptoms. If this is so, then ideally the dating and courtship process should facilitate the modification of those stereotyped attitudes to marriage that research has shown to be very widely held by adolescents.

However, dating is an essentially competitive process, at least in North America (Williamson, 1972). Choice of mate is generally based on the idea of obtaining the best partner available. As we have seen, the criteria in late adolescence for optimal mate choice are determined almost entirely by sex-role stereotypes. The competitive nature of dating, in the context of potent media and peer pressure, serves to reinforce and perpetuate stereotypical mate ideals rather than attenuate them.

Dating is undertaken initially as a risky foray from the safety of a same-sex peer group. The dating partners then report their experiences to their peers, often adding material to impress. Adolescents with a strong need for peer support and approval will tend to focus on the stereotyped aspects of their dating experiences, and will tend to select and maintain dating partners on the basis of sex-role stereotypes. Those with a more clearly defined sense of identity and individuality are more likely to reject stereotypes and instead search for genuine intimacy and understanding within an egalitarian or companionship-oriented relationship.

As adolescents' social groups form and reform, they come to reflect sex-role-stereotyped themes to a greater or lesser degree. That minority of couples and individuals who have embarked on a search for genuine intimacy, sharing, and understanding will tend to mix with similar people. Such social groups enhance the opportunity for departure from sex-role stereotyping, since members can learn from each other and give each other support and encouragement. In contrast, that majority of individuals and couples who seek, consciously or unconsciously, to preserve stereotyped ideas about male–female relationships tend to mix socially with others having a similar outlook, so that stereotypes are reinforced and perpetuated.

Clearly, dating that increases the capacity of those involved to relate in an open, honest, nonexploitative manner to the opposite sex is a useful preparation for marriage. During the dating phase of their lives, people who experience dating as an opportunity to enrich their understanding of opposite-sex peers are also likely to acquire a clearer picture of themselves as individuals in a complex, competitive social arena. They will learn more about their personal strengths and weaknesses. Concurrently, they will clarify or develop their occupational status and potential. They will adapt their recreational, sporting, and leisure interests to those of their regular dating partners, thereby learning about the give-and-take that is essential for a harmonious relationship.

Perhaps most important, they will acquire a fairly accurate judgement of their status in the marriage market. Their physical attractiveness and their capacity to relate to, empathize with, amuse, entertain, and impress members of the opposite sex will be fairly well established. Their ambitions, character, personality, and their socioeconomic status and potential will become more adequately defined. Thus, in their early 20s, they will be in a relatively good position to select a marriage partner on the basis of mutual respect and understanding, broadly defined aspirations, interests and personal philosophies, and an awareness of the need for empathy and flexibility in their marriage relationship.

In contrast, those who have had their stereotyped attitudes to the opposite sex reinforced and consolidated by their dating experiences will be handicapped in their search for genuine marital harmony. Since the stereotype obscures the individual, those within highly stereotyped relationships cannot achieve genuine intimacy and sharing until their stereotyped images of each other have been replaced by pictures of real people.

Those who have avoided or been deprived of the opportunity of dating will also be disadvantaged in their search for a compatible marriage partner. Although they may not always have strongly stereotyped views of the opposite sex, they may instead be almost completely ignorant of gender issues. They bring this ignorance, often combined with misconceptions and idiosyncratic fantasies, into their search for an ideal marriage partner. This makes the fulfillment of their search for true marital harmony as improbable as that of the man or woman who seeks a marriage relationship based on stereotyped ideas of the opposite sex.

THE COURTSHIP PROCESS

The intricacies of the courtship process have been extensively studied by the sociologist Bernard Murstein (1970). Although he is but one of many original and thought-provoking contributors to this field, his work is particularly relevant to the relationship between marriage and mental illness.

Murstein suggests that young adults possess an *ideal self*, which is an image of how they would like to be; and an *actual self*, which is an image of how they see themselves in reality. In well-adjusted young adults, the ideal and actual selves are not only very similar, but are determined mainly by the conventions of society. Although Murstein does not suggest it himself, recent research has suggested that images of the ideal self are strongly influenced by sex-role stereotypes (Ruble, 1983). Murstein has shown that young adults initiate and maintain courtships primarily with those who have attitudes and personal adjustment levels similar to their own; as courtship progresses, the partners' attitudes become increasingly similar, and they become more accurate at predicting each other's views in certain areas.

Poor adjustment and psychological problems and symptoms are strongly associated with a large discrepancy between actual self and ideal self. Although poorly adjusted young adults are often able to initiate dating relationships with well-adjusted peers, such relationships rarely proceed to the courtship stage. According to Murstein, this is primarily because the rewards of such a relationship for a well-adjusted person are less than the costs of maintaining it. Thus, the well-adjusted young adult will disengage early from a relationship with a poorly adjusted dating partner, and seek one who is better adjusted. The effect of this on the abandoned, poorly adjusted partner is to lower even further his or her self-confidence and to increase the gap between ideal and actual self.

Thus, the poorly adjusted young adult becomes the victim of a vicious cycle: Repeated rejection by dating partners of superior psychological adjustment leads to a progressive lowering of self-confidence and self-esteem, and to an increasing gap between the ideal self and the actual self. As a result, the ideal self, or sex-role stereotype, is increasingly overvalued. Similarly, sex-role-stereotyped attributes become overvalued as criteria for the ideal mate.

Ultimately, dating may cease altogether, or be replaced by brief, impersonal sexual encounters. Alternatively, the poorly adjusted young adult may settle for a regular dating partner of similar adjustment, even though such a partner, on objective criteria, falls short of the stereotyped ideal. Murstein has provided considerable evidence for this process: For example, he showed that courting couples made good progress in their courtship only if they scored at similar levels on a questionnaire measure of psychological adjustment.

Clearly, the competitive nature of dating makes it likely that those with poor psychological adjustment will come to progressively overvalue sex-role stereotypes as a basis for mate selection.

COURTSHIP AND INTIMACY

An ideal courtship allows the couple to reach a stage of genuine intimacy in their relationship: Ideas, feelings, fantasies, hopes, dreams, and expectations are shared freely and openly, so that the couple can make a reasonably accurate prediction of their long-term compatibility in marriage. Murstein's data suggest that this occurs to only a very modest extent during the average courtship. For example, the men in his study got no better at estimating their partners actual selves as courtship progressed, although they became more accurate at estimating their partner's ideal selves. Women, however, increased their accuracy in estimating their partners' ideal and actual selves. Furthermore, throughout the courtship process, both partners tended to overestimate each other's actual selves; in other words, they made more favorable judgments about each other than they did about themselves. Men made more errors of this kind than did women.

This mutual idealization is central to the courtship process, since it equates with the sense of being "in love." However, it requires mutual deceit and pretence in that the idealization is based on both partners' obscuring or denying personal idiosyncrasies and attitudes that are incompatible with the sex-role-stereotyped ideal.

That these pressures toward deceit create significant problems even in well-educated, sophisticated young adults is clearly demonstrated in a study by Davidson (1981), who examined the conflict generated by the contrast between traditional gender stereotypes and the emergent feminist perspective. She concluded that "men think women demand that men be active; women think men demand that women be passive. Both claim an internal desire to change and yet they feel reciprocal pressures to behave in traditional ways. The unfortunate irony is that men and women force each other into pressures and pretence, thus perpetuating stereotypical roles and the 'myths' of gender differences" (p. 346).

Thus, even well-adjusted young adults enter marriage with substantial obstacles to mutual honesty and intimacy. Because the idea of being "in love" is based on mutual idealization and denial of nonstereotyped personal attributes, romantic love is in itself a barrier to genuine intimacy and mutual understanding. This is particularly so when romantic love is overvalued by one or both partners, or regarded as the main or sole basis for the marriage.

SUMMARY AND CONCLUSIONS

I have reviewed evidence showing that a great majority of contemporary adolescents and young adults have highly stereotyped attitudes toward marriage and mate selection. The competitive nature of dating makes it difficult to relinquish these stereotypes, and many young adults marry with relatively stereotyped attitudes and expectations.

Given this high level of stereotyping and rapidly changing social expectations about sex roles, sex-role strain and conflict are almost inevitable early in the course of marriage. These strains and conflicts increase the chance of psychological symptoms emerging in the more vulnerable of the two marriage partners. However, the likelihood of this is reduced if the couple have a mutually supportive, emotionally intimate relationship with good communication between them. Although rigid adherence to a sex-role stereotype, particularly in the husband, is a potent obstacle to shared communication and problem solving, personality factors are equally important in this respect. Where negative personality factors and rigid adherence to stereotyping coincide, the likelihood of effective communication and problem solving within marriage is remote.

Persisting failure to resolve sex-role strain and conflict often leads to psychological symptom formation, although the precise nature of the symptoms is determined primarily by genetic, constitutional, and childhood learning factors. Alternatively, the marriage may be disrupted by separations or end in divorce.

Those with poor object relations and related types of psychological maladjustment are particularly likely to overvalue sex-role stereotypes in mate selection, and to cling to them rigidly within marriage. Assortative mating markedly increases the likelihood of marriage between two people who overvalue sex-role stereotypes. Conversely, marriage between individuals with a nonstereotyped perspective occurs more often than would be expected by chance (Orlofsky, 1982).

In a marriage between two people with severely impaired object relations, primitive psychological mechanisms such as splitting and projective identification combine with sex-role stereotyping to bind the marriage partners together. This process is often consolidated by the development of psychological symptoms in one partner. Precisely how this occurs will be elaborated in Chapters 4 and 5.

Future research in the area of sex roles will become increasingly difficult as a general awareness emerges about the social undesirability of publicly endorsing sex-role-stereotyped attitudes. As a result, there will be an increasing tendency for research subjects to "fake good," and report untruthful attitudes to sex roles. Thus, research findings of nonstereotyped attitudes need to be regarded with circumspection unless the influence of social desirability (and unconscious denial) on responses is adequately allowed for.

CHAPTER FOUR

Psychological Symptoms Resulting from Marital Interaction

The emergence of psychological symptoms as a result of marital interaction is by no means confined to marriages based on matching psychopathology or overt maladjustment in one or both partners. It may occur when seemingly well-adjusted people choose marriage partners in response to the competitive nature of modern society. As a result of pressures to excel in everything they do, many people of average or superior social adjustment choose their marriage partners as if they were taking part in a competition. In their anxiety to secure a mate of maximum social appeal, they overvalue criteria such as physical attractiveness, popularity, and apparent conformity to stereotypes about desirable personality traits and attributes. When, after marriage, the genuine personal attributes and aspirations of each partner are revealed, these may depart radically from stereotyped ideals. Failure of the couple to negotiate this early challenge to their marital harmony can lead to the development of psychological symptoms in one or both partners.

Thus, marriages that contribute to the development or maintenance of psychological symptoms in one or both partners fall into two broad categories which I have termed "status-oriented" and "symbiotic." Status-oriented marriages are contracted by people with adequate or superior premarital social adjustment: Symptoms emerge from the failure of the couple to deal with personal and cultural pressures to compete and to excel. Symbiotic marriages are contracted by people with poor premarital adjustment: Symptoms emerge when the partners fail to obtain from each other the gratification of the conscious or unconscious needs that initially determined their mutual attraction.

Creating these two broad categories of status-oriented and symbiotic marriage facilitates description and analysis of this complex area. In reality, there is a considerable overlap between the two categories, and the relevant population characteristics are distributed in a range of modes in addition to the categorical (bipolar).

STATUS-ORIENTED MARRIAGES

Modern North American society is intensely competitive, based as it is on the idea of free enterprise and the equal opportunity of all to achieve wealth through personal endeavor. A person's value in modern America is determined largely by his or her occupational or economic status. This is equally true of Australia and Canada, although the situation in the United Kingdom is somewhat different. Here, traditional class structures still have considerable influence on social status. Thus, an impoverished aristocrat has very high social status whereas a successful entrepreneur of working-class origin might enjoy little social status in spite of obvious wealth. Indeed, such a man would often be sneered at as *nouveau riche* by the upper middle class and envied and resented by the working class.

People who describe themselves as working class still comprise a great majority of the population in the United Kingdom. Most of them identify strongly with working-class values that have evolved and consolidated over many centuries; they reject middle-class values as snobbish or inflated. Thus, social pressures toward upward mobility and the creation of personal wealth are somewhat less than in America, and British society as a whole is less competitive. Although excellence is highly regarded and sought after by the British, it is not directly linked with social and economic status, but valued for its own sake. However, the situation is rapidly changing in Britain, with increasing numbers of Britons, aspiring toward middle-class status. Inevitably this will increase the overall level of competitiveness in society and create social problems similar to those that are now widespread in North America and Australia.

Competitive Husbands

In North America and Australia, to be a well-adjusted young man is to be competitive in almost every aspect of social, occupational, and sporting activity. The personal and societal benefits of this competitiveness are unarguable. The powerful incentive to function at optimal effectiveness stimulates young men toward excellence, the achievement of which brings a sense of personal fulfillment as well as improved socioeconomic status. Society as a whole benefits enormously from the wealth created by successful businessmen, and from the creative endeavors of scientists and others who are motivated by a competitive drive toward excellence. However, an excessive or unmodified tendency to compete may have an adverse effect on personal relationships in general, and on marriage in particular.

The average age at which men marry in English-speaking countries is now about 25. By the age of 30, most married men have at least two young children, and a substantial mortgage on a house. Competitive pressures dictate that the house must be the best that the couple can afford, so that the mortgage will be the largest that their income can accommodate. However, they will probably be relying on a single income, since traditionally the presence of infants or very young children prevents the wife from working.

To the financial burdens of a large mortgage and dependent wife and children will be added those of furnishing the home and running one or two cars. Once again, competitive pressures demand the highest possible standards of furniture and general decor in the home, and the most expensive vehicles compatible with the family income. It is no coincidence that the main thrust of advertising is directed toward young married couples, for they are at a very critical and sensitive time of their lives, and particularly vulnerable to outside influences. They are at the beginning of the great adventure of marriage and family life, and their attitudes toward it will be strongly influenced by the romanticized, stereotyped hopes and expectations that advertising promotes. Combined with the general competitiveness of society, these idealized hopes and dreams make the couple highly susceptible to media, advertising, and peer pressures to live at the very limits of their income.

The power of the media to influence social attitudes and behavior was demonstrated in a study by Mamay and Simpson (1981). These authors analyzed, in the context of the viewing audience, 207 television commercials that depicted female roles. They concluded:

> The Black civil rights movement led to rapid racial desegregation of television commercials, but the woman's movement has not had a comparable effect. Women are less liberated, and sex roles more differentiated, in the commercials than in real life. . . . The technological rationalization of housekeeping . . . casts men in the role of housekeeping experts because of the stereotypes that men are better able then women to understand mechanics and science. . . . Commercials blend two images that lower the woman's status to that of menial labourer and servant: (1) housekeeping as a complex technological process with men as the experts, and (2) children as self-centered consumers. . . . These television commercials are intended to sell products, not describe social life. But it is likely that they help to perpetuate stereotypes of "woman's place" (p. 1231).

Reciprocally, these media pressures reinforce the male sex-role stereotype. Early in his marriage, the husband is under enormous pressure to earn as much as possible. Whether he is a salesman, a factory worker, a professional man, a blue-collar worker, or running his own business, he will be compelled to work extra hours in order to maximize his income. He may have to make career decisions based purely on short-term earning power, perhaps sacrificing longer-term career prospects and thereby creating within himself a sense of conflict over meeting his own personal needs, hopes, and expectations as opposed to the economic needs of his family.

If he is exceptionally competitive and ambitious, he may take on extra work commitments that do not immediately improve his income, but that lay the groundwork for future promotion. For similar reasons he may attend evening classes. If he has been a successful sportsman at high school or college, excellence at competitive sports will have become an important aspect of his life style and physical and emotional well-being. He will naturally seek to continue taking part in sporting activities.

All these pressures and demands upon him are taking place at a time when he is most needed at home. This adds further stress and conflict to his life, because his wife and young children will resent his lack of involvement with them, even though they may understand that his absence from them is enforced by the demands of his work. If his wife lacks the support of parents, relatives, or close friends, she will be struggling virtually alone to raise two or more young children. The relentless demands of child raising, combined with the stereotyped expectation that she keep the home and perhaps even the children in an impeccable state of order and cleanliness, may lead her to develop symptoms of depression and anxiety. This will in turn add to her husband's burden, since he will be required to help and support her in her emotionally distressed or disabled state.

Looked at objectively, modern marriage might almost be designed quite deliberately to create the maximum possible stress on young men and their wives and families. Once this is understood, it becomes possible to comprehend the very high rate of early marital breakdown. Indeed, the really astonishing fact is not that so many marriages break down in the first few years, but that so many survive.

Wives Who Compete by Proxy: Complementary Marriage

I suggested in Chapter 2 that it is only very recently that women have been confronted by the challenge of competing directly with men. Historically, women have competed directly mainly with other women, usually within hierarchical social structures that prevented or defused extremes of open conflict or rivalry. These traditional social structures were largely destroyed by the Industrial Revolution, which rapidly created a new, urban society. As a result, men and women were brought together in overcrowded cities that lacked a social or geographical framework for structuring relationships between the sexes. To protect themselves from male aggression, married women collectively identified with men's idealized image of them as dependent, unassertive, homely, and nurturing. From this emerged an increasing tendency for men and women alike to accept a sex-role-stereotyped view of male–female relationships.

English-speaking countries have now been predominantly urban for over a century. Gradually, nonstereotyped ideas of male–female relationships are emerging and consolidating. However, the fiercely competitive nature of modern society is hindering the development of nonstereotyped alternatives, because competitiveness between men strongly reinforces the male sex-role stereotype, and conversely. As we have seen, many women still identify with the stereotypes originally imposed upon them by men.

The female sex-role stereotype forbids competitive, aggressive behavior and attitudes. It assumes that women lack these attributes. In reality, most women have strong aggressive and competitive drives that they habitually repress, suppress, or deny in the face of matching drives in men that are even stronger. This means that married women often can find only an indirect expression of their aggressive and competitive drives. They achieve this by identifying unconsciously with these attributes in men. In this way, such women express their aggressive and competitive drives vicariously, or by proxy, through the achievements and exploits of their husbands.

This adds yet another burden to the young married man. Because high socioeconomic status symbolizes the successful expression of "male" competitiveness and aggression, his wife may strongly identify with the symbols of success. Her unconscious need to be surrounded by status symbols will be powerfully reinforced by media and advertising, generating the following tyrannical vicious cycle.

The greater the demands on the husband to earn money, the more time he will be away from home exercising his stereotyped male attributes of competitiveness and aggression. This will confine his wife increasingly to the domestic, and elevate the need for vicarious gratification of her aggressive and competitive drives through her husband's exploits and achievements. Thus, she will increasingly identify with the symbols of "male" success, placing further pressure on her husband to earn money to pay for them. Her identification with status symbols, and her husband's provision of them, will be powerfully reinforced by media and advertising pressures. Unchecked, this vicious cycle leads ultimately to the almost complete absence of the husband from a home that has become a shrine for the worship of status symbols, totally empty of the human warmth, caring, and sharing that the couple once hoped to achieve. It is this barren environment that sets the stage for the emergence of psychological symptoms in one or both partners.

The effects of this type of marriage relationship on the mental health of men was richly illustrated in a paper by Bird, Martin, and Schuham (1983), aptly titled "The Marriage of the 'Collapsible' Man of Prominence."

The study is based on 16 men who presented for psychiatric treatment in a state of acute crisis or emotional collapse. On an index of social position, these men scored at the 99.8th percentile. Five were presidents of major corporations; three were senior health professionals; two were attorneys, one of whom was a politician; and four were highly successful businessmen. Their mean annual income was higher than 99.5 percent of all U.S. wage earners, as determined by the 1980 census data. All were viewed by the community as wealthy and powerful men whose names were easily recognizable in the local media.

During initial psychiatric interviews "each was childlike, expressing profound feelings of helplessness, desperation, inadequacy and confusion. Each had undergone a depressive regression to the point where he no longer functioned in his customary role. . . . Although these patients attributed their regressive reactions to some specific stress or failure in the work situation, exploration invariably disclosed that *the reaction in each had been preceded by attenuation of his bond with his wife and a deeply rooted fear of losing her*" (p. 291; italics added).

The wives, most of whom were also interviewed in depth and took part in couples and individual therapy, were initially "realistic, poised, collected and cool to the point of being distant. . . . *They expressed interest in feminine activities* and had raised their children without major difficulty while engaging in a variety of non-domestic pursuits" (p. 292; italics added).

Without exception, the wives came from families of origin that contained little to promote self-satisfaction, pride in accomplishment, or a sense of personal strength. This led them to be unusual in their capacity for self-effacement and service in the interest of others. However: "When a wife became 'fed-up' with the constant drain of participating in a mother-child unit, she withdrew from the marital relationship and began to take part in personally gratifying activities" (p. 293).

The authors of this important paper adopt an essentially psychoanalytic view in explaining the behavior of the husbands of these women. They emphasize their excessively close attachment to their mothers, their intense need to please, and their failure to individuate because of their mothers' interference in the process of identity formation.

According to the authors, these husbands developed a powerful narcissistic identification with their mothers, and continued to see their mothers as themselves in adulthood. Because of the peripheral family position of their fathers, they did not serve as "healthy identification objects."

The husbands in this study relied heavily on denial to deal with psychological conflicts, and "tended to regress when their primary method of adaptation, a clinging attachment to their spouses, became unavailable. . . . Finally, these men could be described as somewhat effeminate in their interest patterns, an impression which fit with their activities and interests as they emerged during treatment" (p. 292).

The authors recognized the central importance of couples therapy in these cases. However, all husbands and wives were also involved in "intensive, long-term individual psychotherapy" (p. 294). The authors noted that during therapy each wife "had become 'fed-up' with their mate, each experienced a sense of guilt and was tempted to relinquish whatever gains had been made" (p. 294). In contrast, "the husbands were capable of becoming stronger and 'uncollapsible'" (p. 294).

Four of the marriages ended in divorce, and of the remaining 12 marriages, 9 were improved and 3 unchanged. In the 9 improved marriages, both spouses were improved in 7 cases. These results suggest that the effects of intensive, prolonged therapy were of limited effectiveness and perhaps destructive in some cases. A divorce rate of 25% over a year or two is much higher than would be expected by chance, and the improvement rate in the marriages that remained intact is not much greater than that reported by psychotherapy waiting-list patients who receive no active treatment.

In my view, the seemingly poor treatment outcome is attributable to the authors' adherence to a psychoanalytic model that ignores contemporary views about sex-role stereotypes and conflict. Indeed, the authors make no specific reference to sex-role issues. However, the problems of these couples appear directly related to a gross overvaluation of sex-role stereotypes. Therapy, whatever its stated aims, appears to have consolidated the husbands' stereotypes rather than attenuated them. In consequence, it created, for example, guilt in the wives about their attempts at self-determination and emergence from stereotyped marital roles.

From a sex-roles perspective, social reinforcement of stereotypes and their perpetuation through marital interaction are more potent contributors to the problems of these couples than early relationships with parents. Indeed, the credibility of a purely psychoanalytic explanation is stretched to its limts when we recall that these men are outstandingly successful in a broad social context, and show in many respects a very superior adjustment to the demands of life in contemporary America. *However, these men relied very heavily on their wives to maintain their sex-role stereotyped images of themselves, and decompensated when their wives attempted to emerge from the female sex-role stereotype.* Had therapy focused directly on sex-role issues, it may well have been much briefer and more effective.

Finally, the authors conclude that "the marital relationship of men of prominence is a key determinant of their psychological functioning, and that a breakdown in this relationship results in dire consequences not only for the husband himself, but for the community. . . . We therefore recommend that every effort be made to evaluate the spouse and the marital relationship of the man of prominence with psychiatric impairment as an integral part of his total evaluation" (p. 295).

In my view, these authors have chanced upon a marital pattern that is in fact very common, but that was brought to their attention because of its extreme nature in the couples they observed. Since this type of status-oriented marriage is characterized by an absence of direct competition between the partners, who have complementary but separate roles, I have termed it "complementary" marriage.

Women Who Compete Directly with Men: Competitive Marriage

The history, myths, and legends of English-speaking peoples are almost empty of women who competed directly and openly with men. Anglo-Saxon history and legend are made of men competing with men, in battle or in polemic. Women played essentially supporting roles.

Very recently, this has changed. As more and more women have entered the work force and achieved varied status in business, industry, the professions, and in academic life, they have increasingly come to compete with men in a direct and open manner. The central cause of this change has undoubtedly been the creation over the past 40 years of new jobs that do not require physical strength, although most are boring and repetitive. In factories other than those in traditional male-dominated industries such as automobile production, assembly lines are attended mainly by women. Routine jobs in typing pools and most secretarial and stenographic jobs are still held primarily by women, whose role is essentially that of handmaiden.

Although women's jobs in industry are generally menial, subordinate, routine, and of low status, they have nonetheless created an opportunity for women to meet together and to reconstruct the collective influence that was removed from them in the social upheaval that followed the Industrial Revolution. This, together with the economic independence that goes with employment, has enabled them to begin to challenge the stereotypes imposed upon them by men.

Unfortunately, many young women still regard employment simply as a brief interlude to be endured between high school and early marriage. As a result, their experience in the work force does not create an opportunity for their stereotypes to be significantly modified. However, increasing numbers of young women are becoming ambitious and competitive in their own right, either in high school or college or as a result of constructive and rewarding employment experiences. They have committed themselves to employment on a middle- to long-term basis rather than perceiving it as a brief, unrewarding interlude in their lives. Out of this commitment grows skill, competence, status, and increased personal self-esteem. Many job-oriented women are as dependent on their work for a sense of value and purpose in their lives as are a majority of men.

Perhaps most important, a woman's commitment to work outside the home creates the chance for her to compete directly with men. Equal-opportunity legislation has meant that very few jobs are now restricted to men, and even fewer to women. There is no more effective way of breaking down sex-role stereotypes than for a woman to demonstrate clearly and unarguably that she is equal or superior to a man in a job that, traditionally, has been within the male stronghold. Even if women do not achieve much status themselves, there are today few offices and factories of any size that are without some fairly high-status women. These successful women provide role models for ambitious, competitive women who have not yet risen far up the employment ladder.

Women who are committed to the work force face the following profound challenges when they marry and have children.

To begin with, they must decide whether or not to relinquish work in favor of child rearing. Since they are nearly always ambitious, well-organized people who set high standards for themselves in the pursuit of excellence, they bring these attitudes into child rearing. They often believe that to be excellent mothers for their young children, they must be full-time mothers. Thus, they frequently sacrifice their employment outside the home, and with it the main source of their self-esteem and personal well-being.

In sacrificing their jobs, they generally also sacrifice their social support system. In today's mobile society, comparatively few working people can preserve day-to-day access to old friendships, so that most rely heavily on friends and acquaintances made at work. Much of their leisure, social, and recreational life is therefore based on their work. The loss of this social support system when they stop work can have a devastating effect on their personal well-being.

Under normal circumstances, pregnancy and childbirth are very demanding both physically and mentally. Most women experience some "post-maternity blues", and about 20–25% experience moderate to severe depression in the year after childbirth (Watson, Elliot, Rugg, & Brough, 1984). This depression may be increased or prolonged if it is concurrent with retirement from the work force and its ensuing loss of self-esteem and social support system.

Even if they fully recover from the demands of pregnancy and childbirth and adjust to the loss of their jobs, other major problems confront them in their early child-raising years. As well-organized and energetic women, they complete their household duties in a small fraction of the time available. Because they have successfully challenged and overcome many of the constraints of sex-role stereotyping, they often find the company of other full-time mothers boring and frustrating. Their previous commitment to work has helped to expand their horizons beyond the purely domestic, and they do not wish to spend hours discussing children, husbands, and domestic matters. Thus, they cannot easily recreate a viable social network to replace the one they lost when they stopped working. In the absence of supportive parents or other relatives, they may become socially isolated, coping almost alone with boredom, frustration, and the demands of raising young children. A common result of this is the development of depression and other psychological symptoms.

Competitive Women and Sex-Role Conflict

Although there is less sex-role stereotyping in the marriages of directly competitive women than in the marriages of women who compete by proxy, it is still a major problem. Because strong commitment to work is a central theme in their lives, competitive women tend to marry men who share this attitude, and who are generally even more competitive and ambitious than they are. Such men usually deny sex-role stereotyped attitudes, but their fierce drive and ambition is often the product of powerful sex-role conditioning. Consciously, they reject attitudes based on sex-role stereotypes, but unconsciously they are wedded to a male sex-role stereotype, at least with regard to the importance of work and achievement in their lives.

Thus, even if they are genuinely sympathetic to their wives' problems in adjusting to a domestic role, they are usually too busy working to be able to give much practical help. Since they are at the early stages of their careers, or may have low-paid jobs, even very long hours may not generate sufficient income to provide for luxuries. In particular, baby-sitters may be financially beyond the couple. In the absence of friends and relatives willing to help out, this stops the wife from going out in the evenings, compounding her sense of isolation and confinement.

Gradually, competitive women in this situation come to envy and resent their husbands for the freedom and fulfillment they obtain from their work. This creates tension within the marriage that may result in the wives losing the sympathy and support of their husbands. This underlines even more strongly their lack of a social support network, and, in addition, makes them feel that their domestic role is not valued or appreciated. As a result, profound conflict occurs in these women about whether to preserve their full-time domestic role or return to the work force. This sex-role conflict may be of sufficient intensity to cause severe depression or anxiety symptoms, including panic attacks. If the symptoms become consolidated as a psychiatric disorder requiring treatment, this reinforces the patients' sense of inadequacy and powerlessness, and decreases the likelihood of early resolution of sex-role issues.

Because this type of status-oriented marriage is characterized by direct competition and conflict between the partners, I have termed it "competitive" marriage.

Young Married Women as Symptom Bearers

There is a great deal of evidence to show that young married women have a very high level of psychological symptoms and psychiatric disorder (Berg, Butler, Houston, & McGuire, 1984; Briscoe, 1982; D'Arcy, 1982). At greatest risk are married women who have young children and are unemployed because of their child-care and domestic commitments: One major survey (Tennant, Bebbington, & Hurry, 1982) found that 25% of such women had a definite psychiatric disorder, and this finding accords with those of other surveys. Over 90% of these women complained mainly of anxiety symptoms or depression, usually in admixture. Work outside the home dramatically reduced the risk of psychiatric disorder: Only 9% of women so employed had a definite psychiatric condition.

To be classified as having a definite psychiatric disorder, women must report severe, troublesome psychological symptoms. If symptoms of mental distress are included, the proportion of young, unemployed married women who report significant psychological symptoms becomes as high as 40% (Berg *et al.*, 1984). This proportion is so high that it almost defies credibility. But, because the data from the increasing number of studies in this area are based on well-designed research, they are almost certainly accurate.

Further analysis of data obtained in surveys of psychiatric disorder in the community yields a fairly clear and consistent overall picture. Lack of outside employment, the presence of young children in the home, and the absence of a close, confiding relationship with the husband are the three major risk factors in married women. Nearly half of the women who report all three risk factors have a definite psychiatric disorder.

However, as Henderson *et al.* (1981) have pointed out, the absence of a close, confiding relationship does not necessarily cause the development of psychological symptoms. It is possible, for example, that the presence of psychological symptoms causes a deterioration in the marriage relationship, so that wives feel unable to confide in their husbands. A circular relationship is perhaps most likely, with psychological symptoms reinforcing marital disharmony and marital disharmony reinforcing the symptoms, establishing a vicious cycle. However, there is evidence that the relationship between unemployment and psychological symptoms in married women is causal: Women who arrange suitable child-care and return to the work force generally report a substantial decrease in psychological symptoms. Conversely, women who reluctantly or involuntarily stop work to resume full-time child care and domestic commitments generally report an increase in psychological symptoms.

Whatever the precise factors that cause psychological symptoms in unemployed married women with young children, their husbands appear immune to them. Overall, married men have *less than one-third* of the prevalence of psychiatric disorder than married women (Tennant *et al.*, 1982). Thus, at a time when their wives are often experiencing profound psychological distress, husbands are generally enjoying good psychological health— unless they, too, are unemployed, in which case the likelihood of them developing a psychiatric disorder more than doubles.

These findings support the idea that work outside the home is the single most powerful contributor to mental health in both men and women. Young married men are protected from psychiatric disorder because they are employed. Even if their jobs are boring and routine, they are sustained by the idea of supporting a dependent family. Sex-role stereotyping supports and confirms men in their role as breadwinner, with its built-in assumptions of meaning and purpose in life. However, the same process of sex-role stereotyping creates profound conflict within married women who want to work outside the home, but who feel they should sacrifice their personal needs for the sake of children and husbands. Often, their reward for this sacrifice is to become the victims of distressing, disabling anxiety symptoms and depression that, once established, confirm them in their positions of isolation and powerlessness.

Sex-Role Conditioning in Complementary Marriages

In spite of the hidden social pressures upon them, a majority of complementary marriages survive, and many of these appear to be based on a reasonably happy and fulfilled marital relationship. In only a minority of cases do significant psychological symptoms emerge within complementary marriages. The extent of sex-role conditioning seems to be a major factor in determining whether or not this occurs. Because sex-role-stereotyped attitudes are so deeply ingrained in English-speaking society, they are transmitted unconsciously, and it is this that gives them their enormous power to influence the behavior and attitudes of children and adults alike. They are generally internalized without question and become a fundamental aspect of the growing child's personality and view of the world.

Intensive and systematic sex-role conditioning is in many ways highly adaptive to modern society. It facilitates unquestioned and persisting competitiveness in men, and powerfully reinforces nurturing behavior in women. It guides and stabilizes the conduct of the first few years of marriage: Husband and wife accept their predetermined sex roles without major conflict within or between themselves. Because their respective roles overlap so little, there are comparatively few opportunities for them to come into conflict, and the marriage is conducted reasonably harmoniously. Although the presence of very young children in the home is often demanding, restricting, and frustrating for married women, it is at the same time fulfilling because it creates the opportunity for them to exercise the fundamental nurturing aspects of their sex-role stereotypes.

Thus, symptoms tend to emerge within complementary marriages only when traditional, stereotyped sex roles are challenged or disrupted. A common cause of this is children's attendance at school: This leaves a major gap in the wife's role structure because, in reality, running a modern home efficiently is a part-time job. If excessive sex-role conditioning in childhood leads the wife, her husband, or both, to be unduly rigid in adhering to sex-role stereotypes, then the wife may be unable to adapt to the absence of her children. She may, as a result, develop psychological symptoms, usually of depression or anxiety.

However, most wives within complementary marriages adjust adequately to their children's primary-school years, often by becoming closely involved with school activities. Indeed, without the devotion of such women to a wide range of school-support activities, the functioning of many primary schools would markedly deteriorate.

In a similar fashion, the huge variety of extracurricular sporting, artistic, musical, theatrical, social, and recreational activities undertaken by the average child today would be impossible without the willingness of mothers to permit their lives to revolve around chauffering their children and generally organizing and facilitating these activities. As a return on their investment of time and effort, many mothers obtain the same vicarious sense of achievement through their children's competitive activities as they do through those of their husbands. Whether or not the children actually enjoy this enormous expenditure of their own and their mothers' energy on competitive endeavors is not always considered. Sometimes it seems that the whole complex structure of children's competitive extracurricular activities exists mainly to create meaning and purpose in the lives of underemployed mothers whose days would otherwise be barren and empty.

It is only later, when their children become relatively independent, that such women may no longer have a valid focus for their care-giving and nurturing drives, and no adequate opportunity for vicarious gratification of their competitiveness and aggression. If they are unsuccessful in finding alternatives, then they are likely to develop psychological symptoms. For example, Radloff (1980) found that depression among married women increased markedly in the 40–64-year age group only in those who remained unemployed outside the home. Since a return to the work force after child rearing is completed is a major adaptive move in many married women, it is not surprising that its absence was strongly correlated with depression. The presence or absence of children in the homes of older married women was not significantly correlated with depression, underlining the importance of the employment variable.

Age and Sex-Role Issues in Married Women

Although lack of employment outside the home appears to be a potent contributor to the development of psychological symptoms in married women of all ages, sex-role issues change as the reproductive and child-raising cycle unfolds.

In younger women with dependent children, sex-role conflict and strain are major contributors to psychological symptoms. Older women with teenage children can resume paid employment without substantial interference to their maternal roles. Those who fail to do so are often constrained by excessive sex-role conditioning, so that it is sex-role stereotyping, rather than sex-role strain or conflict that contributes to their adjustment failure and the subsequent emergence of psychological symptoms.

This pattern of events may be largely attributable to generational differences. Married women now in their 40s and 50s were exposed to more rigid sex-role conditioning than women now in their 20s and 30s. When the present generation of young mothers enters its mature years, it is likely to be less constrained by sex-role stereotypes than the previous generation. This should progressively reduce the incidence of psychological symptoms in older married women. However, this decrease may be outweighed by an increased incidence of symptoms in younger married women as they grapple with endemic sex-role strain and conflict.

SYMBIOTIC MARRIAGES

Up to this point, this chapter has focused primarily on social factors relevant to the formation of psychological symptoms in married people. The remainder of the chapter will focus mainly on psychological and interpersonal factors.

In discussing the marriages of those with major problems of social and personal adjustment, which I have termed "symbiotic marriages," I will rely primarily on the modified object relations model outlined in Chapter 3.

Projective Identification

Central to an object relations perspective on pathological interaction within marriage is the concept of "projective identification," first named by Melanie Klein in 1946 (Zinner & Shapiro, 1972). Since then, the phenomenon has been repeatedly described by marital and family therapists with a wide range of theoretical perspectives. Its essence has been admirably summarized by Zinner and Shapiro (1972):

> (1) The subject perceives the object *as if* the object contained elements of the subject's personality, (2) the subject can evoke behaviours or feelings in the object that conform with the subject's perceptions, (3) the subject can experience vicariously the activities and feelings of the object, (4) participants in close relationships are often in collusion with one another to sustain mutual projections, i.e. to support one another's defensive operations and to provide experiences through which the other can participate vicariously. (p. 525)

Zinner and Schapiro emphasize first, that the subject interacts with the projected part of himself or herself in the object as if he or she had in fact *internalized* the self-part; and, second, that *active efforts* must be made by the projecting subject to involve the recipient object as a collusive partner in conforming to the way in which he or she is perceived by the subject.

Dicks (1963) has suggested that, paradoxically, many marriages based on projective identification continue because of the partners' drive toward personal growth and integration. Such marriages are contracted because of each partner's unconscious wish to integrate their lost or projected parts by finding them in the other partner. However, this wish is countered by an equally powerful unconscious wish to preserve a collusive, mutual defense against the painful process of personal integration and individuation.

Ultimately, the full richness and complexity of marriages that are sustained by projective identification can be understood only in a clinical context. Thus, the next section of this chapter is based on a detailed description and analysis of original case material.

Case 1: "Machismo Unmasked"

The case of Joseph and Rachel illustrates a marriage in which the husband's sense of personal identity was based on a male sex-role stereotype, constantly reinforced by his wife's dependency of him.

JOSEPH

Joseph, age 35, came from a very disturbed family background. His father had been incarcerated in a psychiatric hospital after attempting to strangle Joseph's mother when Joseph was aged 3. The family had not seen him since. It appeared that Joseph's father had suffered from a form of schizophrenic disorder and had lost touch with reality at the time he attempted to strangle his wife.

Joseph was raised by his mother and his brother, who was 12 years his senior. He had no other siblings and his mother did not remarry. Family relationships were characterized by extreme ambivalence. Joseph's mother and his brother alternated between extreme aggressiveness and gross oversolicitude toward each other, and they both related to Joseph in a similar way. Thus, Joseph internalized a confusing mixture of positive and strongly negative attributes from his mother and brother.

A poor student, he left school at 15 and obtained employment as a construction worker. His social life revolved entirely around drinking in the company of unskilled laborers like himself, and he took great pride in his capacity to drink large amounts of beer, claiming a personal record of 30 pints in one day. He hated spending any time on his own, and entirely avoided introspection. His view of himself coincided with a crude male sex-role stereotype that was reinforced by his drinking companions, his chronic gambling, and the macho ethos of the construction industry. Beyond the stereotype he had no sense of personal identity whatsoever.

When sober, he was very quiet and reserved, and could be extremely charming. Although good looking and attractive, he had formed no serious sexual relationships with women up until the time he met Rachel. They married, after a brief courtship, when he was 23 and she somewhat older.

RACHEL

Rachel's father had died of cancer at the age of 52 when she was 20. He was a strikingly quiet and withdrawn man with whom Rachel had never had a close relationship. In contrast, Rachel's mother was noisy, garrulous, aggressive, intrusive, and dominating. Rachel recalled no gestures or words of affection from her mother throughout her childhood, but she had vivid memories of episodes during which her mother vilified and humiliated her without apparent justification. Although her father, even if present, was too emotionally withdrawn to offer her sympathy and understanding at these or other times, he was never aggressive toward her. Thus, she came to value him greatly as a source of passive reassurance and comfort.

When her father died, Rachel was entirely unable to mourn his death. Her capacity to experience and express emotions had been powerfully inhibited by her mother's aggressive domination of her, and she had never learned about the normal, spontaneous expression of grief from her family or others. Thus, she suppressed, repressed, and denied all her feelings of sadness and anger about her father's premature death.

Rachel's personal adjustment before her father's death was characterized by poor individuation and autonomy and a powerful, ambivalent identification with her mother. His death consolidated this pattern of maladjustment. Rachel, therefore, felt unable to manage on her own, and continued to live with her dominating mother, whose behavior toward Rachel became even worse after her husband's death.

THE MARRIAGE

Rachel met Joseph at a local party. His quiet, reserved behavior and certain mannerisms were strikingly reminiscent of Rachel's father, although she did not recognize this at a conscious level. Instead, she experienced an immediate and powerful attraction toward Joseph who, in response to Rachel's obvious interest in him, remained uncharacteristically sober, finally plucking up the courage to ask her out.

During their brief courtship, Joseph was a model of charm and gentlemanly behavior. So strongly attracted to him was Rachel that she entirely overlooked his very limited conversation and rather unsavory friends. Joseph in turn was so elevated by Rachel's attention—she was a very attractive woman—that he cut down his drinking and gambling and no longer sought out the company of his barroom companions.

Their marriage was hastened by Rachel's strong desire to get away from her mother. Predictably, the marriage was disastrous from the honeymoon on. Joseph was incapably drunk on the wedding night, so that consummation did not occur. Even when sober, Joseph's sexual approaches were fumbling and inept, matching Rachel's almost total ignorance of sexual matters. They never discussed these sexual difficulties, and sexual intercourse between them remained an infrequent and unsatisfactory event.

A few months after the honeymoon, Joseph's behavior changed dramatically. He insisted that Rachel stop her work as a sales assistant in order to be a full-time housewife. So uncharacteristically forceful and aggressive was

Joseph in his views on this, that Rachel reluctantly agreed to his demands. Soon after she stopped work, Joseph began to accuse her of infidelity: At this stage, sexual activity between them was negligible because of Joseph's heavy drinking and Rachel's increasing hostility toward him. Joseph would shout: "If you're not having sex with me you must be having it with someone else," and fierce arguments would occur when Rachel denied his allegations.

Joseph began coming home from work at odd times to "check up" on Rachel. If she was out, he would cross-examine her intensively on her return. Any inconsistency in her account was met by his angry accusations of her unfaithfulness. In reality, she had no inclination toward sexual infidelity, and was never actually unfaithful to her husband. Nonetheless, his accusations became more frequent and intense, and on several occasions he struck her during related arguments.

Because of her very low self-esteem, and her belief that she could not manage alone, Rachel endured Joseph's increasingly brutal and aggressive behavior toward her. She coped by becoming housebound, unable to travel more than a few hundred yards from home unless accompanied either by her mother or by Joseph himself. If she attempted longer journeys alone, she developed acute anxiety symptoms and panic attacks. Although inconvenienced by Rachel's housebound state, Joseph welcomed it as confirmation of his view that married women belonged "at the kitchen sink" and were invariably "up to no good" if out alone. Most important, once Rachel was virtually housebound, Joseph was protected from his fears that she might, during her journeys alone, meet someone better able than he was to gratify her sexual and emotional needs.

Over the next two years, Rachel bore two daughters to Joseph. This consolidated her position as a virtual prisoner within the home and the marriage. She ceased to fantasize about escaping from Joseph's influence: Doubting her ability to manage alone, she believed that the chances of surviving independently while burdened with two infant daughters were even more remote. Thus, she reluctantly accepted her fate. Joseph's brutality and aggression to her were kept at bay as long as she remained housebound and willing to accommodate his every wish. In fact, she did not see a great deal of him, since he invariably went drinking or gambling after work and at weekends with his fellow workers and local friends. His adjustment still relied on a total identification with a crude male sex-role stereotype that was reinforced by Rachel's complete dependency on him—a dependency that Joseph himself had created.

When her daughters were aged 9 and 10, Rachel found the courage to seek professional help for her problems. She had at last come to believe that she could survive without Joseph, mainly because her daughters were now old enough to offer her practical help, support, and encouragement.

By the time she came to see me, Rachel had been diagnosed as severely agoraphobic, a label that she had in fact applied to herself several years earlier after reading an informative article in a women's journal. She had received extensive drug treatment for this condition, to no avail. By blaming her housebound state on an illness, she had been able to overlook Joseph's contribution to her condition; this helped to keep her anger and frustration toward him at manageable levels. Thus, she neglected to inform me at first of Joseph's abnormal jealousy and his subjugation of her. Instead, she emphasized her love for him.

I interviewed Rachel and Joseph at some length, both as a couple and individually, and explained in detail my approach to the treatment of agoraphobia. This involved assembling a group of five or six people with agoraphobia and encouraging their shared attempts at overcoming their fears. Much emphasis was placed on groups traveling and shopping together, since this created the opportunity for them to confront their fears in real life. Both Rachel and Joseph agreed that this approach made sense, even though it was extremely challenging.

Rachel responded very well to treatment. She particularly valued the chance of mixing with others who had symptoms similar to her own, and with whom she could share the task of overcoming long-standing and disabling fears. The friendships she made in the group sustained her not only during therapy, but afterward, since she maintained contact with several group members. This provided both an incentive and a supportive structure for maintaining and increasing the gains she had made during therapy. Within a month of starting treatment, Rachel was virtually free of agoraphobia and felt more confident about herself than for many years.

The effect on Joseph of these changes in Rachel was dramatic. Instead of reacting in a positive way to Rachel's improvement, he became anxious and irritable. He tried in various ways to sabotage her treatment, but, with the support of the group, she was able to continue. When it became clear that Rachel was determined to overcome her fears, Joseph became increasingly agitated, and suddenly, in the middle of one night, he became acutely psychotic, losing touch with reality. He jumped out of bed and began running about the house, raving about the Mafia, whom he said were, among other things, going to cut off his arms. He kept this up for over an hour, searching in cupboards and in bushes outside for tape recorders and other evidence of a plot against his life. Rachel was able to reassure him enough to get him back to bed, exhausted, in the early hours of the morning.

The next day, Rachel took Joseph to their family doctor, who started treatment with major tranquilizers and referred Joseph to a local psychiatrist. Gradually he settled down, but for several months he continued to believe there was a Mafia conspiracy against him. He frequently heard voices, and refused to eat certain foods because he believed they were poisoned. One year after Rachel's recovery, Joseph himself had virtually recovered, and had resumed his previous life-style based largely on a crude male sex-role stereotype. However, he felt increasing dissatisfaction with this, and began to search for new interests and companions of a less stereotyped nature.

COMMENT

This case richly demonstrates the interaction between projective identification and sex-role stereotyping.

Rachel had denied and "split off" the assertive, independent "masculine" part of herself as a means of adapting to her mother's attempts at total domination and control of her. Her view of men was based on an idealization of the male sex-role stereotype, and she felt intensely attracted to Joseph as the epitome of this. Once married, she projected the denied "masculine" aspects of herself onto Joseph and obtained vicarious gratification through his stereotyped enactment of them. At a conscious level, when Joseph was not mistreating her, she either felt "in love" with him, or sought to nurture him.

Joseph had split off the "feminine" aspects of himself, which were based on his identification with his mother. He projected these, representing the "bad object," onto Rachel, dominating, controlling and vilifying her as the container thereof. Particularly noteworthy are his constant accusations of infidelity. These represented a denial of his powerful feelings of libidinal attachment to his mother, which he projected onto Rachel, and then ruthlessly and unceasingly attacked. Joseph's conviction that Rachel was unfaithful was an alternative to his feeling that he himself had betrayed his mother through a transfer of libidinal attachment and dependency onto Rachel. Unconsciously, Joseph felt enormous guilt and fear about abandoning his primitive emotional attachment to his mother.

Rachel's agoraphobia consolidated and reinforced the couple's stereotyped relationship and protected Joseph from fears that Rachel might abandon him. Once Rachel recovered and became more assertive and independent, Joseph's adjustment was shattered. He could no longer control Rachel's behavior and utilize her as the recipient of his projected "bad object" or unwanted "feminine" attributes. This precipitated a psychotic reaction in which the "bad object" was represented by the persecuting Mafia who were plotting his destruction.

The importance of genetic factors is highlighted here. Joseph's father had developed a schizophrenic disorder, and presumably Joseph inherited his father's tendency to develop psychotic behavior under acute stress. With a different genetic loading, Joseph may well have developed, for example, a panic disorder or a depressive condition.

Gradually, Joseph adapted to the changed marriage relationship and began to construe the world in less stereotyped terms. That the marriage survived all the above difficulties underlines the power of interlocking psychopathology to maintain the marital bond.

Case 2: The Private Eye and His Wife

The case of Damion, 33, and Roxanne, 31, illustrates the interaction between projective identification and sex-role conflict.

DAMION

Damion's mother was a chronic invalid. Throughout his childhood, she had suffered from "giddy spells," palpitations, fainting attacks, and migraines that had often confined her to bed. At these times, she could not bear noise. Damion was required to look after her. As a result, he was rarely allowed to go out and play with other children, or to receive friends at home. His sister, three years younger, had less responsibility, and Damion was required to look after her as well, which added to his sense of frustration and resentment.

Damion's father was a large, florid, hearty but aggressive man who had devoted himself to a successful career in the police force. He spent little time at home except when his wife was particularly ill. At such times, he was torn between a sense of duty to look after his wife and a wish to further his career. This conflict made him tense and irritable, and he frequently abused Damion, who at such times felt displaced, and rejected by both his parents.

Damion entered adolescence with very low self-esteem, having internalized his father's negative views of him. He was, however, determined to prove that he was at least as good as his father, and worked hard at school, getting good grades. After graduation he applied to join the police force, but was rejected, mainly on physical grounds. He decided instead to become a private investigator. His father's contacts in the local police were helpful, and he was already quite successful when, at the age of 26, he married Roxanne.

ROXANNE

Roxanne described her mother as: "caring and loving on the outside but cold and rejecting underneath . . . she basically didn't want us children around . . . whenever I've really needed her, she'd let me down." After marriage, her mother had not worked outside the home.

Of her father she said: "He's a very deep person who never showed any emotions. I used to go to him with my problems, because my mother wouldn't listen. But I never got any sympathy, only advice about how I should pull myself together."

With this style of parenting, Roxanne grew up with average social skills but feeling unloved, unwanted, and basically inadequate, constantly afraid of failing to live up to the high standards she set herself. She did well at school and obtained a job as a junior secretary in a large financial institution. Because of her well-organized, conscientious, rather driven approach, she gained rapid promotion and was in a position of some responsibility when she married Damion.

THE MARRIAGE

Roxanne felt strongly that motherhood was a full-time job, and stopped working when her first child, a girl, was born 15 months after her marriage. Over the next 4 years, she had 3 more children.

Her intense premarital attraction to Damion had been based on the fact that, unconsciously, he reminded her of her father. Since Damion was more outgoing than her father, and a busy, successful young man, she believed that he would give her the warmth, care, and support that she had craved from her father, but had never received. Sadly, after their marriage, her hopes and expectations were not met. So determined was Damion to compete with his father that he became obsessed with professional ambitions. He attended numerous conferences and courses about the latest surveillance technology and related matters. He was out late most nights and at weekends, either cultivating contacts or pursuing investigations. Although his business prospered, his marriage deteriorated.

Roxanne became desperate for warmth, affection, and support, a craving made all the stronger because she was coping virtually alone with the enormous emotional and physical demands of four young children. When Damion proved unable to meet her needs, she became resentful and withdrawn. Her standards of child and domestic care fell precipitantly.

Damion needed Roxanne to be warm, loving, and caring toward him when he was at home: Working so hard, he felt strongly that he should be waited on hand and foot in his few moments of relaxation. Therefore, he in turn withdrew from Roxanne when she failed to meet his needs.

Roxanne began to develop anxiety symptoms that were somewhat similar to those that plagued Damion's mother. Instead of reacting with sympathy to Roxanne's symptoms, Damion became angry, shouting "You should go and have your head examined," or similar suggestions. She sought help from her family doctor, who put her on tranquilizers. These gave her transient relief, but added to her feelings of uselessness and inadequacy.

One day, Damion was contacted by the police and told to return home immediately. On arrival, he found several policemen in the house, which was in a state of utter chaos. The contents of drawers were spilled everywhere, furniture was broken, the television smashed, and many of Roxanne's clothes ripped and slashed. Roxanne explained that two men had entered through the back door, seized and bound her, and then searched the house for money. Unable to find any, they had threatened her and wrecked the house in frustration.

A major police investigation was undertaken, with no results. Certain inconsistencies between Roxanne's story and the evidence emerged. Finally, she admitted that she had fabricated the whole story, and that she herself had wrecked the house in a fit of rage.

THERAPY

Because of Damion's good reputation and relationship with the local police, Roxanne was able to avoid prosecution on the condition that she underwent psychiatric evaluation and, if necessary, treatment. When I saw her, she was understandably depressed and anxious. It emerged that she had, for some two years, elaborated fantasies about being raped and assaulted by strangers who broke into her home. The end point of these fantasies was Damion's successful rescue of her and arrest of the criminals. On several occasions, these fantasies had become so powerful that Roxanne had enacted aspects of them in real life. She had slashed and torn her underwear, knocked chairs over, and created a domestic scenario of forced entry by an intruder who violently raped her. However, she had on each occasion removed the "evidence" and tidied the home before Damion returned home.

It seemed that unconsciously Roxanne had sought to gain Damion's attention by herself becoming one of his clients, and in this way receiving some of the passionate interest that he directed toward his work.

Her fantasies had become reality in the wake of the outburst of destructive rage to which her habitual use of tranquilizers may well have contributed: There is scientific evidence that aggressive outbursts are more likely after ingestion of the benzodiazepine tranquilizers that she used (Rosenbaum, Woods, Groves, & Klerman, 1984). Surveying the damage, she had been unable to resist inventing a story that put the blame on criminals.

I involved Damion in Roxanne's therapy. Initially he was very aggressive toward Roxanne, believing that her behavior indicated a major mental illness. However, the couple came fairly quickly to understand the reasons behind Roxanne's "extraordinary" behavior. Damion gradually reduced his working hours and became more supportive and appreciative of Roxanne. She in turn became more loving and caring toward him. Thus, they ceased their sulky, hostile withdrawal from each other, and began to meet each other's cravings for mutual affection and support. At the end of therapy, their relationship was much improved, and Roxanne was free of psychological symptoms. The couple felt confident that they would grow in their capacity to meet each other's needs.

COMMENT

Damion's adjustment in early adulthood was based largely on an identification with the male sex-role stereotype. Healthy identification with his mother was made difficult by her chronic invalidism, which contributed to his need to suppress and deny his own "feminine" aspects. This in turn made it extremely difficult for him to provide the care and affection that Roxanne craved: Instead, he blamed and attacked her for having psychological symptoms.

Roxanne's stereotyped, idealized view of marriage and motherhood meant that she found herself caring for 4 young children virtually single-handedly. In reality, she was more suited by personality and disposition to full-time employment outside the home than to the role of a full-time mother and housewife. Out of this dilemma emerged profound, but unconscious, sex-role conflict.

Unable to adequately repress or constructively express the assertive, independent "masculine" aspects of herself, Roxanne relied on projective identification. Her elaborate and intense fantasies allowed her to perceive her husband as an idealized "warrior" who rescued her from assault and rape and punished her assailants. Tragically, her attempts to bring fantasy into reality caused Damion to become more, rather than less, critical and rejecting of her.

It is unlikely that individual psychotherapy for Roxanne would have altered Damion's anger toward her, or his belief that she had a serious mental illness. Indeed, had she been offered intensive individual psychotherapy—an option that I initially considered myself—Damion's negative attitudes toward her would probably have hardened (Hurvitz, 1967). Since the marriage was already in considerable trouble, it may well have foundered. Alternatively, the couple might have been driven back into their stereotyped roles and attitudes. However, relatively brief couples therapy focusing on sex-role issues allowed a sustained improvement not only in Roxanne's symptoms, but also in the marriage.

Case 3: The Reluctant Nurse–Wife

The case of Karl, 44, and Cheryl, 47, illustrates the emergence of Karl's psychological symptoms within a sex-role-stereotyped marriage, and the way in which the symptoms themselves came to represent the "bad object."

KARL

Karl was the youngest of four: he had three older sisters. His childhood had been characterized by an intense, ambivalent relationship with his overcontrolling mother, who had never permitted him to express any anger or frustration toward her. She totally controlled Karl in a subtle way by gently but firmly invalidating almost everything that he attempted to do. Ostensibly she allowed him a measure of independence, but whenever he attempted to make a decision for himself, she undermined and contradicted him. However, she did this in a smiling, loving way, so that Karl came to confuse love with ambivalent, controlling overprotection.

As a child, Karl idealized his father, whom he regarded as a kind of visiting superman; visiting because his job involved extensive travel interstate, and he was rarely at home; and a superman because he appeared to be independent, assertive, and fun loving, traits that Karl craved to possess but that were denied him by his mother.

Because Karl's father was mainly absent and there were no other adult relatives readily available, Karl had no one to encourage him toward independence. As an adolescent, he was solitary, spending his free time at home reading, studying, watching television, and listening to music. Inside himself he experienced a confusing mixture of feelings, especially toward his parents. He felt inferior and uncomfortable in the presence of peers, but when alone he sustained himself with the fantasy that he was superior to them, a fantasy that relied heavily on sex-role stereotyped ideals and aspirations.

An average student in high school, Karl became an apprentice auto mechanic after graduation. At the age of 21 he married Cheryl after a 9-month courtship. At an unconscious level, he was seeking in her a mother who would look after him without being overcontrolling and undermining. In return, he would provide for all her material and financial needs by dint of hard work. Karl assumed that in due course he would become the successful manager or owner of a large garage or automobile engineering concern.

CHERYL

Cheryl was the oldest of six: she had four younger brothers and a younger sister. Both her parents were unaffectionate, emotionally controlled, and very strict. They expressed occasional approval of Cheryl, but only when she earned it by performing well at some defined task. Far more often, they criticized and abused her for making mistakes or for performing her various tasks inadequately. Cheryl's mother was disinclined to domestic activities. As the oldest child, Cheryl was given increasing responsibility for managing the house and looking after her younger siblings. Since she received a measure of parental approval only after completing her duties well, she came to believe that love and affection had to be earned, and were never offered freely or unconditionally. She entered adolescence feeling that no one could possibly value her for herself, but only for what she did for them. Her sense of identity depended entirely on the idea of looking after others and sacrificing her own personal needs. In that sense, she identified totally with a female sex-role stereotype.

Not surprisingly, she became a nurse, a profession that she greatly enjoyed and to which she was dedicated. Karl attracted her because he elicited within her a nurturing, care-giving response and appeared to appreciate her attempts to "mother" him. This powerfully reinforced the sex-role stereotyped view that she had of herself.

THE MARRIAGE

After the first of their two girls was born, Cheryl interrupted her nursing career to become a full-time mother. She redirected her powerful nurturing and care-giving impulses away from Karl and nursing, and focused them on her two daughters. As a result, they were grossly overprotected. Karl coped with the decrease in her "mothering" of him by absorbing himself in his work: The money he earned from overtime at his auto mechanic's job was much needed at this stage of the family life cycle.

All went fairly smoothly until Karl was 33, at which time the girls were aged 7 and 9. Karl had been in the same job for 8 years, but had not achieved the senior management status that he had been led to anticipate on joining the business. Instead, a manager was brought in from outside. Karl greatly envied and disliked this man. His lack of promotion caused him to evaluate the success in life he had so far achieved, and he found that he had fallen hopelessly short of the stereotyped aspirations of his adolescence and early 20s.

Karl became depressed and anxious. Cheryl responded to these changes in Karl by increasing her nurturing of him. In a sense, this was a welcome opportunity for her to redirect her nurturing impulses away from the girls, who were striving to become independent and resisting Cheryl's overprotective style of parenting. However, Cheryl had developed a strong ambivalence about the idea of nurturing Karl: She had come to construe his weeping spells and anxiety attacks as "unmanly." When he failed to improve after a few weeks, she became angry and resentful toward him, although she was reluctant to express this directly. When Karl had weeping spells or complained of anxiety symptoms, she alternated between meeting his demands for "mothering" and ignoring or rejecting him. Occasionally she even shouted "pull yourself together, you creep," or words to that effect. This profoundly distressed Karl, since up to that time he had idealized Cheryl as an endlessly patient, loving, and caring mother substitute.

Karl was unable to acknowledge his rage toward Cheryl, let alone express it: The years of conditioning by his mother against the expression of anger toward her had been only too successful. However, his deeply buried rage emerged as panic attacks of such severity that he visibly shook. Karl was intensely frightened by these attacks, during some of which he thought he was going to die. Naturally, Cheryl felt compelled to respond with solicitude, which had the effect of powerfully reinforcing Karl's symptomatic behavior.

By now, there was a great deal of tension in the marriage and this, combined with Cheryl's unpredictable responses to Karl's requests for "mothering," raised his anxiety levels even further. Cheryl's cold withdrawal and thinly veiled hostility to Karl was replaced by care and concern only when he had a major panic attack, or when he was so troubled by depression or other symptoms that he talked of suicide. Unfortunately, Cheryl's generally sympathetic responses to such dramatic symptoms served only to reinforce them, setting up a vicious cycle that perpetuated both the marital tension and Karl's symptoms.

This state of affairs continued for 11 years. Karl sought medical treatment and saw numerous physicians and psychiatrists over this period. None of them addressed the marriage. Instead, he was treated with tranquilizers and antidepressants, with no lasting benefit. During the 6 months before I saw him, he was in danger of losing his job because of the amount of time he took off sick.

THERAPY

Since Karl's drugs were clearly unhelpful, the first step in therapy was to withdraw them. This was a huge challenge for Karl, but he coped with the highly distressing withdrawal symptoms, and 1 month after stopping his drugs he felt better than he had for several years. Cheryl was invited to support him through the withdrawal process as a constructive and valid expression of her nurturing impulses.

The remainder of therapy focused on identifying and changing those marital interactions and attitudes that reinforced Karl's symptoms. After 3 months of weekly conjoint therapy sessions, he had virtually recovered, at which time Cheryl herself suddenly became depressed. She revealed that although she resented Karl's symptoms, she welcomed his dependency on her, since it made her feel loved and needed. I suggested to Cheryl that now that Karl had recovered and the children were almost grown up, a return to nursing might be timely. She rapidly found a suitable job, and her depression lifted. One year after therapy, Karl and Cheryl were both well, and described their marriage as reasonably harmonious, although there was still considerable room for improvement.

COMMENT

Karl's psychological symptoms emerged when, in his mid-30s, he realized that he was most unlikely to achieve the stereotyped occupational aspirations that had sustained him thus far. His severe anxiety symptoms and bouts of depression were directly reinforced by his wife's behavior, and indirectly reinforced by tranquilizers and other drugs that perpetuated his sense of helplessness. Gradually, he came to blame the symptoms for all his problems. His fear of panic attacks became profound, totally dominating his life.

Unconsciously, his symptoms represented the denied, split-off, "feminine" aspects of himself—the "bad object." Because feelings of anxiety and depression were incompatible with his sex-role stereotyped view of himself—and also with Cheryl's view of acceptable masculinity—they were increasingly construed by the couple as mysterious and uncontrollable manifestations of a major psychiatric disorder.

Conjoint therapy that focused on sex-role issues allowed the couple to reconstrue Karl's symptoms in terms of their excessively rigid adherence to sex-role stereotypes. As Karl improved, Cheryl's role as his nurse–wife was threatened, and she understandably became depressed. However, her symptoms resolved rapidly once she resumed her nursing career outside the home.

Case 4: The Poltergeist Mystery

The case of Judith, 37, and Henry, 40, illustrates the power of projective identification to help preserve marriages over long periods of time in the face of enormous difficulties.

JUDITH

Judith came from a family background of gross emotional deprivation. An only child, she was sent, at the age of 6, to a boarding school, where she felt abandoned, lonely, and bewildered. Her father, a successful businessman, deserted the family when Judith was 7 and went to live in another state. She recalled being constantly criticized and humiliated by her mother throughout her childhood. For example, on one occasion, her mother insisted that a male friend examine 9-year-old Judith's genitals, to see if they were "normal," after her mother had found her masturbating. Repeatedly, Judith's mother told her that she hated her because she reminded her of Judith's father. Her father had said the same thing to Judith regarding her mother shortly before he left.

Judith's mother relied on threats, lies, false promises, and seductive blandishments to get Judith to cooperate with her. However, she always denied these lies and deceits. As a result, Judith came to equate love with denied deceit and lying, inconsistency, and confusion. Although she mistrusted her mother, she lived in the hope that one day they might achieve an honest, trusting relationship. Judith's problems were compounded by the fact that her mother was constantly accusing *her* of lying, even though Judith insisted that she always told the truth.

Very concerned about social status, Judith's mother would not let her play with local children, so that Judith grew up socially isolated. Her mother ruthlessly suppressed, with beatings and other punishments, any expressions of anger by Judith, who as a result learned to totally repress all her angry feelings.

At 19, Judith married a man 6 years her senior. It rapidly emerged that he was an alcoholic, and he frequently abused her physically and verbally. Because she was convinced that she could not manage alone, and because she loved her husband, who was highly remorseful after his excesses and promised to change, she endured the marriage for 14 years, leaving when her only child, Wallace, was 13 and hence old enough to be a supportive companion. In spite of her bad marriage, she had never experienced psychological symptoms severe enough for her to seek treatment.

At 36, two years after her divorce, she married Henry, then aged 39.

HENRY

Henry's family background was as disturbed as Judith's. He and his brother Hank, 8 years his junior, were brought up by their mother virtually single-handedly. Henry's father was a cold, distant, punitive, and very paranoid man. Although absent a great deal and uninvolved with Henry's upbringing, he would often have angry outbursts during which he would accuse Henry of stealing, mislaying, or damaging some of his property. Henry's father had a workshop at the back of the house where he attempted to fix automobiles as a hobby. Since he was constantly mislaying tools and equipment, Henry was frequently and unfairly blamed for this, and punished or persecuted as a liar if he denied responsibility.

Henry's mother behaved very sadistically toward him, ostensibly for his own good. For example, when he was 3 or 4, she often took him to a busy shopping center, where on several occasions she deliberately hid from him. This caused the little boy intense fear and panic. Then, when he was on the point of being "rescued" by another adult, she would reappear and say she had done it for his own good, to teach him how important it was not to become separated from her. Henry's mother played numerous other sadistic tricks on him, and then either denied them or said that she did them for his own good. He was not permitted any expression of anger or frustration toward her, and was not allowed to bring friends home or play on the street, so that he grew up in a state of social isolation and emotional repression. He came to believe that love was equated with sadistic tricks that were either denied or justified as good.

An above-average student at school, Henry obtained higher technical qualifications and got a job as a technician in a large laboratory, where he stayed for many years, eventually becoming a senior technician with some managerial responsibilities. He lived alone and had few sustained social contacts other than with his brother and mother until he met Judith.

THE MARRIAGE

Judith was attracted to Henry because he seemed responsible, reliable, sober, and considerate—the complete opposite of her first husband. She believed that he would treat her with respect and help create a stable family framework for her and Wallace, who was then just 16. Henry was attracted to Judith because she appeared vivacious and full of life: He hoped that she would enliven and fill his rather dull, empty existence.

Henry owned his own home, which was large but needed extensive renovations. Judith had some savings, which were used to restore and redecorate the house and buy new furniture. The house stayed registered in Henry's name alone. The first year of the marriage was reasonably harmonious, apart from some arguments between Henry and Wallace.

At the start of the second year, strange things began to happen in the house. On several occasions, the front and back doors were found wide open when Judith got up in the morning. Judith was sure she had locked and bolted them before going to bed. During the night, vases were moved to the edge of the mantlepiece, and objects were moved in the kitchen and family room. The alarm clock and the oven timer went off at unexpected times, often in the early morning. The telephone directory was found deeply slashed. Books and other objects were mysteriously misplaced, damaged, or hidden. Mud or grease smears were found on carpets and walls in the morning. A plastic gnome in the garden was found on its side with its hands and feet cut off. These and other incidents occurred over a period of 3–4 months. Henry blamed Wallace, who, as a result, went to live elsewhere. But the episodes continued, and Henry then blamed Judith, saying that she was mentally ill and did not know that she was in fact doing all these things herself. Judith then started talking about a poltergeist, and considered arranging an exorcism. First, however, she came to see me because of acute anxiety about these mysterious happenings, and fears for her sanity.

THERAPY

I suspected that Henry was the "poltergeist," and that, at one level, his motives were to get Judith to leave the house either through fear or by making her "crazy." Judith had herself suggested this to Henry who had denied it vigorously, as he did to me when I discussed the problem with him. He pointed out that many events attributed to the poltergeist happened during the day, when he was proven to be at work and hence could not possibly be implicated. For example, Judith went out for 2 hours (she was working only part-time and was at home quite often) and found on her return that the furniture in the family room had been rearranged. On another occasion, she returned to find the telephone off the hook, and there were several other bizarre incidents. Henry was so convincing in his denial of responsibility that I almost ceased to suspect him.

Therapy entered a stalemate until Judith returned from work one day much earlier than usual and discovered Hank, Henry's brother, hiding in the bathroom. It was then impossible to hide the truth. Hank admitted that he and Henry had been responsible for the mysterious happenings, and that they had done it just as a "joke." When confronted, Henry admitted his role in the deception.

Surprising as it may seem, once Judith had got over her initial anger, she forgave Henry and agreed to continue the marriage on condition that ownership of their house was transferred to both their names. Eighteen months later, they were still together, and Judith was free of symptoms, although the house remained in Henry's name only.

COMMENT

Judith had endured 14 years of marriage to an alcohol-dependent man who brutalized and degraded her, but she did not develop any major psychological symptoms during this period. Presumably, at some level, such a degrading relationship met aspects of her psychological needs.

In terms of object relations theory, her first husband, when drunk, became the "bad object." Through projective identification, his violent behavior had provided Judith with vicarious gratification of her own deeply buried aggressive impulses. At the same time, their marital interaction recapitulated Judith's relationship with her mother, within which Judith had been the helpless victim of sadism and violence.

When he was sober and remorseful, Judith idealized her first husband as a "good object." Thus, he was, in her eyes, either impossibly good or impossibly bad. Since in reality he could sustain neither posture, it was perhaps inevitable that he oscillated constantly between the two, obscuring the fact that both "good" and "bad" coexisted within him. Such a dynamic appears common in the marriages of women who remain married to domestically violent men with alcohol problems, or who repeatedly marry such men.

Surviving her first marriage for 14 years without developing significant symptoms is perhaps also a reflection of Judith's basic "ego strength" or psychological robustness. However, after only 15 months of her second marriage to Henry, Judith developed a severe anxiety state.

Henry was not a drinker. Indeed, Judith was attracted to him precisely because of his sober, controlled, reliable, and stable posture. Clearly, her marriage to Henry recreated aspects of her childhood. Like her mother, he often lied to and deceived her, at the same time denying it and falsely accusing *her* of being the liar and deceiver.

As marital tension and conflict increased, Judith was unable to turn Henry into a "bad object" and use him as a repository for her repressed and denied aggressive impulses and feelings. Thus, the poltergeist became acceptable as the "bad object." But such a notion profoundly challenged Judith's adjustment: Either she was imagining things—and hence crazy, as Henry insisted—or there existed a supernatural world, which was extremely frightening to her. Out of this delemma emerged acute anxiety symptoms, for which she sought my help.

Henry also was recreating aspects of his childhood through marriage to Judith. Identifying with his punitive, paranoid father, he was unconsciously getting revenge on his sadistic mother by persecuting Judith as her proxy. In this re-creation of his relationship with his mother, he, and not she, was the one who played sadistic tricks in the guise of love. Judith, in her angry confrontations with Henry, became his "bad object," to be rendered harmless by the attribution of craziness.

Undoubtedly, Henry's treatment of Judith was partly the result of his equating love with playing sadistic tricks: He always claimed, with conviction, to love Judith very much. But he was able to idealize her as a "good object" only when she totally aquiesced with his views and wishes. When initially discussing his marriage with me, and in general with colleagues at work, he presented himself as caring devotedly for a much-loved but sick wife; he entirely overlooked the fact that he himself had been a major contributor to his wife's illness.

Even after Henry's contribution to her symptoms was exposed, Judith wished to continue with the marriage. This underlines once again the power of interlocking psychopathology in maintaining the marital bond.

DENIAL OF MARITAL CONFLICT

In all four of the above cases, the designated patient presented with *personal psychological symptoms*. Both Rachel (Case 1) and Karl (Case 3) had received extensive drug treatment for their symptoms before coming to see me.

Neither had previously mentioned any marital difficulties to their doctors, and no previous attempts had been made to elucidate the marital context of their symptoms.

The general willingness of doctors to prescribe drugs or individual therapy for psychological symptoms without examining their marital context is a major contributor to symptom maintenance in cases such as these: It consolidates the symptoms as a displaced focus of denied marital conflict. Precisely how this occurs is discussed in the next chapter.

Because of their habitual denial of marital problems, patients such as these are rarely offered couples therapy. Should it be offered, it is often refused by one or both partners, or embarked upon with extreme ambivalence or reluctance. This creates special problems in therapy that will be addressed in Chapter 9.

CHAPTER FIVE

Marriage, the Medical Model, and Psychiatry

STEREOTYPING THE MENTALLY ILL

Just as there are widespread stereotypes of marriage and motherhood, so there are widespread stereotypes of mental illness. Progress in eradicating deeply ingrained sex-role stereotypes from English-speaking societies has been slow, and progress in removing stereotypes of mental illness has been even slower. Although there are parts of America where it has become socially acceptable to be "in therapy," a majority of Americans remain ignorant and prejudiced about the mentally ill. There is also an element of fear, powerfully reinforced by those rare but newsworthy episodes of murder, sometimes bizarre or multiple, by people who are subsequently recognized by the courts to be insane. Such reports contribute to an exaggeration in the popular mind of the connection between insanity and extreme violence.

It is often difficult for mental health professionals to acknowledge the extent of popular prejudice against the idea of mental illness. Their own prejudices and stereotypes have been attenuated or removed entirely by daily professional contact with the mentally disturbed. As a result, they may ignore or underestimate the importance of popular stereotypes in determining an individual's response to a psychiatric diagnosis, or the impact on a marriage of one partner's psychological symptoms. Both with particular cases and more generally, an understanding of the relationship between marriage and psychological symptoms requires a comprehension of the nature and intensity of personal and popular stereotypes about mental illness. These are best understood in the context of a brief historical review.

Historical Attitudes to Mental Illness

Historically, attitudes to mental illness have been characterized by a dichotomy between popular and medical perspectives. Although mental illness requiring treatment was clearly recognized by physicians in the 15th and 16th centuries (Schoeneman, 1982), mental illness as such was not widely recognized by the general public. People who would now be recognized as suffering from psychiatric disorders were commonly thought to be possessed by the Devil or evil spirits. A proportion of such people, mainly women, were regarded as witches, and executed. However, a majority of confessions to witchcraft appear to have been extracted under torture from women who were free of significant mental illness. Thus, the official demonology and witch hunts of the 15th and 16th centuries represented primarily the persecution of women rather than of the mentally ill.

Although the idea of mental illness became generally accepted in northern Europe during the 17th and 18th centuries, the treatment of mentally ill people was usually harsh and unsympathetic. In the few mental hospitals that existed, conditions were generally deplorable. For example, at the Bethlem Hospital in London, England, the public paid to come and observe the lunatics as a popular entertainment. The inmates were kept in conditions of indescribable squalor, often in chains, with straw as bedding and no washing or toilet facilities. "Treatment" included floggings, purgatives, emetics, immersion in icy cold water, and confinement in straitjackets.

It will be recalled from Chapter 1 that the English Poor Law Act of 1601 was promulgated as a basic welfare facility. Since the mentally ill were generally dispossessed, their care became the responsibility of the local parishes. Out of this emerged pressure for more systematic and humane treatment of the mentally ill, in response to which William Tuke opened the York Retreat in 1796. Here, patients were treated with kindness and understanding, and the emphasis was on rehabilitation through constructive work or occupational therapy. The use of straitjackets and other forms of physical restraint was discouraged, as was the use of the more vigorous physical treatments such as purgatives and emetics.

Although these enlightened principles were retained as a basis for treating the mentally ill, later mental hospitals were generally much larger than the York Retreat, and they rapidly became little more than dumping grounds where the mentally ill could be conveniently isolated from the rest of society. This is exemplified in many American cities and most notably in London, England, which by the late 19th century was ringed at a distance of 8–12 miles by numerous large mental hospitals. Many contained 2,000 beds or more. Because these hospitals were so large and isolated, it became difficult for them to sustain the enlightened approach initiated by William Tuke. Instead, they were run on a strictly authoritarian, hierarchical basis. Physical restraints were reintroduced. The sexes were segregated behind locked doors. Containment rather than rehabilitation became the rule. The high walls that surrounded these isolated "insane asylums" powerfully reinforced public fears and stereotypes of mental illness.

Although significant advances were made in treatment during the 1930s and 1940s, these were often misused: Electroshock (electroconvulsive therapy or E.C.T.), heavy and prolonged sedation, and even lobotomy, were used to control disturbed patients, or as threats to maintain discipline and conformity. Patients who refused to conform were moved to the locked wards of the severely disturbed as a disciplinary rather than a therapeutic measure. Thus, the aim of most large mental hospitals became not so much to treat patients on an individual basis but more to confine them with the minimum of trouble to the staff until they either recovered spontaneously or lapsed into chronic, harmless madness.

In the 1950s, it became evident that much of the chronic mental illness within the large mental hospitals was partly a product of institutionalization. Life as a patient in a large mental hospital destroyed personal initiative and responsibility. Patients became totally dependent on the institution and lost the desire or the ability to manage in the outside world. Increasing awareness of this led to the contemporary emphasis on closing down large mental hospitals and developing psychiatric treatment facilities in the community and in general hospitals. Although numerous teething problems have occurred, these moves to establish community-based psychiatric treatment facilities now have great impetus. In many cities, the old, large mental hospitals have been closed down or greatly reduced in size and have been replaced by innovative, effective, community-based programs. Although community treatment is not necessarily cheaper than institutionalization, it should ultimately reduce the demand for psychiatric services through its emphasis on prevention and early therapeutic intervention.

Clinical Effects of Stereotypes about Mental Illness

A historical perspective helps to explain the persistence of popular stereotypes about mental illness. Traditionally, social attitudes to the mentally ill have ranged from the persecutory to the unsympathetic, and it is only very recently that we ceased to incarcerate the mentally ill behind the high walls of isolated insane asylums. The combination of ignorance, fear, and prejudice about mental illness generates a profound reluctance on the part of many people with psychological symptoms to accept that their symptoms have a psychogenic basis. Similarly, spouses may seek to deny that their partner's symptoms have their origins in the psyche. In such circumstances, one or both partners may cling fiercely to the idea that the symptoms have a physical basis, and the need to prove this may become central to the patient's relationship with the medical profession.

Such activities by patients fall within the framework of abnormal illness behavior, a relatively new field of study pioneered by Pilowsky (1978) that is fast expanding. However, as Singh, Nunn, Martin, and Yates (1981) have pointed out, abnormal illness behavior cannot exist without "abnormal treatment behavior" on the part of physicians—behavior that is to a large extent determined by their own prejudices and stereotypes about mental illness.

Research emphasis to date has been overwhelmingly patient-oriented and thus has obscured the contributions of physicians to the problem.

However, abnormal illness behavior interacts powerfully with marriage relationships, as illustrated, for example, in Chapter 4. Thus, problems in the patient–spouse relationship are often compounded by problems in the doctor–patient relationship, and conversely. Hence, marital and doctor–patient relationships become inextricably interwoven as symptom-perpetuating factors. In order to understand precisely how this occurs, it is necessary to clarify modern medical views on mental illness.

PSYCHIATRY AND MEDICINE

Because psychiatry is a branch of medicine, the "medical model" is central to psychiatrists' ideas about mental illness. There is great controversy surrounding the medical model of mental disorder, particularly at the level of sociological theorizing. Clinical psychologists have tended to replace the medical model with ideas based on learning theory, and many social workers actively reject it as unhelpful in their attempts to deal with clients' problems. I propose to argue that a rigid adherence to the medical model by mental health professionals can be a potent contributor to the development and maintenance of psychological symptoms in married people. In order to elaborate this viewpoint, it is necessary to define the medical model and examine its scientific basis. I have been struck by how many psychiatrists uncritically accept the medical model of psychiatric disorder, and by how many psychologists and social workers tend to reject it without a clear understanding of its nature and origins. For these reasons, what follows is derived from basic premises.

Psychiatric Diagnosis

Modern psychiatry relies on the principle of accurate diagnosis along medical lines. Medical diagnosis is based on the presence of symptoms, physical signs, and objective evidence of structural or biochemical abnormalities. In medical disorders, symptoms and signs are usually elicited with a high degree of reliability. A presumptive diagnosis can generally be confirmed on the basis of positive radiographic, bacteriologic, or biochemical findings. Appropriate treatment may then be instigated on empirical grounds or in relation to an understanding of the disease process. The basic assumption, of course, is that *diseases have a cause or causes that are clearly definable in terms of specific organic, structural, or biochemical abnormalities.* Treatment is aimed at removing or ameliorating these abnormalities and their causes through the use of drugs, surgery, radiotherapy, or immunologic techniques. This is the essence of the medical model, and is the definition on which I will base my use of the term in this book.

Although a formal diagnosis along medical lines underpins modern psychiatry, an adequate scientific basis for this infrastructure remains to be established. For example, the reliability with which psychiatric symptoms can be elicited has until recently been low, with more disagreement than agreement between raters about even the more common symptoms and signs (Grove, Andreasen, McDonald-Scott, Keller, & Shapiro, 1981). The consequent poor reliability of psychiatric diagnosis led to the development of standardized diagnostic schemes such as those in the *DSM-III*, and the use of these by trained personnel has undoubtedly increased the reliability of psychiatric diagnosis. However, attempts at increasing reliability generally reduce validity, and this explains why the level of agreement between different diagnostic schemes is disappointingly low (Dean, Surtees, & Sashidaran, 1983). Thus, the validity of psychiatric diagnosis remains a major problem in contemporary psychiatry.

Furthermore, in spite of a great deal of research over many years, few consistent structural or biochemical abnormalities have been found in any nonorganic psychiatric disorder. Recent research developments in the area of affective disorders, for example the Dexamethasone Suppression Test (Rabkin, Quitkin, Stewart, McGrath, & Puig-Antich, 1983), are very promising. Few would disagree that underlying neurophysiological abnormalities contribute substantially to the symptoms of schizophrenic disorder. Evidence is steadily accumulating for biochemical abnormalities in patients with panic disorder. Nonetheless, the idea of a structural or biochemical *basis* for a great majority of psychiatric disorders remains essentially an article of faith. This does not, of course, exclude the possibility that a physical basis for the major psychiatric disorders will *ultimately* be found: but believing in something that might happen as if it has already occurred is an act of faith, not of logic.

Inconsistencies such as these create the opportunity for a total rejection of psychiatric diagnosis as currently practiced (Frank, 1975):

> We have to throw off the conceptual shackles of ways of approaching data borrowed from the physical sciences and medicine which serve us ill. We have to think . . . from the point of view of the interpersonal as well as the intrapsychic, not just as regards the manifest behavior. . . . Our system of classification in psychiatry has proven to be: full of sound and fury, signifying nothing. . . . Indeed, it is frightening to think that we clinicians hold to beliefs about behaviours which are invalid, much as do our patients. (p. 80)

Such statements overlook the enormous practical value of psychiatric diagnosis. In spite of valid concerns about the scientific basis of psychiatric diagnosis, it has not yet proven possible to find an adequate practical alternative. In my view, it is the discrepancy between the practical utility and the scientific credibility of psychiatric diagnosis that is primarily responsible for problems in its application.

Those whose concern is mainly with theoretical models of human behavior must necessarily expose any logical or scientific inconsistencies that are inherent in psychiatric diagnosis. For those who struggle daily to treat or manage people suffering from major psychiatric disorders, psychiatric diagnosis and the medical model are often essential concepts. Little wonder that such people often react overdefensively when attacks are made upon a fundamental premise of their work. Even those who are not actively involved in the therapy or management of serious psychiatric disorders, but who embrace the medical model in the context of research or teaching, may react overdefensively if their basic assumptions are challenged.

Such defensiveness often leads to a compensatory overvaluation of psychiatric diagnosis and the medical model in clinical practice, teaching, and research. This overvaluation takes many forms, including a literal belief in psychiatric diagnosis, or a total, exclusive reliance upon it to guide treatment and management (Hafner, Lieberman, & Crisp, 1977). However, a literal or exclusive belief in psychiatric diagnosis requires distortions of perception and logic that can be sustained only by constant rationalization and justification. The interaction of such professional attitudes with the personal constructs and marital systems of patients with psychological symptoms may perpetuate these symptoms in ways that will now be discussed.

HOW THE INTERACTION OF PSYCHIATRIC AND MARITAL SYSTEMS MAINTAINS SYMPTOMS

Preserving Hope in the Psychiatrist

As Berman and Lief (1975) have pointed out, the medical model is so deeply ingrained in the training of doctors that it becomes an unquestioned, fundamental assumption that is hard to relinquish. This background factor is a powerful contributor to the overvaluation of the medical model by many psychiatrists.

An additional, potent reason, which is rarely acknowledged, derives from the psychiatrist's need to preserve a sense of therapeutic hope and optimism, particularly when dealing with difficult cases. The necessity for this is underlined by evidence that nearly one quarter of practicing psychiatrists have little confidence in their ability to help patients with major or recurring psychiatric disorders (Hafner *et al.*, 1977).

Severe psychiatric disorders are profoundly distressing to the patient, and psychiatrists must find ways of ameliorating the impact of this distress upon themselves. Otherwise, in the course of prolonged or intimate contact with such patients, they risk becoming depressed or otherwise dysfunctional. Furthermore, many patients with severe psychiatric disorders come from tragic or grossly deprived backgrounds: To hear an open, honest account of their lives is often heartrending and may move the most experienced psychiatrist to tears.

Thus, it becomes essential at times to shift the focus of enquiry or therapy away from the past, and to concentrate instead on the here and now. Unfortunately, many severely disabled psychiatric patients have *current* personal, interpersonal, or marital problems that are not only highly distressing, but virtually inaccessible to change. In these circumstances, it is profoundly difficult for the psychiatrist to preserve the idea that he or she can usefully help the patient. But it is vital to sustain that belief: Otherwise the psychiatrist risks becoming hopeless about his or her work and may withdraw entirely from constructive efforts to provide help for those patients most in need of it.

In such difficult circumstances, the medical model sustains the psychiatrist's hope in several ways. Because it validates the idea of a mental illness with a genetic or biochemical basis, the patient's past and present misfortunes, conflicts and problems become much less relevant. This protects the psychiatrist from the pain—and the mental effort—of having to link the patient's tragic personal history, and unendurable but seemingly unmodifiable present problems, with his or her current psychiatric symptoms. The symptoms themselves can then become the main focus of inquiry and treatment by drugs. The use of drugs validates the idea of a mental illness, and conversely, so that a circular, self-reinforcing process is established. If patients do not respond to drug treatment, or relapse in spite of it, this failure can be attributed to an insufficiency of medical science and knowledge rather than to the personal shortcomings of the psychiatrist. Furthermore, the hope is preserved that a greater understanding of the biochemical basis of mental illness will allow new drugs to be developed, increasing the chances of curing intractable or relapsing patients.

The overvaluation of drugs in treating persisting psychiatric disorders leads to prescribing habits that are logically and scientifically untenable. For example, two recent surveys of long-stay, mainly psychotic patients in typical large psychiatric hospitals (Edwards & Kumar, 1984; Holden, 1984) showed that over 80% were receiving major tranquilizers, and that over half of these were on two or more different types concurrently. Over 50% of the patients were receiving anticholinergic drugs to counter the parkinsonian side effects of their neuroleptic medication.

Prescribing patterns such as these are still the rule in mental hospitals, even though there is now good evidence that many patients with persisting psychotic disorders are not helped, and may be hindered, by long-term treatment with major tranquilizers (Marder, van Kammen, Rayner, & Bunney, 1979). Even where major tranquilizers are indicated, less than 20% of patients require antiparkinsonian drugs (Edwards & Kumar, 1984).

Preserving Hope in the Patient

Just as the medical model may protect psychiatrists from a sense of personal responsibility for their treatment failures, so may it protect psychiatric patients from the idea that they are personally responsible for their symptoms and related problems. Severely disabled psychiatric patients generally have very poor self-esteem and profound, often insoluble, personal, marital, or interpersonal problems and conflicts in addition to their psychiatric symptoms. Although their unresolved problems and conflicts may be the main cause of their psychiatric symptoms, to confront them about such problems while treating severe, distressing symptoms is to risk plunging them into utter despair. Instead, it is vital to diminish their sense of guilt, hopelessness, and personal inadequacy. Encouraging such patients to believe that they are mentally ill relieves them of their sense of personal failure: They can attribute all their problems and symptoms to an *illness* that has been thrust upon them by circumstances beyond their control or responsibility. At the same time, they can share their psychiatrist's hope of a cure through the use of drugs and medical treatments. Since such a cure requires no great effort on their part, they are able to rest and regain their equilibrium within an undemanding, protective hospital environment. However, unless on recovery or improvement they are encouraged to deal with the real basis of their symptoms, they are likely to relapse. Unfortunately, treatment based on the medical model generally ceases when the patient's symptoms resolve. Thus, relevant family and marital conflicts and stresses are rarely examined, and the patients are usually left with the idea that they are suffering from a medical illness over which they have no personal control, and for which they have no personal responsibility.

Denying the Marital Context of Psychiatric Disorder

From the above it is clear that in the case of severe psychiatric disorders, there are numerous reasons for the interpersonal aspects of the patient's problems to be ignored or denied. In the treatment of married patients, who are a majority in nearly all adult psychiatric disorders, the denial of marital factors is a major but largely unacknowledged contributor to the chronicity or recurrence of patients' symptoms (Goldstein & Chambless, 1981; Kohl, 1962). This denial of marital factors is self-reinforcing. For example, many patients with severe psychiatric disorders repeatedly relapse, even when on medication. This is particularly true of patients who have required more than one admission to a mental hospital or general hospital psychiatric unit. This high relapse rate has been rather cynically termed "the revolving door policy," and is a major cost factor in the provision of mental health services.

When such patients are readmitted to the hospital, they generally improve markedly within a few days. Since readmission usually coincides with a change of medication, it is the psychotropic drugs that get the credit for the patients' improvement, although in reality this is often attributable to their removal from marital or family stress and conflict. Thus, with each readmission, the medical model becomes progressively overvalued at the expense of attention to marital and interpersonal factors. Ultimately, it become virtually impossible to reverse this process, even if the relevance of marital factors finally becomes apparent to those responsible for the patient's treatment: Having been strongly conditioned to a medical model, both patient and spouse naturally resist alternatives, particularly if these evoke feelings within them of fear, confusion, anger, or guilt.

Although these self-perpetuating events and attitudes are most relevant in severe psychiatric disorders, similar processes, somewhat attenuated, occur in less severe conditions. Implicit in the medical model is the one-to-one doctor patient relationship. In psychiatry, this perspective is reinforced by the psychoanalytic emphasis on intrapsychic rather than interpersonal confict, and by the related belief that seeing members of the patient's family will dilute the central therapeutic power of the transference (Berman & Lief, 1975). As a result, the marital contribution to symptom maintenance is often overlooked during individual psychodynamic psychotherapy, the process of which may exacerbate marital problems and related symptoms. Unless the spouse is actively involved in therapy, individual psychotherapy may become interminable, or deterioration or breakup of the marriage may occur (Hurvitz, 1967). Sometimes, psychological symptoms develop in the untreated spouse, complicating the marital situation further.

Because of the therapist's preoccupation with the patient's individual psychopathology and transference issues, these harmful effects of therapy are often either not acknowledged, are attributed to the patient's "resistance" to therapy, or are rationalized by the therapist as an inevitable consequence of the patient's personal growth and development.

The Impact of Psychotropic Drugs on Marital Interaction

Although the effects of psychotropic drugs on marital interaction largely coincide with those of the medical model in general, there are some specific influences that merit consideration.

Not only does the prescription of drugs reinforce the medical model, but it generates a strong expectation of symptomatic improvement in patient and spouse. Although the patient may have been warned, for example, about the likelihood of side effects with tricyclic antidepressants, the spouse may be unaware of this possibility. A substantial number of patients find these side effects unacceptable, and stop taking the drug. It is not unusual for the spouse to react to this with frustration and anger, either toward the patient for abandoning attempts at recovery, or toward the doctor for making the patient worse. Similar reactions toward the doctor may occur when, as is very common, the patient relapses on withdrawal of a therapeutic drug regime. Such reactions in the spouse or the patient may not only exacerbate marital problems, but may also make it impossible for the patient to maintain a therapeutic relationship with the treating physician.

The use of benzodiazepines may have adverse effects on marital interaction. It is now well established (Ashton, 1984) that many patients become dependent on these drugs even in relatively low dosage. Drug withdrawal is a particular problem with the shorter acting benzodiazepines such as oxazepam. As the drug effects wane, usually 2–4 hours after a tablet is taken, many people experience what may be termed "mini-withdrawal symptoms," that are very similar to the symptoms of anxiety for which the drug was taken in the first place. Because they are unaware that a waning drug effect is responsible for the resurgence of unpleasant symptoms, these people believe that their underlying disorder is getting worse. As a result, they increase their dosage of oxazepam, setting up a vicious cycle that can lead to chronic use of the drug, sometimes in very high dosage. In such circumstances, drug withdrawal is a profoundly challenging task for which the patient may need admission to hospital.

Grappling with the distressing and disabling side effects of benzodiazepine dependency inevitably has adverse effects on marital interaction. The spouse may come to regard the patient as "weak" or inadequate because of their dependency on drugs, reinforcing negative attitudes that may already exist toward the patient's symptoms. Use of benzodiazepines disinhibits the expression of aggressive impulses (Rosenbaum *et al.*, 1984), and the associated outbursts of rage may have devastating effects on a marriage.

Many of the above problems are illustrated in the following account by a woman who had been on moderate doses of diazepam (Valium) for several months:

> I started to become withdrawn, insecure and confused and suffered bouts of depression together with uncontrollable outbursts of rage. . . . I was prescribed many different forms of antidepressants, hypnotics and tranquillisers to take with the Valium. None of these had any lasting good effects, in fact I gradually became worse instead of better. The relationship between our G.P. [family doctor] and myself broke down. . . . During one particularly bad spell, my husband dragged me to psychiatric in-patients. . . . During the weekly sessions it was suggested I drop my dose of Valium . . . but then things became much worse. My confidence began to wane dramatically—I could not go out or be left on my own. My husband finally had to give up his job, as I spent most of my time begging him to come home as I was frightened. . . . My doctor advised me not to drop Valium any more (I was down from 15 mg to 4 mg) as I was suffering from chronic anxiety and needed some form of sedation. What both of us did not realise was—I was in tranquilliser withdrawal. (Ashton, 1984, p. 1135)

After a further year, which the patient described as "hell for me and my family," the dependency/withdrawal syndrome was recognized and treated. Once she had adjusted to a drug-free state, the patient became virtually symptom free.

Lithium carbonate is, of course, invaluable in bipolar affective disorders, particularly in treating manic episodes and preventing their recurrence. It may also prevent or diminish the severity of depressive episodes in bipolar disorders. Since it is so dramatically and unequivocally effective in true bipolar disorders, it tends also to be used in cyclothymic disorders, where it is of doubtful effectiveness.

Because of its potentially dangerous side effects, blood levels of the drug must be frequently monitored until they have stabilized within a range that is both safe and therapeutic. Even after stabilization, which may take several months, blood levels should be checked regularly. This involves visits to medical clinics and venepuncture, so that the use of lithium carbonate powerfully reinforces the medical model and the idea of an illness beyond the patient's control or responsibility. Although bipolar disorder undoubtedly has biochemical and genetic contributors, it also has a substantial psychological and interpersonal component. Marital and family interaction can be critical in precipitating manic or depressive episodes, and thus in perpetuating the disorder (Mayo, 1979). However, excessive reliance on the medical model inhibits patients, their spouses, and their psychiatrists from examining and modifying these important marital and family aspects of the condition. If they believe that bipolar disorder is a mysterious illness of biochemical/genetic origin, to be treated primarily or exclusively with drugs, then they are unlikely to do justice to alternative or supplementary treatment approaches.

Behavioral Therapies and Marital Interaction

Although behavioral therapies are still conducted mainly by clinical psychologists, increasing numbers of psychiatrists are being trained in their use. Behavioral therapies are held by their main protagonists to be based on learning theory, although there is disagreement about this. However, behavior therapists are virtually unanimous in their agreement that transference is largely irrelevant to the process of therapy. In this and several other ways, their approach is fundamentally different from that of psychodynamically oriented therapists.

Learning theory is based mainly on experiments conducted on laboratory animals, particularly white rats. Virtually all these experiments have been carried out on individual animals, so that behavior therapy has evolved in a social and interpersonal vacuum. Thus, albeit for different reasons, behavior therapists are often as blind to relevant marital factors in therapy as are insight-oriented therapists. Joseph Wolpe (1970) and Arnold Lazarus (1976), both influential clinical behaviorists, have emphasized the importance of marital factors in treating seriously disabled patients. However, this aspect of their work appears to have been disregarded by a majority of behavior therapists. To date, books and journals on behavior therapy have largely ignored the marriage relationship as a factor in perpetuating psychological symptoms. Fortunately, this omission is now being remedied; there is a progressive trend towards integration of behavioral and marital techniques in contemporary behavioral approaches to persisting psychiatric disorders in married patients (Falloon, in press).

THE LACK OF RESEARCH INTO THE MARITAL CONTEXT OF PSYCHIATRIC DISORDER

Just as an overvaluation of the medical model may become self-perpetuating in everyday clinical practice, it may become so in psychiatric research. Methodological factors are important here.

In accordance with its medical aspirations, psychiatric research has been based on empirical science, an approach that favors the study of comparatively large groups of patients so that appropriate statistical calculations and inferences can be made. This is especially true of studies that compare different treatments. Understandably, most psychiatrists are more impressed by the results of large-scale clinical studies than they are by anecdotal reports based on a few cases. Unfortunately, there are numerous unresolved methodological problems in the application of empirical science to an investigation of psychiatric disorders. Of these, the problem of *selection bias* is the most relevant to the present discussion.

Selection Bias

The problem of ensuring that research populations are at least broadly representative of clinical populations has been virtually disregarded by clinical research workers. As a result, they have come to underestimate the importance of marital and interpersonal factors in generating and perpetuating the more common psychiatric disorders.

Although most large-scale treatment studies are rigorous in reporting the number of patients who drop out of therapy, few report the number of those initially referred who refuse to participate or are rejected because they do not meet operational diagnostic criteria for inclusion in the study. As stricter diagnostic criteria have evolved, the number of patients who fail to meet them has increased.

Miller, Strickland, Davidson, and Parrott (1983) found that of 44 patients referred for a study of schizophrenic disorder, 38% did not meet the inclusion criteria, and 32% refused to participate. Only 13 of the original 44 were actually enrolled in the study. Of 56 patients referred for a study of depression, only 15 (21%) were finally enrolled. In both studies, several statistically significant differences in demographic data were found between the patients who actually enrolled and those who did not.

The effects of selection bias are well demonstrated in studies of agoraphobia, which can be regarded as a clinical paradigm for moderate to severe anxiety neurosis (Hallam, 1978). The psychiatric literature on agoraphobia is notable for opposing views on the role of marriage in precipitating or perpetuating the disorder. Psychotherapists generally emphasize the central role of marital factors (Chambless & Goldstein, 1981; Fry, 1962; Goodstein & Swift, 1977; Holmes, 1982; Quadrio, 1983; Schwartz & Val, 1984; Webster, 1953). In contrast, clinical researchers either disregard the marriage relationship (Sheehan, Ballenger, & Jacobsen, 1980; Zitrin, Klein, Woerner, & Ross, 1983), or explicitly reject its relevance (Buglass, Clarke, Henderson, Kreitman, &Presley, 1977; Cobb, Mathews, Childs-Clarke, & Blowers, 1984; Rapp & Thomas, 1982).

These differences between therapists and research workers occur primarily because they deal with different populations. As the *DSM-III* points out, agoraphobia often coexists with depression, anxiety, ruminations, minor checking compulsions, and social phobias. Depression has a particularly strong association with agoraphobia (Bowen & Kohout, 1979), and Clancy, Noyes, Hoenk, and Slyman (1978) observed that the presence of depression reduced the responsiveness of agoraphobia to treatment. However, the level at which associated symptoms are regarded as disorders requiring treatment in their own right is essentially arbitrary. Clinical researchers routinely *exclude* patients with significant symptoms and problems in addition to their agoraphobia (Buglass et al., 1977; Sheehan et al., 1980; Zitrin et al., 1983) whereas psychotherapists routinely accept such complex cases as part of the reality of clinical practice.

In one of the few studies reporting relevant data, Jannoun, Munby, Catalan, and Gelder (1980) found that only 28 of 53 patients referred to an experimental behavioral treatment program for agoraphobia actually started therapy. Because therapy involved spouses, the rejection or refusal rate of 47% is higher than the probable average of 30–35%.

In addition to the estimated 30–35% of patients who refuse treatment or are excluded because they have significant additional symptoms and problems, about 25% of patients drop out of large-scale drug and/or behavioral studies of agoraphobia (Mavissakalian & Michelson, 1982). Thus, on average, less than 50% of patients initially referred actually complete treatment.

It is well established that patients with major symptoms and personality problems in addition to their agoraphobia tend to have unsatisfactory marriages, and that poor marital adjustment is strongly associated with a negative response to treatment (Hafner, 1982a; Milton & Hafner, 1979). Excluding patients with "complex agoraphobia" leaves mainly uncomplicated cases comprised of people with good marital adjustment and a fairly normal personality who are likely to respond well to unimodal or bimodal drug and behavioral therapies. In such cases, marital factors do not have any obvious effects on treatment outcome.

In failing to acknowledge that they are dealing primarily with an unrepresentative population of uncomplicated cases, clinical researchers have mistakenly generalized their findings to the entire population of agoraphobia sufferers. As a result, drugs and behavior therapy have become overvalued in the treatment of agoraphobia. In reality, a majority of patients with agoraphobia seen by therapists in routine clinical practice are complex cases that do not generally respond to unimodal or bimodal therapies. Instead, they require a multimodal approach, of which direct attention to the marriage is often a crucial feature.

A similar process appears to have contributed to an overvaluation of drugs and cognitive–behavioral therapy in the treatment of depressive neuroses, with a reciprocal undervaluation of multimodal and couples approaches to therapy.

A diagnosis of pure anxiety disorder or depression is made in only about 20% of psychiatric cases seen in a *primary care setting* (Goldberg, 1984). A great majority of cases are comprised of a mixture of anxiety, depression, and somatic symptoms. Thus, by the time pure cases of anxiety or depression reach psychiatrists, they are already highly unrepresentative of the total population of patients with neurotic disorders.

Most large-scale clinical research into anxiety disorders and depression is carried out in major centers, usually with established treatment programs. To be referred to such programs, patients must presumably be readily identifiable by their physicians as having a well-defined disorder, and this represents yet another selection filter. As we have seen, a further filtering process occurs when patients with significant additional symptoms or problems are excluded; and when they exclude themselves because they regard a relatively inflexible unimodal therapy as inappropriate, or because of personality or marital problems. Dropping out of the program represents the final phase of the selection process.

Thus, patients who actually complete therapy in research programs are a very highly selected population. Yet it is from such unrepresentative patients that clinical researchers generalize their findings to the total population.

It should now be clear that this rigorous and extensive selection process reinforces and consolidates the system of psychiatric diagnosis and hence psychiatrists' reliance on the medical model. Highly specific diagnostic categories such as those espoused in *DSM-III* create a demand by researchers for patients who fit neatly into them. There is no doubt that such pure, uncomplicated cases exist, but they are comparatively rare. However, because they are highly overrepresented in research populations, clinical researchers come to regard them as fairly typical of the total population.

Furthermore, since such patients generally respond well to unimodal treatment programs, research workers usually become highly enthusiastic about their particular treatment approach. This enthusiasm often spreads to their associates, and usually leads to the establishment of the program as a local resource. This helps to perpetuate the researchers' illusion that most patients fit neatly into highly specific diagnostic categories and respond well to unimodal drug or behavioral therapies.

Circular processes such as these are occurring in many major research centers, so that clinical research becomes less and less relevant to the realities of routine clinical practice. Fortunately, there are those who are aware of this problem. For example, Barlow (1981) suggested that "at present, clincial research has little or no influence on clinical practice" (p. 147). Tyrer (1984) has argued strongly for the retention of the broad diagnostic category "anxiety neurosis," pointing out the problems inherent in the restrictive categories espoused by *DSM-III*. However, the momentum of clinical research based on strict operational diagnostic criteria is now so great that nothing short of a revolution in psychiatric thought seems likely to modify it.

This places a responsibility upon clinicians to disseminate more widely and vigorously their understanding of the complex realities of general psychiatric practice. It is to be hoped that this will lead to a more general awareness of the crucial role of personality and marital factors in initiating and perpetuating the more common psychiatric disorders. A greater willingness to adopt a multimodal approach should emerge from this. Although such an approach often relies heavily on drugs or behavioral techniques, these are used only when the full complexities of the patient and his or her marital and personal problems are acknowledged and understood.

INTERACTION OF MEDICAL AND MARITAL SYSTEMS IN SYMPTOM FORMATION

The Primary Care Physician

To this point, discussion has focused on the interaction between psychiatric and marital systems. However, a great majority of psychiatric disorder is treated in a primary care or general practice setting, and most referrals to psychiatrists are initiated by family or primary care physicians. Thus, the way in which primary care physicians deal with psychiatric disorder in their patients is crucial as an alternative or precursor to formal psychiatric treatment.

The exposure of medical undergraduates to psychiatry varies greatly between training institutions. In some, psychiatry is given perfunctory attention, whereas in others it is a highly developed aspect of medical undergraduate training. Most psychiatric textbooks written primarily for medical students assume the basic validity of the medical model in psychiatry, and ignore or gloss over any problems in this assumption. Thus, unless their teachers emphasize alternatives, medical graduates tend to construe psychiatric disorders in medical rather than interpersonal or experiential terms. Their prejudices and stereotypes about mental illness are modified according to the extent and nature of their exposure to psychiatric patients, which ranges from extensive to minimal.

These differences in training experiences, together with personality factors, contribute to the great variation among primary care physicians in the proportion of psychiatric disorder that they diagnose in their patients. A recent survey of 45 American family physicians (Goldberg & Huxley, 1980) showed a range of 0–85%, with a mean of 39%. Other recent surveys in America and the United Kingdom reveal considerably lower proportions, with an overall average of about 15–20% of patients diagnosed as suffering primarily from psychiatric disorders.

It is of great interest that these patients do not usually present to their physicians with psychological or emotional symptoms: Recent research in America and the United Kingdom has shown that the complaints of over 50% are primarily physical (Goldberg & Huxley, 1980). The patients' emphasis on physical symptoms may influence primary care physicians' diagnoses: When these were compared with the diagnoses of experienced psychiatrists, the physicians substantially overdiagnosed purely somatic complaints and underdiagnosed depression (Goldberg, 1984; Mann, Jenkins, & Belsey, 1981).

A reluctance among family practitioners to record a psychological basis for physical complaints was also demonstrated by Beaber and Rodney (1984). Although nearly one-third of 109 consecutive clinic attenders scored at moderate or high levels on a self-report measure of hypochondria, *none* of these was diagnosed by their physicians as suffering from hypochondriasis. Routine laboratory investigations had been ordered for 90% of the moderate to high scorers, as compared with only 53% of the low scorers. Of the 6 patients who scored highest, the case notes of only one referred to psychosocial problems. The authors suggested the possibility that "the most pathological somatisers create the greatest amount of physician denial, or nonacknowledgment. High scorers may simply increase the physician's concern about the possibility of true physical disease" (p. 46).

However, the range of accurate psychiatric diagnosis by primary care physicians in general is very wide, with some doctors detecting all cases, and others less than 10%. Overall, primary care physicians detect psychiatric disorder at a level some 10% lower than the 25–30% that is recorded in studies that use strict operational criteria. Of that 25–30% of patients with primary psychiatric disorder, about 70% experience a mixture of anxiety symptoms, depression, and somatic complaints.

It is not yet fully understood why patients who experience a mixture of anxiety and depression together with somatic symptoms should emphasize the latter to their primary care physicians. However, prejudice and fear about mental illness is undoubtedly one potent reason for the reluctance of patients to present with psychological symptoms. Another reason derives from the belief of most patients that their physician expects them to present with physical rather than psychological complaints.

Although the primary care physician may have diagnosed a psychiatric disorder, he is unlikely to communicate this to the patient (Marsh, 1977). The reasons for this are complex, but include the likelihood that patient and doctor share the same prejudices against mental illness. Instead, the doctor is likely to "reassure" the patient that there is nothing physically wrong with him or her, and, rather inconsistently, prescribe a psychotropic drug. Such drugs currently account for 20% of *all* prescriptions, and nearly half of these are for the tranquilizing benzodiazepines (Mann *et al.*, 1981). This tacit collusion between doctor and patient to deny the existence of a psychological or stress-related disorder has repercussions that interact with the patient's family and marital systems.

Denial of Marital Conflict and Its Repercussions

It is well established that neurotic symptoms in general, and depressive neurosis in particular, are strongly associated with marital dissatisfaction and conflict (Birtchnell & Kennard, 1983; Sims, 1975). The persistence of marital problems is significantly associated with poor outcome (Rounsaville, Weissman, Prusoff, & Herceg-Baron, 1979a, 1979b). Thus, in denying or minimizing the psychological aspects of their disorders, patients are also denying associated marital conflicts and difficulties. This denial is reinforced either by the conscious collusion of physicians, or by their failure to recognize and deal with the psychological aspects of the patient's disorder.

In these circumstances, patients typically return to their physicians repeatedly, because their symptoms continue in spite of medication. Continued attention to the symptoms reinforces them as a displaced focus of personal, marital, family, or work-related dissatisfaction and conflict. Since the doctor has already colluded with the patient in denying the psychological or stress-related aspects of the symptoms, it becomes increasingly difficult to reconstrue them in nonorganic terms.

In the early stages of this process, the commonest symptoms include headaches; feelings of faintness, unsteadiness, dizziness, and unreality; trembling of the limbs; excessive perspiration; breathing and swallowing difficulties; nausea; diarrhea, and excessive frequency of passing urine; blurring of vision; pains in the neck, shoulders, chest, and abdomen; disturbances in mood, memory, and ability to concentrate; and sleep disturbances. Since most of these symptoms can be caused by a sinister illness such as cancer or heart disease, their persistence is often a source of increasing concern to both patient and doctor. Particularly if the patient's behavior is anxiety provoking, a conscientious doctor will seek to exclude any sinister underlying disease, even if he or she still suspects that the disorder is primarily psychological in origin. The doctor will therefore probably order some routine blood tests and basic radiographic or electroconductive investigations. These will reveal, with a high degree of certainty, whether or not there is a sinister basis to the symptoms. In virtually all cases of stress-related or psychogenic disorder, the results of these investigations are normal. The doctor is then able to reassure the patient: "Don't worry, there is nothing wrong with you." Inconsistently, a prescription for a tranquilizing drug will often be offered at the same time.

Unfortunately, this type of reassurance has an effect opposite to that intended on a significant number of patients with stress-related symptoms. They *know* that there is something wrong with them, or they would not have presented their symptoms to the doctor in the first place. Thus, the doctor's "reassurance" confuses them, and leaves them with three options:

1. The doctor or his investigations are in error, and a sinister or, it is to be hoped, a benign cause for the symptoms has been missed.
2. The symptoms are psychological or "imaginary" in nature.
3. The doctor has discovered a fatal disease, but, in order to protect the patient from this knowledge, is lying about the test results.

The commonest way in which the patient deals with the dilemma presented by options (1) and (2) is to seek more tests and investigations from the same or a different doctor. The patient's aim is to prove that there is a physical basis for his or her very real, persistent, and troublesome symptoms.

This is the start of the *illness-confirming* aspects of "abnormal illness behavior." Repeated medical investigations are almost invariably normal, and the patient is "reassured" by the doctor that there is nothing wrong. As a result, the patient becomes more and more puzzled, confused, and frustrated. This increases the stress upon the patient and hence the severity of the stress-related symptoms. The doctor senses the patient's frustration and often unconsciously responds to it in an irritated manner, suggesting, for example, that the patient's symptoms are "psychological." If this or a similar term is used without thorough explanation, or in an angry or dismissive fashion, it infuriates most patients with stress-related disorders. Such patients generally equate "psychological" with "imaginary" at best, and "crazy" at worst. Since they believe that they are not crazy, and know that the symptoms are real, they redouble their efforts to prove that the symptoms have a genuine physical basis. This reinforces the whole circular process, which may continue for many years, with hostile, nonconstructive attitudes hardening on both sides.

Some patients devote a very considerable amount of time and energy to illness-confirming behavior, all with the aim of proving that their symptoms have a genuine organic medical basis. For a few, this appears to become their mission in life, ultimately encompassing hundreds of consultations with many different doctors from a wide range of specialties. Sadly, the more such patients complain about the distressing nature of their symptoms, the more likely are doctors to regard them as troublesome hypochondriacs with "imaginary" symptoms.

Option (3) presents a different challenge to the patient, overlapping somewhat with option (1), since in both instances the patient is fearful that a fatal illness underlies their symptoms. Such patients are in an impossible position. Their persisting symptoms suggest to them a sinister physical origin that has been missed or denied by their doctor. If, however, these symptoms do *not* have a physical basis, then they must, according to their own illness model, be psychological. This idea evokes fears of madness. Thus, neither choice is acceptable, and so these people are forced to pursue a third alternative: the search for a *benign* organic basis to their symptoms. Inevitably, they are not reassurred by repeated negative findings of physical or biochemical investigations, which serve only to maintain their illness-confirming behavior. The normal distribution curve inevitably yields a proportion of marginal or false-positive test results, and these (particularly if the investigations are repeated) serve as powerful reinforcers of the patient's search for a physical basis to their symptoms.

When the fear of a sinister underlying illness becomes central to the patient's illness-confirming behavior, the diagnostic label of hypochondriasis is often applied. However, fears of underlying physical illness are also very common in patients with anxiety disorders. For example, Buglass *et al.* (1977) found such fears in 16 out of 30 agoraphobic women, but in none of the normal control group.

The Marital Repercussions of Illness-Confirming Behavior

At least one-third of patients who present to their family physicians with anxiety disorders and depressive neuroses develop illness-confirming behavior and become chronic attenders, often interminably (Dunn, 1983; Kedward, 1969; Mann *et al.*, 1981). This 8–10% of the average physician's overall population of patients contributes as much as 20–25% to the total number of consultations. Not only do these long-term patients tend to have persisting marital, interpersonal, and general adjustment problems, but they also have matching personality problems (Murphy, 1976). Recent research into the marital context of severe anxiety disorders (Hafner, 1983a, 1984a, 1984b, 1985a, 1985b; Hafner & Ross, 1983) has suggested that in female patients, who comprise a substantial majority, personality abnormalities and a sex-role stereotyped marriage relationship interact as symptom-perpetuating factors.

As I suggested in Chapter 3, women with a poorly developed sense of personal identity tend to overidentify with the female sex-role stereotype. This represents an abandonment or postponement of the search for personal identity and self-determination. Such women seek to marry sex-role-stereotyped men to protect and support them. However, once married to such a man, it soon becomes clear that the strength of his identification with the male sex-role stereotype makes the marriage relationship inflexible. As the woman matures and tries to abandon her stereotyped perspective, seeking greater autonomy and self-determination within the marriage, her husband resists these changes. He deeply but unconsciously fears his wife's moves towards autonomy and self-determination, since they lessen her dependency upon him, threatening to expose the fact that his personal adjustment relies upon a rigidly stereotyped marriage relationship. Since his fears are ultimately irrational, his attempts to undermine his wife's moves toward independence are illogical, inconsistent, and confusing. However, since his wife has already defined herself as unusually dependent on her husband, she finds it extremely difficult to resist his demands that she remain dependent on him, however irrationally, inconsistently, or illogically these are expressed.

Often, the wife develops psychological symptoms in relation to the conflict between her wish for greater autonomy and the demands of her husband that she remain dependent and subservient. However, because this conflict is mainly unconscious, she experiences her symptoms as mysterious, unpleasant and frightening phenomena over which she has no control. Seeking explanation and reassurance, she presents them to her family doctor. Since her symptoms are a product of stress deriving from denied, ill-defined, or unacknowledged marital conflict, she will now in all likelihood be caught up in the circular process of illness-confirming behavior. As a result, her symptoms will gradually become a displaced focus for her marital conflicts and dissatisfaction.

Instead of grappling directly with issues of power and control in the marriage, she can use her symptoms to exercise some power indirectly. For example, the disability caused by her symptoms may prevent her from carrying out certain domestic tasks or from functioning socially. This forces her husband to be more involved in family tasks, and circumscribes his life beyond the domestic. Thus, a measure of role sharing is achieved. But, because it is compulsory rather than the result of a voluntary reappraisal of marital roles and stereotypes, it is resented by both partners and contributes to their mutual hostility.

In such circumstances, the patient's symptoms gradually become central to marital interaction. This is associated with a subtle shift in the role of the doctor, who now serves mainly to substantiate and validate the patient's symptoms. At a conscious level, the patient's repeated approaches to the medical profession reflect a genuine wish for relief from distressing and disabling symptoms. Furthermore, as long as she believes that she has an illness that can ultimately be cured, she is able to preserve hope for the future. In addition, she gets a measure of support and encouragement from doctors and others in her struggle to cope with the symptoms: Symbolically, this represents to her an acknowledgement of her overall struggle to transcend stereotypes and become an individual in her own right.

Unconsciously, her repeated approaches to doctors have a different purpose. The repeated failure of doctors to cure her symptoms is highly frustrating to the doctors concerned. As authority figures, usually male, doctors symbolize the arbitrary control and power that her husband seeks to assume over her. Thus, she gets unconscious gratification from defying or obstructing the doctor's deeply felt wish to cure her. Perhaps most important, the doctor's validation of her symptoms as an illness protects her from intrapsychic and marital conflict: Because of her illness, for which she is not personally responsible, she *is* totally dependent on her husband, and could not leave the marriage even if she wished to do so. Thus, she has no choice but to obey her husband, and to bury her conflicts about power and autonomy so deeply within her that they cease to be a disturbing influence.

In nonstereotyped marriage relationships also, personality abnormalities and sex-role conflicts may interact to precipitate psychological symptoms (Hafner, 1983a, 1984a, 1984b). Once the patient's stress-related symptoms have been confirmed by the primary care physician as medical–organic rather than psychological–interpersonal, the patient's incentive to examine marital or other relevant stresses and conflicts is markedly reduced. If the symptoms persist, problem-solving activities are directed toward finding a medical cure rather than resolving background problems. As a result, the couple may abandon attempts at constructive, shared, problem-solving activities, instead handing over responsibility for the patient's symptoms to medical "experts."

The failure of medical treatment increases frustration both within the doctor–patient relationship and within the marriage. This increases the need for illness-confirming behavior, since the doctor is likely at this stage to express frustration by irritably implying or stating that the problem is psychological. These views may be transmitted to the patient's spouse. In any event, since the patient's symptoms are likely to be very variable, the spouse also is likely to refer to them in moments of anger or irritation as psychological or "imaginery," and to suggest at the same time that the patient needs merely to "pull herself (or himself) together." Thus, both within marriage and within the doctor–patient relationship, the patient needs to prove that his or her symptoms are "genuine." In effect, this means proving that they have a physical basis, thereby perpetuating the vicious cycles that surround and maintain illness-confirming behavior.

Therapeutic Interventions

Marsh's (1977) landmark study showed that when family physicians systematically replaced the routine prescribing of drugs for minor ailments with brief counseling and education about the likely origin and nature of symptoms, worthwhile clinical and economic benefits emerged. For example: "A common finding too has been that when no prescription is offered the patient seems more ready to declare the real problem that bothers him—for instance, a psychiatric or marital problem."

Catalan, Gath, Edmonds, and Ennis (1984) carried out a study that was similar to Marsh's, but of a more rigorous experimental design. Although they found no overall benefits from withholding anxiolytic medication in treating minor affective disorders, there were clearly no overall disadvantages. In particular, the patients who were denied anxiolytic medication made no increased demands on the doctors' time during the six-month follow-up, an important finding that invalidates a frequently stated justification for the regular use of anxiolytics in treating minor psychiatric disorders in family practice.

However, there are many pressures on family physicians to prescribe anxiolytic drugs when these may not be strictly indicated, and sympathetic, insightful counseling does not coincide with the main interests or skills of all general practitioners. Even if appropriate counseling was offered routinely as an alternative to anxiolytic medication, many patients would prefer drugs to the challenge of grappling with marital or personal problems that appear profoundly difficult or insoluble. Furthermore, a proportion of patients reacts overdefensively when confronted about interpersonal or intrapsychic problems and conflicts that are deeply repressed or strongly denied. In such circumstances, attempts at counseling are likely to be counterproductive unless they are handled very skillfully indeed.

Clearly, a greater awareness among primary care physicians of the ways in which they may unwittingly contribute to psychological symptom formation or maintenance would prevent a significant amount of chronic psychiatric morbidity. As noted earlier, a vast majority of identified psychiatric disturbance is treated in primary care setting; each year, the average family physician refers only about 5% of his or her psychiatrically diagnosed patients to psychiatrists (Goldberg & Huxley, 1980). Another 5% is referred to medical specialists, usually with the aim of eliminating a possible organic basis for their somatic complaints. This subgroup is particularly prone to developing persistent abnormal illness behavior, which, once firmly established, is often extremely difficult to reverse. Andrews *et al.* (in press) have developed some useful guidelines for the management of such cases.

CHAPTER SIX

Marriage and Affective Disorders

The *DSM-III* category "affective disorders" comprises major depression, dysthmic disorder (or depressive neurosis), bipolar disorder, cyclothymic disorder, and atypical variants of both depression and bipolar disorder. Most of this chapter is devoted to depression because it is far more common than bipolar or cyclothymic disorders.

COMMUNITY STUDIES OF DEPRESSION

Two recent American studies have made a major contribution to our knowledge of the prevalence and treatment of depression in the community.

Weissman, Myers, and Thompson (1981) surveyed a representative sample of 510 adults in New Haven, Connecticut, over a 2-year period. They used the Research Diagnostic Criteria of major and minor depression, which broadly coincide with the *DSM-III* criteria.

The point prevalence (or current rate) for overall psychiatric disorder was 15.1%, of which depression comprised 5.7%. This confirmed previous findings in the United States, the United Kingdom, and elsewhere that depression is among the most common psychiatric disorders in the community.

Only 34% of those with a diagnosis of depression had received treatment from a mental health professional at any time during the previous year. Of those who had not, about one third had approached other professionals such as members of the clergy, nurses, and nonpsychiatric social workers. A surprising 65% of those depressed subjects who had not seen mental health professionals over the previous year had visited nonpsychiatric physicians *more than six times* during the same period.

Of those with a diagnosis of depression, 55% had been treated with psychotropic drugs over the previous year. Only 17% of those had received antidepressants, the remainder receiving minor tranquilizers (35%) or hypnotics (17%). Women were more than twice as likely than men to have received any kind of treatment for depression over the previous year.

A second community study by Roberts and Vernon (1982) broadly supported the findings of Weissman *et al.*, although Roberts and Vernon found that only 21% of those with a diagnosis of depression had sought help from mental health professionals over the previous year.

Weissman, Myers, and Thompson (1981) reviewed a number of studies that suggested that although about 20% of patients attending general medical or primary care physicians are depressed, this is recognized in less than one half of cases. Depressed patients who are not recognized as such, or who are inappropriately treated, often make heavy, extended, and expensive demands on general medical services.

Barnes and Prosen (1984) reported data showing that the frequency of depression among patients attending primary care physicians is probably higher than the 20% detected by Weissman, Myers, and Thompson. In their own study, Barnes and Prosen found significant depression in 33% of 1,250 patients attending 37 general practitioners. Reviewing similar studies, they found an average rate of over 40%. Although many patients were suffering from depression in conjunction with major or minor illnesses, the authors pointed out that there is nonetheless great scope for improving the recognition and treatment of depression in a general practice setting.

This point was underlined by Kedward (1969), who found that over 50% of patients with a psychiatric disorder who were attending primary care physicians had a *chronic* psychiatric condition, most commonly depression. A majority of these patients were unimproved over 3 years.

Even after psychiatric treatment, a substantial proportion of patients remains chronically depressed. Bothwell and Weissman (1977) found that only 31% of women had fully recovered 4 years after treatment for an acute depressive episode, and that 26% were as symptomatic as when they first came for treatment. It is noteworthy that marital problems and frictions persisted even when patients became free of depression.

In a recent review, Weissman and Akiskal (1984) reported data suggesting that depression becomes chronic in about 20% of cases, and that a majority of these remain treatment resistant for several years or longer. They suggested that "evidence for the possible efficacy of psychotherapy in chronic depression is indirect and sparse. . . . chronic depressions are not only inadequately treated, but . . . there may be an iatrogenic contribution to a chronic denouement as a result of inappropriate prescription of sedative hypnotics as the sole treatment modality." They added that the marriages of chronically depressed patients "were dysfunctional in that, despite serious friction, neither reconciliation nor divorce were contemplated" (pp. 25–26).

Weissman and Akiskal's (1984) findings were substantiated in a naturalistic study by Barrett (1984), who followed up for 2 years 169 people meeting Research Diagnostic Criteria for depression. Of these, 73% were women.

Although none of the subjects were planning to enter treatment at the start of the study, 53% in fact did so during the subsequent 2 years. There was no relationship between outcome and the type of treatment received, and those who received no treatment improved as much as those who did. Of 27 subjects who had a diagnosis of chronic depression, 63% were unchanged or worse after 2 years. Of 6 subjects who had a major depression superimposed on chronic depression, all were unchanged or worse 2 years later.

Chronic Depression: A Major Community Problem

If we accept a current rate or 6-month prevalence for depression in the community of between 5–7% (Myers *et al.*, 1984; Weissman, Myers, & Thompson, 1981), and if we accept also that about one fifth of those cases are chronic and treatment resistant, then at least 1% of the population is suffering from chronic, treatment-resistant depression at any point in time. In the United States alone, this represents over 2 million people.

Although Weissman and Akiskal (1984) underline the importance of marital factors in perpetuating chronic depression, they and Barrett (1984) point out that the condition has hitherto been linked primarily with personality disorder. This reinforces the idea of individual therapy, so that marital factors tend to be overlooked.

While personality is clearly important in chronic depression, it interacts powerfully with marital factors. Clinically, marital and personality factors are often so inextricably linked with each other and with overt symptoms, that it is essential to deal with all three concurrently. Spouse-aided therapy (Chapter 9) creates a framework within which this therapeutic challenge can be addressed.

MARRIAGE AND DEPRESSION

It is now well established that a diagnosis of depression is made about twice as often in women as it is in men (Goldman & Ravid, 1980; Myers *et al.*, 1984; Weissman & Klerman, 1977).

That this sex difference is not found in young, unmarried adults was demonstrated by Parker (1979). However, Parker found that young unmarried women rated themselves as much more likely than young single men to develop depression in the face of interpersonal problems such as "being rejected or distanced in a relationship," "the break-up of an important relationship," or "a fall-off in support to my self-esteem."

He predicted that sex differences in depression might emerge over time, "as males and females take up roles allied to their sex, which offer different social responsibilities and which may have varying capacities to increase vulnerability to depression" (p. 130).

That the social roles and responsibilities of marriage and full-time motherhood are strongly associated with overall psychiatric disorder in women has been established in previous chapters. Evidence to be outlined shortly suggests that this applies equally, or more so, to depression. Furthermore, a recent major longitudinal community study of depression and anxiety disorders has suggested that the prevalence of these conditions is increasing in married women with dependent children (Murphy, Sobol, Neff, Olivier, & Leighton, 1984).

The date in Murphy *et al.*'s study were obtained from interviews with a representative sample of over 2,000 people from "Stirling County" in North America in 1952 and 1970. The point prevalence for depression and anxiety disorders combined was 12.5% in 1952 and 12.7% in 1970. In 1952, the prevalence rates for depression and anxiety disorders were almost equal at 5.3 and 5.0% respectively. In 1970 the prevalence of depression had increased to 5.6%, whereas that of anxiety disorders had fallen to 4.6%. Admixtures of depression and anxiety accounted for the residual percentages.

Although the *overall* prevalence of depression and anxiety did not increase significantly between 1952 and 1970, the *age-specific rates for women changed substantially*.

In 1952, the prevalence for women was lowest (less than 10%) between the ages of 30–39, rising to nearly 20% between 40–49 and peaking at over 30% between 60–69. In 1970, the prevalence rate was lowest (less than 5%) between the ages of 18–30, *peaking between 30–39* (about 18%), and thereafter decreasing slightly.

Prevalence rates for women aged 30–39 were *lower* in 1952 than those for men of the same age. In 1970, the prevalence rates for women aged 30–39 was nearly 150% *higher* than men in the same age group.

In concluding their study, Murphy *et al.* ask: "With the image of the working woman now firmly planted, have young women who are bound to their homes by small children or lingering tradition become especially vulnerable? Are some among them the working mothers of young children who are finding the effort to keep a foot in each of two worlds is a situation that takes away whatever advantages outside work may hold for others?" (p. 996).

By asking this question, the authors imply that work outside the home is destructive to the mental health of married women, which is contrary to almost all the available evidence. This perspective overlooks, for example, the challenge and possible benefits of more equal role sharing between male and female parents.

In reality, by far the most likely reason for the dramatic rise in depression and anxiety in women age 30–39 is an increase in sex-role strain and conflict deriving primarily from continuing idealization and stereotyping of the maternal role.

Evidence obtained more recently than 1970 suggests that the female preponderance of depression in younger married people may still be increasing. Heins (1978) reviewed data on those married people who were diagnosed as suffering from depression when they sought psychiatric treatment for the first time at a public hospital.

He found that between the ages of 26–45, only 35 married men were diagnosed for every 100 married women. However, between the ages of 51–65, 71 men were diagnosed for every 100 women. In only one age group, 51–55, were married men diagnosed as depressed more often than married women (57 versus 46 new cases per 100,000 of married people).

The most obvious interpretation of these data is that marriage and parenthood protects men from depression, whereas it has the opposite effect on women. This appears to be particularly true when the employment variable is taken into account. Married women who work full-time report levels of depression that are similar to those reported by fully employed married men (Briscoe, 1982; Tennant *et al.*, 1982). Single men who are employed report levels of depression that are somewhat higher than those reported by single, employed women. This trend becomes most evident in single men over age 35. The level of depression rises greatly with unemployment in both men and women, whether married or single. Thus, the balance of evidence suggests that it is the *combination* of marriage and lack of employment outside the home that is most potent in causing depression in married women. Although the presence in the home of children younger than 12 is strongly associated with depression in married women, it does not in itself appear to be a major cause of depression: It is a risk factor mainly because it prevents married women from working outside the home.

MARITAL INTERACTION AND DEPRESSED WOMEN

Although lack of employment outside the home appears to be a major contributor to depression in married women, there are many other possible contributing factors, of which a highly significant one is the absence of a close, confiding relationship with the husband (Tennant *et al.*, 1982). The quality of the marital relationship becomes even more important once psychiatric help for depression has been sought (Bothwell & Weissman, 1977; Rounsaville *et al.*, 1979a, 1979b). A majority of depressed married women who are assessed by psychiatrists have significant marital problems and conflicts. Their depression is likely to lessen only if their marital difficulties are improved or resolved.

Impairment of the marriage relationships of clinically depressed women is evident in many areas (Heins, 1978). There is a reduction in the amount of affection and an increase in the amount of overt or indirect hostility and criticism; there is an increased struggle for control and dominance within the marriage; and there is less cooperation and shared problem-solving activity, with a related increase in husband-dominated interactional patterns. Interestingly, the latter has been reported even when the husband is the depressed patient.

For reasons outlined in previous chapters, sex-role issues have been grossly underrepresented in clinical and research reports on depression. In order to counter this, sex-role stereotyping and conflict are highlighted in the following case histories.

Case 1: Beauty and the Beast

The title "Beauty and the Beast" has been chosen because the folktale of that name reflects certain themes that can be found in this case, particularly that of a woman confined in a "house–castle" by a mysterious, frightening creature who professes adoration for her.

LOUISE

Louise was 48 when she came to see me complaining of moderate to severe depression over the previous 4 years. Her *DSM-III* diagnosis was dysthmic disorder. The onset of her depression coincided with the departure from home of her younger son, then aged 21, to whom she was very close. Her older son had left home 18 months previously, but she had been little affected by this because her relationship with him was less close.

Louise's family background was very sad. Her mother had consistently tormented, criticized, and humiliated her from early childhood: "She was cruel to me, but only when we were alone. She'd torment me until I was screaming and thumping myself, and then she'd tell me to calm down, and pat me. I had to do housework the whole time. If it wasn't perfect when she came home, she'd hit me really hard about both ears. She had a violent temper. I always got the blame for everything, but my younger brother was spared (Louise had one brother who was 3 years her junior). My mother was always telling me I was stupid, especially in front of others, laughing at me and ridiculing me. She was rude and ill-mannered, but I was always trying to cover up for her. She even used to attack my father: I remember once blood streaming down his face. I grew up with the idea that one person had to dominate another in marriage. My poor father, he died a broken man. . . . And yet, there was good in my mother; she was hard and strong. She had a dreadfully sad, tragic life."

Although rather ineffectual and often absent, Louise's father had done his best to protect her from her mother's cruelty. Louise said of him: "He said he loved me; he was the only person who understood me and cared for me, but he never showed it, I think because mother resented his affection for me."

Louise showed much insight into the reasons for her marriage to Arnold when she was 20 and he 23: "It was the only way I could get away from my mother. I hated her, yet I loved her. She had such power over me. She totally dominated me, so that I couldn't think for myself. She made all my decisions for me. She even took all my money when I went out to work. Because of the way she treated me, I was ripe for the plucking by a man like Arnold. He took over where mother left off. I thought I was marrying a nice person who'd take care of me, but he turned out to be all the things I hate in a person. I've had a miserable marriage from the word go. I would have divorced him years ago for mental cruelty, but I didn't want to deprive the boys of their father. He was a weak, insignificant father, but I figured a weak father was better than none. I guess really I stuck it out because it was the proper thing to do. I had obedience drilled into me as a child, and I carry things out to the bitter end. I've put the family before myself for all these years."

ARNOLD

Arnold came from a family that placed great emphasis on propriety and correctness in manners and conduct. This tradition was powerfully maintained by his father, who ruled the family in a rigidly autocratic manner, and rarely displayed any warmth or affection. Nonetheless, Arnold had a very high regard for his father, almost to the point of idealization, and also for his family's name and tradition, which he referred to as if they were part of a dynasty.

Arnold's mother was harsh, dominating, and rejecting, relying on threats, harassment, or emotional blackmail to secure Arnold's obedience as a child. In particular, she would often offer him a choice of activity, food, or clothing to wear, and then indicate her displeasure with his choice, at the same time insisting that he adhere to it. Thus, he found his mother inconsistent and confusing as well as dominating, and was unable to relate to her with any warmth or affection. Indeed, he felt that neither parent acknowledged him as a person, but merely as a nuisance to be controlled and endured.

When he met Louise, who was an attractive woman, he immediately experienced a strong desire to protect and take care of her.

The couple's initial marriage contract was based on a seemingly straightforward stereotype. Louise would bear and raise children, preferably sons, to continue Arnold's family dynasty. She would be an obedient, loving, dutiful, and faithful wife, carefully managing his house–castle. In return, Arnold would protect her, care for her, and financially support her.

However, serious problems emerged soon after their marriage. For example, when Louise tried to express views of her own, Arnold would often shout her down, and she would end up "a shaking, trembling wreck." To avoid arguments, she began to agree automatically with Arnold (just as she had learned to do with her mother). She began to identify with Arnold's attempts to belittle her on these and other occasions: "I put myself down and agreed with Arnold, rather than constantly feel angry with him. He turned me into a weakling, and I was disgusted with myself for letting it happen."

Gradually she became less self-confident and more dependent on Arnold, who was clearly gratified by her dependency on him. While professing his love and adoration of her, he nonetheless insisted on her absolute obedience. There was little communication between the couple. According to Louise, Arnold was "like a person with a wall around him. No one can get through. He's incapable of any kind of emotion or affection."

When the two boys started high school, Louise took her driving test and began for the first time to develop some social and leisure interests of her own. However, Arnold was rude or offhand to people she invited home and because of this (or so Louise believed), they stopped visiting. If she and Arnold went out together, Arnold constantly criticized and belittled her, particularly in front of others, so that she avoided going out with him.

Although he denied it, Arnold resented her going out alone, since she was then beyond his control. He undermined in various ways her confidence about traveling alone, pointing out traffic dangers, complaining about the high price of petrol and car maintenance (Louise had no income of her own), and often mislaying Louise's car keys at critical times. Although unable to prove it, Louise was convinced that on occasions he tampered with her car so that it would not start. In the face of Arnold's denials about these and other mysterious events, Louise thought at times that he was trying to drive her crazy, and she feared for her sanity. Here it will be recalled that Louise's mother used to torment her in childhood until she went "crazy," and would then reassure her with a pat on the head.

Louise developed anxiety symptoms when driving, which reinforced her fears that she might lose control of the vehicle and have an accident. This led her to stop driving when alone. Thus, she became virtually housebound—an isolated prisoner in her husband's "castle." Matters became even worse when financial problems developed as a result of Arnold's habitual gambling.

Louise's dislike and hatred of Arnold reached an extraordinary intensity: "I'd actually be sick if he touched me. I couldn't bear the sight of his clothes or anything about him. They just made me sick, nauseated." In her eyes, he had truly become a mysterious, frightening beast. Her disgust with him had reached phobic intensity.

However, as long as her younger son was at home, Louise was able to endure these problems. Only after he left did she become seriously depressed and seek the help of her family physician. Louise was age 44 at this time.

MEDICAL TREATMENT

Louise complained to her family physician of depression and anxiety symptoms. She did not mention her long-standing marital difficulties because she was convinced that her doctor would not believe her account of them. He had met Arnold and had told Louise that he had been very impressed by him. Arnold was indeed an impressive figure. Tall, distinguished in appearance, and with a military bearing, he charmingly created an image of the utmost respectability and tolerance. Had Louise revealed his true behavior toward her, it would certainly have strained her credibility in her doctor's eyes.

Thus, Louise's doctor treated her for the "empty nest syndrome," since her depression had coincided with her son's leaving home. For nearly 4 years he prescribed for her a range of antidepressants and tranquilizers, with no real benefit. It was only by chance that he learned about Arnold's gambling habit, and the resulting financial difficulties that had plagued Louise over the years. While questioning Louise about this, the whole story came out. Shocked by her account, Louise's doctor urged her to leave the marriage. This she did clandestinely some months later, with the reluctant help of her younger son. However, both her sons criticized her for leaving their father alone, and refused to visit her in her small flat. She lasted only 5 days before returning to Arnold.

For a while, matters improved. Arnold was devastated by Louise's departure, and for the first time, she felt he really needed her. However, their relationship soon deteriorated again, and Louise felt increasingly trapped within the marriage, spending hours daydreaming about her much craved "freedom." She became seriously depressed again, and I was asked to see her.

COUPLES TREATMENT

After assessing Louise and Arnold separately, I was able to offer them couples therapy, since both acknowledged marital difficulties that they wished to resolve. Arnold admitted that he was a very poor communicator within the marriage. He expressed concern about his tendency to control and dominate Louise, explaining that old habits took over during disagreements in spite of his attempts to be more reasonable.

After 3 sessions, Arnold found the courage to admit to intense shyness, explaining that this was why he discouraged visitors. Louise was astonished at this revelation, since Arnold had never revealed feelings of vulnerability to her before, and she had assumed that his emotions matched his detached, controlled exterior. Arnold also admitted to a fear that Louise would leave him, and a profound fear of loneliness. He had never been able to discuss his real feelings with Louise because he believed this to be unmanly, and thought that it would cause her to lose what little respect she still had for him. Instead, he had coped with his fears by controlling and dominating Louise, and by undermining her self-confidence so that she was *unable* to leave him, rather than remaining out of choice. However, because Louise had not understood Arnold's motives, which were largely unconscious, his behavior had increasingly alienated her until her fear and hatred of him was more powerful than her fear of managing alone. Thus, with a little encouragement, she was able to leave him, albeit for only a few days. This evoked Arnold's deepest fears of loss and abandonment and contributed to his willingness to become involved in conjoint therapy.

Once Louise and Arnold became able to talk about their real feelings toward each other, their marriage began to improve. Louise came to realize how, from the start of the marriage, she had displaced onto Arnold buried feelings of rage toward her mother, the full intensity of which she was able to acknowledge for the first time in the 6th therapy session. After 14 conjoint sessions, the couple felt able to continue working on their relationship without further help from me.

At a 1-year follow-up, there were still many problems in the marriage, but both were determined to remain together and to continue working at them. Louise was substantially free of depression, and had resumed social and leisure activities outside the home. The couple had resumed sexual intercourse together after a gap of nearly 10 years.

COMMENT

Louise and Arnold's relationship can be explained in terms of sex-role stereotypes and object relations theory. Louise had suppressed her true self, or gender identity, and had come to identify totally with a sex-role-stereotyped view of male–female relationships. She was fearful of being assertive because this evoked frightening feelings of uncontrollable rage that she habitually buried deeply within her and that had combined with her suppressed gender identity to form the "bad object."

Using the mechanism of projective identification, Louise identified unconsciously with Arnold's aggressive behaviour toward her, and obtained vicarious gratification from it. However, Arnold's treatment of her reinforced her buried feelings of rage until they became almost overwhelming in intensity, threatening to escape from repression and control. Sex-role conditioning and fears of managing alone helped to keep Louise in the marriage, within which she felt hopelessly trapped.

Arnold also married with sex-role-stereotyped expectations, but his strong wish to love, care for, and protect Louise disguised an intense need to dominate, control, and subjugate her. In part, this represented his unconscious wish to deal with the unwanted "feminine" aspects of himself that he had projected onto Louise. In doing so, he was also protecting himself from unconscious fears that Louise, like his mother, would seek to dominate, control, confuse, and humiliate him. At the same time, he was displacing his buried anger about his mother onto Louise, just as Louise was displacing such feelings onto him. His rigid adherence to a sex-role stereotype protected him from acknowledging his buried feelings of fearfulness, inadequacy, and vulnerability, but, at the same time, stopped him from discussing them with Louise.

Fortunately, Arnold found the courage to reveal his true feelings during therapy, creating the opportunity for marital rapprochement. As a result, he became increasingly able to reveal to Louise the vulnerable, sensitive, fearful, and dependant aspects of himself that both had traditionally regarded as incompatible with acceptable masculinity. In turn, Louise became more supportive and understanding of Arnold, concurrently developing a sense of personal worth and self-confidence. She became more assertive as she grew less frightened of the rage that was bound up with her buried true self. The couple was able to make slow progress away from a "compulsory" marriage, based on fear and sex-role stereotyping, toward a companionate relationship.

In the original folktale, when Beauty had left the Beast, she eventually returned to find him alone and dying of a broken heart. This evoked from her for the first time expressions of genuine affection, and the tender kiss that transformed the dying Beast into a handsome, vigorous Prince. When Louise left Arnold, he was forced to acknowledge a profound sense of loneliness and incompleteness that, when discussed during therapy, evoked genuine affection from Louise. Thus, Arnold was transformed from a "Beast" into a person who, if not a Prince, was at least an acceptable companion with human rather than stereotyped attributes.

Wider Implications of the Case

The case of "Beauty and the Beast" starkly and clearly illustrates marital problems that, in attenuated form, are very widespread in contemporary English-speaking societies. Marriages based on sex-role stereotypes make enormous demands on mothers, who are expected to be patient, loving, caring, and nurturing to their families while abandoning or postponing their own personal needs, wishes, and aspirations. They are, in fact, expected to be superhuman beings, which most of them are not. In the face of these impossible expectations, many mothers become irritable and frustrated. Cooped up all day with young children, they become rejecting, controlling, intrusive, and dominating toward them. The children cope by burying their own anger and humiliation deeply within them, but when they reach adulthood, their feelings inevitably resurface in an unconscious or displaced manner within their own marriages. Since these marriages are likely to be based on stereotypes, the problem of unconscious hostility within marriage is perpetuated and reinforced across generations. Ultimately, the buried rage may become too great to be contained within the marriage, which as a result may shatter.

Sex-role-stereotyped marriages are based on a strict division of labor and are ultimately sustained by the idea of procreation and childraising rather than the idea of companionship between husband and wife. Thus, when the children leave school and become financially independent, the marriage partners may be unable to adjust. Mothers tend to cling to their children, just as Louise clung to her younger son. When the children finally leave home, their mothers often experience a period of depression. This probably explains Heins's (1978) finding that new cases of depression in women peak in the age group 46–50, which coincides with the period during which a majority of children leave home. Such depression is likely to resolve if the wife finds new interests to sustain her, and if she is able to develop a more open, honest, intimate, and companionable relationship with her husband. Unconscious or displaced anger in either partner is likely to inhibit the development of such a relationship.

Louise's doubts about revealing to her doctor the true state of affairs within her marriage are shared by many other women in similar circumstances. A husband whose public image is of the utmost patience, tolerance and respectability may be a sadistic tyrant in the privacy of his own home. Since his unfortunate wife and children are the only witnesses to such behavior, their accounts may receive little credibility. Moreover, economically and emotionally dependent women who have nothing in their lives except their children and the public illusion of a happy marriage are often profoundly reluctant to acknowledge the truth, even to themselves. Such wives generally deny or obscure their husbands' role in creating a marital climate that causes or perpetuates their psychological symptoms. Even if wives reveal the truth about their husbands' behavior, they may not be believed; worse, they may be accused of causing their husbands' behavior in the first place. Certainly, women with severe psychological symptoms have often been accused by therapists of using their symptoms to exercise tyrannical control over their "long-suffering" husbands.

Jocelynne Scutt (1983) has published a major survey of violence within the family. She amply documents the extraordinary extent to which many women struggle to keep private even dangerous physical assaults by their husbands. Unreported physical assaults upon wives by husbands appear to be very common. If this is so, then the level of unreported abuse that falls short of physical violence is probably very high indeed.

Case 2: Solitary Confinement

The case of Catherine, 27, and Patrick, 28, illustrates a marriage between two ambitious and competitive people. Although before marriage Catherine's social adjustment was superior to that of Patrick, she subsequently became depressed in the context of major sex-role strain and conflict.

CATHERINE

When Catherine came to see me, she explained that she had been very depressed over the past 3–4 months, and had recently experienced suicidal thoughts. Since she did not wish to commit suicide, these thoughts distressed and worried her a great deal, and had led her to seek professional help through her family physician. Her *DSM-III* diagnosis was major depressive episode.

Tears streamed down her face as she described to me the way she felt. I was struck by how puzzled she was about her depression, and how angry she was with herself for being depressed: "Half the problem is I can't work out *why* I'm depressed. It's so *stupid*. I've got all the things I always wanted: a lovely daughter, a beautiful home and a responsible, hardworking husband. There's just no *reason* for me to be depressed. I should be happy, like the other young mothers I see when I go shopping. I get so angry and frustrated with myself sometimes. I guess I blame myself for being depressed, but that probably only makes things worse."

Of her parents, Catherine said: "My mother is a very strong person. She still has a big influence on me. We have a very close relationship, but neither of us are very affectionate toward each other. I resent her at times because she has such a strong impact on my opinions. She's very intelligent, more than I am. Yet she seems to have devoted her life to pampering my father. My father is extremely selfish. I love him, but he's really just a spoiled child, and has continued to be spoiled by my mother. He needs her more than she needs him. Basically, I think he's got an inferiority complex. He left our upbringing to mother, and was called in only for the really bad things. He regarded my sister and I as two precious little beans, but I know he preferred my sister to me."

Catherine's sister Maud was 5 years her senior: "She's much more mature than me, much better adjusted. She's very happily married. We were never close, although we've got a little closer since I left home."

Catherine's mother had a university degree, but had postponed her own career aspirations when she married Catherine's father, a man without higher education who had nonetheless provided adequately for his family by dint of hard work at a rather mundane job. When Catherine started high school, her mother had commenced part-time work in a job of far lesser status than that to which she had originally aspired. There she had remained.

Although Catherine worked hard and conscientiously at school, she was academically poor. This frustrated and disappointed her mother, who sought vicarious gratification of her own academic aspirations through Catherine and Maud. Since Maud was good academically, Catherine was aware of her mother's preference for Maud, a preference which was shared by her father. Constant unfavorable comparisons with her sister contributed to Catherine's negative self-image in childhood and to her poor self-esteem in late adolescence and early adulthood.

Catherine left home at the age of 17 and went to work in the local branch of a department store that had many other branches throughout the state and elsewhere. Here, her conscientious and hardworking approach and her desire to please led to the offer of promotion to a larger store in a city about 100 miles away from her home town. She took advantage of this opportunity and, although only 18, coped well with the move away from home, sharing a flat with some co-workers.

Catherine's acumen in the area of women's fashions was quickly recognized. When, at the age of 21, she met Patrick, she was already a junior buyer and had become highly competitive and ambitious in her field. Although still somewhat lacking in self-confidence, and often feeling inferior to her peers, she had flourished in the context of the new challenges and responsibilities created by her work. To others she appeared animated, cheerful, confident, and outgoing. Her social life was extensive and vigorous.

PATRICK

Patrick was the third oldest of six children. He had never got on well with his father, who had been little involved with parenting, and who tended to be critical and unsupportive of him. Patrick's mother had favored his three sisters, and his two brothers had been favored by their father, ostensibly because of their sporting prowess, which Patrick lacked. Thus, although his mother devoted hersef exclusively to the welfare of her husband and children, Patrick grew up feeling rejected, inferior, and inadequate.

He had worked since the age of 16 as a clerk in the same department store as Catherine, and had achieved modest promotion within the finance section. A lonely, shy, and inhibited young man, Patrick met Catherine at an office party. He had immediately been attracted by her vivacious, sparkling manner. She was attracted by his looks and by his reserve, which gave her the impression of quiet strength and stability. When she was with him, her personal insecurities and self-doubts vanished.

THE MARRIAGE

The couple married after a courtship of about 18 months. During this time, Catherine had continued to derive a sense of security and stability from Patrick's apparent strength and quiet confidence. Patrick's drab, dull life had been transformed by Catherine: He felt enlivened and elevated by her, and, in the wake of her intense sociability, he enjoyed for the first time a fairly active social life.

With a little financial help from their respective families, the couple was able to buy a pleasant home in a good suburb without the burden of excessive mortgage repayments. They both attached considerable importance to material possessions and surroundings, and invested their residual money in good-quality furniture and decor.

In spite of her strong commitment to her job, Catherine craved motherhood. Patrick was almost as enthusiastic about the idea of being a father. The couple discussed parenthood in idealized terms, emphasizing the positive aspects and ignoring problems such as restriction of life-style and financial strains. Catherine spent much time daydreaming about motherhood, which she saw in stereotyped, romantic terms. The idea of being a mother filled her with a warm glow: She believed that having a child would enable her to feel that she was a whole, fulfilled, and contented person for the first time in her life. So powerful and pervasive were her romantic fantasies about motherhood that they completely obscured any doubts she had about leaving her job.

Sylvia was born when Catherine was just 25. The confinement and delivery went smoothly, but after returning home from the hospital, Catherine suffered from "post-maternity blues." Sylvia was a very demanding baby from the start, breast-feeding poorly, crying frequently, and waking repeatedly through the night. In her attempts to meet Sylvia's needs, Catherine soon became exhausted, so that constant fatigue was added to her depressed mood. This made it difficult for her to respond in a positive manner to Sylvia's demands, which, in turn, increased the baby's irritability and frustration. Thus, a vicious cycle was established in which Sylvia became more and more distressed and demanding and Catherine became increasingly exhausted, frustrated, and depressed as she struggled to meet Sylvia's needs.

Patrick was unhelpful at home. He protested exhaustion because of the long hours of overtime he put in at work to make up for the loss of Catherine's income. In spite of his earlier talk about looking forward to fatherhood, he was extremely reluctant to be involved in Sylvia's care. The excuses he used to avoid getting up in the night to attend to Sylvia, or to change her diapers in the evenings and at weekends, were so varied and inventive that Catherine gave up trying to persuade him to help her. Inwardly, however, she nurtured a powerful resentment toward him.

Matters were made worse by the fact that Catherine had no additional help. Her mother had not wanted to come and stay, explaining that she had to remain at home in order to look after Catherine's father. Patrick's mother, who lived about 9 miles from the couple, had offered to come and help at weekends (she worked part-time during the week), an offer to which Catherine had not responded. She did not actively dislike Patrick's mother, but despised her for allowing herself to be dominated and bullied by Patrick's father, whom she disliked intensely because of his critical, insensitive, overbearing, and sexist manner and attitudes. For similar reasons, Catherine disliked Patrick's brothers. As a result, she was anxious to minimize her contact with Patrick's family.

SOCIAL ISOLATION

Catherine's social network had consisted almost entirely of friends and acquaintances at work. None of these relationships was really close or intimate, and within 4 months of Sylvia's birth she had lost virtually all contact with her erstwhile friends. She lacked the energy and the motivation to become acquainted with her neighbors, who made little effort to get to know her or Patrick. Thus, she was alone with Sylvia almost all the time. Increasingly, she felt trapped and isolated at home. She compared her situation to that of a prisoner in solitary confinement, adding that she must be a really wicked person to deserve such a terrible punishment. Indeed, for a person as intensely sociable as Catherine, isolated confinement to the home represented a profound deprivation, and contributed substantially to her depression.

MARITAL DETERIORATION

When Sylvia was about 10 months old, she started to sleep throughout the night and became generally more settled. Gradually, Catherine recovered from her exhaustion and depression. Eighteen months after Sylvia's birth,

Catherine's mood had improved considerably. Although she still had days when she felt depressed and despondent, she had other days when she felt fairly cheerful and animated. However, her relationship with Patrick did not improve. Rather, it deteriorated. The following factors contributed to this.

Patrick's Ambition. It had been made clear to Patrick by his employers that they regarded him as suitable for further promotion, but only if he obtained a degree or diploma in accountancy or business administration. He had become very competitive and ambitious, justifying this on the grounds that his promotion was in the best interests of his family, since it would increase their income. When Sylvia was about 18 months old, he enrolled in a 3-year part-time business course. This required him to attend evening school 3 evenings a week, with about 12 hours additional weekly study. As a result, he had very little time to devote to Catherine, Sylvia, or related domestic activities. Catherine was effectively prevented from pursuing any independent activities outside the home, because the couple could not afford a baby-sitter and Patrick was too preoccupied with his studies on weekends to be able to look after Sylvia. When Catherine pointed this out to Patrick, he agreed that it was regrettable, but insisted that he must be allowed to pursue his studies, since this was ultimately in the best interests of all three of them. Catherine found it hard to disagree with Patrick's viewpoint, but was nonetheless extremely reluctant to accept a continuation of her "solitary confinement."

Divided Loyalties. Catherine's intense dislike of Patrick's father and brothers, and her consequent reluctance to spend time with his family, continued unabated. However, Patrick felt obliged to visit his parents regularly and to meet their not infrequent demands for help and support in family or domestic matters. It seemed to Catherine that Patrick spent more time being a companion to his mother than he did with her, and this aroused a profound resentment within her, particularly as she saw comparatively little of her own mother. She complained to Patrick that his loyalties were with his family and not with her, but Patrick dismissed her complaints as irrational.

Different Coping Styles. When confronted with domestic or personal problems, Catherine favored discussing them with Patrick and trying to formulate problem-solving strategies. If she could not discuss problems, she constantly worried about them, as a result of which their importance to her became exaggerated. In contrast, Patrick coped with problems by denying or dismissing them: He was able to push them entirely out of his mind and to get on with his work or other matters immediately at hand. Thus, he was reluctant to sit and discuss domestic or personal problems with Catherine, and became irritated or angry when she persisted in her attempts to discuss such problems with him. This distressed Catherine greatly, particularly when she tried to describe her depression and related symptoms: Patrick would tend to dismiss these as "imaginery" or "psychological" and suggest that she "pull herself together," go and do some gardening, or find some other activity to distract her from self-preoccupation. While such a personal coping style apparently suited Patrick, he was unable to see that it did not work for Catherine.

Envy of Freedom. Catherine envied Patrick's freedom to leave home for work each weekday. She recalled how her own job had given her a sense of being important and worthwhile as a person, and how much she had thrived on the challenge of working in a busy, competitive environment; she recalled how greatly she had valued her regular paycheck, not just because of the economic independence it afforded her, but because it seemed to confirm beyond question that she was a person of value. Because she was convinced that she had to be a full-time mother to Sylvia, Catherine struggled to deny the adverse effects upon her of stopping work. However, the more she tried to suppress her desire to return to her old job, the more she envied Patrick and his freedom to work outside the home.

When she tried to discuss her feelings about this with Patrick, he was unsympathetic. In fact, he claimed to envy *her*. He did not regard his job as a welcome challenge; instead of equating his work with freedom, he regarded it as constricting and confining. Much of what he did was boring and routine: It was a desire to escape from this that, in truth, was the major reason behind his relentless pursuit of a business diploma. Patrick regarded Catherine's life as potentially idyllic. He saw her as having abundant leisure during the day, and freedom to do a whole range of interesting or entertaining things that were impossible for him because of his commitment to work and study. Given such fundamentally different perspectives, it is not surprising that Catherine and Patrick were totally unable to communicate in this area. This failure of communication generalized to other areas within their relationship.

Maternal Overprotection. Catherine's mother had equated good mothering with rigid, intrusive overcontrol and domination, together with unrealistically high expectations of Catherine. Because Catherine's thinking about motherhood was still based on stereotypes and romantic ideas, she had never seriously questioned the quality of the mothering that she had received as a child. She still dutifully claimed to love her mother, whom she allowed to exercise considerable authority over her, particularly in the matter of Sylvia's upbringing. Thus Catherine unquestioningly mothered Sylvia in the same intrusive, overcontrolling way in which she had herself been mothered. She also set for herself impossibly high standards of motherhood, one consequence of which was her belief that no one apart from her mother and herself could adequately look after Sylvia. As a result, motherhood to Catherine was not only a full-time occupation, but one from which there was no escape, since her mother was too geographically distant and too preoccupied with her husband to be practically involved in her granddaughter's upbringing.

Full-time motherhood made almost overwhelming demands on Catherine. It had deprived her of her much-loved job, which had been her main source of personal fulfillment and self-esteem. It confined her to the home, restricting her access to alternative sources of personal fulfillment and social interaction. And it left Sylvia as her constant, compulsory companion.

Unconsciously, Catherine was full of rage about her situation. However, years of habitual suppression and repression of hostile feelings about her mother had left her unable to deal with angry thoughts, feelings, and impulses toward people who were close to her. She did not permit herself to feel anger and resentment toward Sylvia. Nonetheless, such feelings lay deeply buried within her: After all, were it not for Sylvia, she would now be free to resume her previous happy, fulfilled life-style. When these buried feelings of rage towards Sylvia threatened to surface in her conscious mind, Catherine reacted by invoking the protective stereotype of motherhood and its rituals: She attempted to disguise her rage with an excess of concern and affection toward Sylvia. Her unconscious hostility toward Sylvia emerged as a fear that some harm might befall her daughter: This reinforced Catherine's belief that Sylvia was safe in no one's care other than her own, and consolidated her overprotectiveness.

Thus, another vicious cycle was established: The more Catherine had to bury her unconscious rage toward Sylvia, the more overprotective and concerned about Sylvia's safety and well-being did she become. This restricted further the freedom and independence of both mother and daughter, adding to Catherine's unconscious hostility. At times, Catherine's rage was uncontainable, but she very rarely directed it at Sylvia. Instead, she smashed crockery or shouted at Patrick, which, since he felt an innocent victim, added significantly to their marital disharmony.

THE REEMERGENCE OF DEPRESSION

By the age of 18 months, Sylvia was generally sleeping through the night and was not an unusually troublesome child. In fact, she was an attractive, intelligent little girl with a fairly placid disposition. From Catherine's stereotyped perspective, she had every reason to be a happy, devoted mother: She had a delightful daughter and lived in a pleasant home in a good suburb. Her husband dutifully provided for them and was working extremely hard to improve their financial prospects. Yet she began to descend once again into the despair and depression that had characterized the first year of her life with Sylvia.

Although the reasons for this should now be clear to the reader of this book, they were not clear to Catherine. *Objectively*, she *should* have been depressed: She had lost her job, and with it her main source of personal well-being and her economic independence; she was trapped at home with a demanding infant and no adult company; her marriage lacked communication and warmth, and was full of conflict; and she had no one to whom she could turn for practical and emotional support at those times when she most needed it.

Because of her stereotyped and romanticized attitudes toward motherhood, Catherine failed entirely to perceive that she had good reasons for being depressed. Instead, she blamed herself for not being a happy and fulfilled mother in circumstances that, according to her stereotyped perspective, were ideal. Her reemergent depression was a complete mystery to her. She blamed herself for her seemingly irrational outbursts of anger at Patrick, and came to share his view that she was primarily responsible for their marital difficulties. Patrick was regarded as essentially blameless, which allowed him to adopt a posture of martyred persecution—a posture that he had used in childhood when attacked unfairly by his father.

Both her mother and Patrick reinforced Catherine's stereotyped perspective of motherhood. They agreed that she *should* be happy and fulfilled, and that she had no reason for being chronically depressed and irritable. They did not suggest, for example, that Catherine arrange for child care on one or two mornings or afternoons a week, to help break the vicious cycle of maternal overprotection, buried rage, and depression. Instead, they emphasized the idealized, stereotyped aspects of motherhood, stressing that only Catherine could give Sylvia the maternal love and care that she needed. This left Catherine feeling more and more depressed about her inability to be a contented, responsive, and fulfilled mother.

MEDICAL TREATMENT

In desperation, Catherine sought the help of her family physician, a kindly man in whom she had great confidence. She explained that she had been depressed for the first 10–12 months after Sylvia's birth, which she attributed to the demands of looking after a young infant. She added that her mood and general well-being had improved considerably after Sylvia had reached the age of about 1 year. Then, about 6 months later, just as Sylvia was becoming less demanding and more fun to be with, she had become depressed again. Sylvia was now nearly 2 years old, and she, Catherine, had been depressed for nearly 6 months. She could not understand why.

Her physician had 4 children. He was a devoted family man with a stereotyped perspective on marriage and motherhood that was shared by his wife. He agreed entirely with Catherine that she *should* be happy and fulfilled. Like Catherine, her mother, and Patrick, he could see no reason why a woman with a delightful little girl, living in such an ideal environment, with no financial problems, should be anything but happy and fulfilled. He suggested that Catherine should have another child as soon as possible: This would virtually guarantee her happiness. At the same time, he prescribed some oxazepam to "calm her nerves." Catherine discussed the doctor's remedy with her mother, who was enthusiastic about the idea of another child: She believed that it would help Catherine to relinquish her "selfish" preoccupation with her own problems. Patrick was less keen, suggesting that they postpone a second child until he had completed his studies. Catherine herself was uncertain about the desirability of a second child, but attached great importance to her mother's opinion.

Catherine became more depressed, and her family physician prescribed some tricyclic antidepressants. Although Catherine persevered with them, they did not help. Her reliance on drugs added to her feeling of inadequacy: "I felt a complete failure when I was on drugs. I thought you should be able to sort your own problems out." When it was clear that Catherine had become severely depressed, her family doctor referred her to me. By this time she was beginning to believe that she had a severe mental illness of mysterious origin.

PSYCHIATRIC TREATMENT

Catherine's treatment focused on sex-role issues from the start. With her permission, I interviewed Patrick and then involved him in conjoint sessions. In essence, therapy was aimed at encouraging the couple to view their situation from a nonstereotyped perspective. I pointed out the very good reasons, as I saw them, for Catherine to be depressed. I suggested that although Patrick's ambition and commitment to study would ultimately improve his occupational status and the financial prospects of his family, this was several years away. At present, his preoccupation with study took him away from his family at a time when he was most needed. Nonetheless, Patrick's commitment to study remained unshakable, even though he acknowledged that it was contributing to Catherine's depression. However, he became more sympathetic and understanding toward Catherine and more willing to discuss problems with her. He agreed to spend some time looking after Sylvia on weekends. These changes in his attitudes and behavior greatly improved the marital climate and allowed a significant improvement in Catherine's mood.

Once it became clear that Patrick was not going to reduce his commitment to study, the focus of therapy shifted back to Catherine. Although Sylvia was now a few months past 2, she spent very little time outside the home or with anyone other than Catherine, who remained grossly overprotective of her. Several conjoint sessions were devoted to examining Catherine's buried rage, her overprotection of Sylvia, her depression, the marriage problems, and the circular relationship between these four factors. Catherine came to realize that because of her early childhood conditioning and stereotyped perspective on motherhood, she had been expecting the impossible of herself. She acknowledged for the first time that she had good reasons for being depressed. Instead of blaming herself, she began to search for constructive solutions to her problems.

With some uncharacteristic support and encouragement from Patrick, Catherine was able to arrange for a woman to come and look after Sylvia for 6 hours a week. Sylvia flourished in this new relationship, and Catherine's overprotectiveness began to lessen. Interestingly, Catherine's mother was against this arrangement: If full-time motherhood had suited her, she argued, then it should also suit her daughter! I suspected that, unconsciously, Catherine's mother resented her daughter's newfound freedom to do other things— a freedom that she herself had never had.

When Sylvia was 2 years and 9 months, Catherine resumed working with her previous employers on a part-time basis. Here she was fortunate: So highly had she been valued that she was willingly reemployed part-time in her old job. Few women in Catherine's position have such an opportunity. Predictably, her mother was strongly against her return to work, but Catherine had Patrick's firm support, which helped her to resist her mother's authority. It was fortunate that Patrick was flexible enough to modify his own stereotypes about motherhood sufficiently to realize the necessity of Catherine's return to work. He also welcomed the extra money. Sylvia was happy with the new arrangement: Although she saw a lot less of her mother, the time they spent together was much happier and more fun filled than previously. Furthermore, Sylvia learned a great many useful and interesting things from the woman who was paid to care for her, as well as acquiring, through her, an additional "extended family."

Therapy occupied a total of 13 sessions over 5 months. Out of interest, I kept in touch with Catherine and Patrick for a further 2 years. Within 3 months of resuming part-time work, Catherine's depression lifted completely, and she remained well throughout the follow-up period, during which time the marriage also improved considerably.

COMMENT AND IMPLICATIONS

Catherine is just one of many young married women who become depressed because they fail to acknowledge the realities of motherhood. By clinging to romantic and stereotyped notions about the maternal role, they fail to understand that it is their environment, and the unrealistic expectations that they and others have of them, that are the major contributors to their depression.

This failure to accept the realities of motherhood is rooted in their relationships with their parents, which have left them in adulthood lacking self-confidence and unduly dependent on their mother's authority. This makes it difficult or impossible for them to challenge the stereotypes of motherhood with which they have been imbued. Their husbands almost invariably reinforce these stereotypes: They have much to gain from their wives' selfless and exclusive devotion to motherhood, since it enables them to devote more energy to their jobs and related or independent activities. Because interaction with their husbands represents most of their otherwise barren social life, and because they are depressed or exhausted by motherhood, such wives are strongly infuenced by their husbands' attitudes and opinions. Thus, husbands are crucial in preserving their wives' stereotyped perspective.

When such women approach their family physicians for help, they are likely to be regarded as suffering from a depressive *illness*, to be treated with drugs. This reinforces the idea that there is something seriously wrong *with them*, rather than with their environments and the attitudes to motherhood of those around them. Many continue in a state of depression until their children start high school, or even later. Only when their children are almost independent do they relinquish the idea that their major commitment in life must be to their children and husband. By this time, it may appear too late for them to obtain a really worthwhile or fulfilling job. It may also appear too late for them to embark upon some new challenge in life, such as enrollment in higher education. All too often, they sink into an embittered middle age, fruitlessly seeking the rewards of years of selfless devotion to their children and husbands.

MARITAL INTERACTION AND DEPRESSED MEN

The following case illustrates themes that are commonly reported by married men who present with depression.

Case 3: The Karate Instructor

Charles, 34, and Mary, 32, had personal and marital problems that ostensibly revolved around the expression of sexuality within their relationship. A mutual adherence to rigidly sex-role-stereotyped attitudes contributed to their difficulties.

CHARLES

Charles came to see me complaining of severely depressed mood, excessive fatigue, poor sleep, loss of interest in life, irritability, and thoughts of suicide over the past 2–3 months. In addition, he had been mildly to moderately depressed for at least the previous 2 years. His *DSM-III* diagnosis was major depressive episode superimposed on a dysthmic disorder.

Of his mother Charles said: "She was very attractive. She brought us up on her own because father wasn't there most of the time. She was always there when I needed her. An affectionate, sympathetic woman who wasn't frightened of showing it. I always got on very well with her. She went without a lot so that my sister and I could have the things we needed. She worked on and off serving in the canteen of the local factory."

Charles described his father in quite different terms: "He was never there when I needed him, because of his job, I suppose. We were never close. He was a sergeant major in the army. There were other women in his life. He and mother were always arguing, mainly over money. When he was around, I remember he was always yelling at me for not doing what I was told. Mother sided with me. I really haven't got an image of him—he was around so little.

But I remember that mealtimes with him were for eating, not discussing trivia. He ruled us with the back of a spoon: We'd get rapped hard across the knuckles if we got out of line."

Charles had one sister, 2 years his junior, to whom he was never close. She had married and moved to another state, and they met only at Christmas or occasional family reunions.

At the age of 6, Charles had developed poliomyelitis, which had left him with weakness in his back and legs. As a result, he had been banned by his doctors from participating in any sporting activities. Since he was not particularly good academically, he found no way of compensating for his father's absence and rejection. Thus, he entered adolescence with a very poor self-image and felt inferior and inadequate in the company of his male peers.

By the age of 16, Charles had grown into a tall, well-built, and handsome youth, with no residual disability from his poliomyelitis other than slight weakness in his lower back muscles. Anxious to prove that he was "as good as anyone else," he started attending a gym to build up his muscular strength, and enrolled in karate lessons. To his surprise, he had proved an outstanding student of karate, acquiring the prestigious black belt at the age of 19. Since then, he had remained actively involved in karate, and had been an instructor one or two evenings a week at a local karate school from the age of 25. He had also attended a gym at least once a week.

However, Charles had always worried that his back might cause problems. Four months before he came to see me, his worst fears were confirmed: He sustained a major back injury and had been told by his doctors that he must give up his karate. He was advised also to cease his body-building activities in the gym and to replace them with regular swimming. Since much of his leisure time and interest for nearly 20 years had been devoted to gym work and karate, this was a major crisis for him, and was the main cause of the acute depression that led him to seek my help.

Charles's chronic depression over the previous 2 years had quite different origins. A major cause was his dissatisfaction with his work as a clerical officer in the public service. He had applied unsuccessfully for promotion on several occasions. His work was boring and routine, and the vision of a further 20 years of it filled him with gloom. He had become depressed when he realized that the prospects of significant promotion were remote.

Long-standing marital conflict was an additional major contributor to Charles' chronic depression. The couple's marital and sexual difficulties will be discussed shortly.

MARY

Mary herself had sought psychiatric treatment for depression when she was 25, about 7 years before I saw her. Therapy had helped her to understand the basis of some of her own problems, which she recounted to me during our interview.

Mary's family was characterized by a rigid adherence to sex-role stereotypes. Of her mother she said: "I never took much notice of her. She was just there. She did things for me. She never worked outside the house, never had a life of her own. My picture of her is standing ironing on wash day."

Mary's father was a long-distance truck driver and often absent on trips. At weekends he generally went fishing, to the hotel, or to local sporting events. He was uninvolved in domestic or child-raising activities, but nonetheless exercised absolute authority in the home. Mary found it impossible to describe him as a person.

From the age of 12, Mary had functioned as a maidservant to her father and three older brothers. Her younger sister had helped her a little, with her mother contributing less and less on the grounds of poor health and general exhaustion. Gender apartheid in the household was total: None of the males was expected to do any housework whatsoever, whereas Mary was required to cook, clean, wash, and polish for many hours after school and on weekends.

Mary recalled having no sense of individuality or personal identity during adolescence: She saw herself exclusively in terms of a sex-role stereotype based on domestic servitude. Any feelings of resentment and injustice were buried so deeply within her that she was completely unaware of them. Although she felt inferior and had a negative self-image, this was because she was female rather than because of any more specific psychological deprivation or trauma. She had been systematically conditioned to believe that women were second-class citizens, to be dominated and controlled by men on whom they waited hand and foot. In late adolescence, her expectations in life revolved entirely around getting married and having children.

THE MARRIAGE

Charles and Mary had married when he was 22 and she 20. For Mary, marriage had been a simple and total transfer of dependency from her parents onto Charles, whom she expected to provide all her material needs. For Charles, marriage had been a partial transfer of dependency from his mother onto Mary, whom he expected to provide sexual, domestic, and emotional support services.

Charles had a very high sex drive and wanted sexual intercourse with Mary nearly every day. Mary was much less interested in sex and claimed that she would be happy to dispense with it altogether. This created a major dilemma for Charles. He wanted the same kind of caring, concern, affection, and honesty in his relationship with Mary that he had enjoyed with his mother. This made him most reluctant to deceive Mary about sexual liaisons outside the marriage. Furthermore, he found distasteful the idea of sex without emotional involvement, and was concerned that if he started an affair, he would become so emotionally involved that his marriage would be threatened. Since he loved Mary and the two young sons who were born within the first 3 years of the marriage, the idea of breaking up his relationship with Mary was totally unacceptable to him.

Although Charles masturbated occasionally, obtaining some relief from sexual tension, he disliked masturbation and found it emotionally frustrating. It was therefore not an acceptable supplement or alternative to sex with Mary. Thus, he was frequently in a state of sexual frustration. This made him irritable and prone to shouting at Mary, which in turn made it less likely that she would accommodate him sexually, thereby setting up a vicious cycle of sexual frustration and marital conflict.

Charles endured chronic sexual frustration for nearly 4 years. He then had an affair. His worst fears were confirmed: He found himself increasingly emotionally entangled in the relationship, even though he had agreed with the woman, who was unmarried, that mutual sexual gratification must remain the primary basis for their meetings. Charles became tortured by guilt. After 4 months of clandestine sexual encounters, he could bear his guilt no longer, and confessed all to Mary. Not surprisingly, Mary was devastated. She threatened to leave the marriage. Only through abject apology and pleading was Charles able to persuade her to stay.

Subsequently, although Charles had sworn to have no further affairs, and was determined to keep his promise, Mary's lingering resentment toward him made her even more reluctant to make love. Furthermore, she idealized him much less, and became increasingly reluctant to wait upon him hand and foot. The marriage deteriorated further, and Mary became depressed. Fortunately, she responded to the psychiatric treatment mentioned previously, emerging from it with a much stronger sense of personal and gender identity. She began to modify her sex-role-stereotyped perspective on marriage, and became more assertive. At the age of 28, when both the boys were at school, she got a part-time job, which she enjoyed.

Charles kept his promise not to have another affair, but his sexual frustration increased. He felt driven into a series of casual sexual encounters, opportunities for which were created by his position as a karate instructor. Although these left him feeling guilty, he found guilt easier to bear than constant sexual frustration. Charles felt profoundly deprived of affection within the marriage. When Mary started part-time work, he acutely felt the loss of his privileged, powerful position as sole income earner. He began to question the whole basis of his marriage, feeling that he was getting nothing out of it, and staying married only because he hoped for an improvement in his relationship with Mary and because of his love for the boys. When Charles came to see me, he felt that he had nothing worthwhile in his life.

PSYCHIATRIC TREATMENT

Since Charles's depression was so intimately bound up with his marital and sexual problems, couples therapy was indicated. However, a major obstacle to this was the presence of Charles's casual extramarital liaisons. Ostensibly,

146

Mary was ignorant of these. I explained to Charles that although I would abide by his wish to keep these from Mary, I would in effect be colluding in his deceit of her. This would make me feel uncomfortable during therapy, and would undoubtedly hinder my effectiveness as a therapist. Nonetheless, Charles wished to proceed with couples therapy, to which Mary was agreeable also.

It rapidly emerged that Charles's sense of masculinity and potency depended greatly on his role as a karate instructor. Furthermore, a sense of physical strength and fitness, maintained by his gym work, had been central to his self-image for nearly 20 years. Once Charles realized this, he was able to understand why he had become so acutely depressed after his incapacitating back injury. His depression was a reaction to the sudden and probably permanent loss of the main source of his psychological well-being and self-esteem. Given his dissatisfaction with his job and his marriage, it was not surprising that he felt that there was nothing worthwhile in his life.

Charles's first real task in therapy was to mourn the loss of the symbols of his masculinity and potency. Before he could begin, he had to give himself permission to weep freely and openly, something that for years he had denied himself because it was incompatible with his stereotyped view of manhood. Mary spontaneously came to his aid here, stressing that she would think more, and not less of him, if he were able to express his feelings of sadness and loss. Thus, he began to transform his depression into sadness and grief, and the tears came. For several weeks he spent much time thinking about himself, his life up to that point, and his successes and failures. He discovered within him great anger and disappointment about his father. He realized that as a child he had never really had a father and that he must accept this and work through the associated feelings of anger and sadness.

As he worked through his grief, Charles gradually became less sad. During therapy he came to realize that his lack of promotion at work was due mainly to his ambivalent attitudes to those in authority, onto whom he had transferred his unconscious feelings of anger and disappointment about his father. His relationship with Mary improved greatly as he became able to share with her his innermost feelings. For the first time, Mary felt that there was real communication between them. Her habitual anger toward Charles, which was partly a transference of buried hostile feelings about her own father, became less as she understood more about Charles's problems and conflicts.

After 14 sessions of conjoint therapy over a period of 5 months, Charles had mainly worked through his grief, and was able to accept his life as it was. To his surprise, he was much less tormented by sexual frustration. He realized that much of his desire for frequent sex had been linked with a need to prove his masculinity in terms of a sex-role stereotype. Now that his sense of masculinity was more realistically founded on an acceptance of both his "male" and "female" attributes, his urge for sex had diminished.

The reduction in Charles's and Mary's anger toward each other allowed a sustained improvement in their marriage. Mary became more sexually responsive to Charles, and they began to share regular sexual intercourse, which both enjoyed, although it was still less frequent than Charles desired.

I followed up Charles and Mary for 2 years. During this time Charles gained promotion at work, which he began to enjoy. The marriage remained fairly harmonious, and Charles had no recurrence of his depression. He had replaced his gym and karate interests by joining a pistol shooting club, a pastime that allowed him to work off or displace anger and frustration without further injury to his back. This was a reminder of the limited scope of my therapeutic endeavors: Although Charles's attitudes had changed fundamentally in several areas, there were many aspects of his basic personality that had been untouched during therapy.

IMPLICATIONS OF THE CASE: THE MID-LIFE CRISIS

It is not uncommon for men in their mid-30s to become depressed in the context of a need to appraise the progress of their lives up to that point. This has been called the "mid-life crisis," a phenomenon that has been described and discussed at length by O'Connor (1981). One drawback of his book is its assumption that the mid-life crisis is almost exclusively a male phenomenon. In fact, many women also experience a powerful need to reappraise their lives around their mid-30s, although their preoccupations generally differ in content from those of men.

In men, the mid-life crisis has a great deal to do with the male sex-role stereotype and its emphasis on competitiveness and achievement. Most young men have dreams of success and recognition in their work, and of wealth and social prominence. Few achieve these early hopes and expectations. Around the age of 35, most men begin to face up to the fact that they are not going to be anything other than fairly ordinary. For many, this realization is acutely painful, and involves a period of grief and withdrawal from life. During this time, old hopes, dreams, and fantasies must be relinquished and mourned, to be replaced by more realistic ones.

Failure to resolve the mid-life crisis may cause difficulties later. Many men disguise their despair and anguish through excessive use of alcohol, which creates its own problems. Others develop chronic depressive or anxiety symptoms. If these become diagnosed as an illness, they may become an excuse for failure to "succeed" in life: Thus, being "ill" is an alternative to a sense of personal failure. In such circumstances, treatment of symptoms alone, using drugs or behavior therapy, is likely to be unhelpful and may even be destructive.

Although confrontation and resolution of the mid-life crisis often requires a great deal of courage, it has its rewards. Energy that is redirected from the struggle to compete for occupational status and recognition can be put to good use elsewhere. Men discover creative aspects of themselves. Married life often becomes more intimate and satisfying. As personal goals become more realistic, they are more likely to be achieved, bringing a sense of personal fulfillment. However, it is misleading to regard the mid-life crisis as the only obstacle to fulfillment and contentment. Of course it is not. Many of the issues first dealt with during the mid-life crisis must be confronted repeatedly for many years afterwards. But, having overcome the supreme challenge of the mid-life crisis, subsequent crises can be tackled with more insight and confidence.

MARRIAGE AND MANIA

Manic and hypomanic episodes are highly distressing and disrupting to the close relatives of the afflicted person, who are in a no-win situation: The more they try to control or protect the manic person, the more angry and resistant does he or she become. The close relatives, particularly the spouse, have to manage the social and financial repercussions of the manic episode. Where a hypomanic episode has been prolonged, such repercussions may be financially crippling or socially devastating. During sustained hypomanic episodes, the afflicted person may be persuasive, credible, and charismatic, entering into complex and interlocking financial agreements that are unrealistic but nonetheless often legally binding. The loss of family assets or even bankruptcy may result. More commonly, expensive and unnecessary goods are purchased on credit, leaving the spouse with major problems in returning them or otherwise coping with the resulting debts. Concurrently or alternatively, a hypomanic person may permanently alienate friends and relatives through offensive or otherwise socially unacceptable behavior.

Confronted with such repercussions, even the most devoted spouse might well have reservations about remaining married to someone prone to manic or hypomanic episodes. It is not surprising, therefore, that patients with bipolar disorders have a divorce rate that is substantially higher than normal (Lesser, 1983). It is widely assumed that those spouses who remain married to patients with persisting bipolar disorders are unusually patient, tolerant, and long-suffering. Although this is often true, such spouses would be superhuman if they did not harbor, at some level, considerable resentment and hostility toward their afflicted partners for the problems they have created. The medical model powerfully inhibits direct expression of this hostility: by labeling the hypomanic episode as part of an illness, the afflicted person is protected from blame or responsibility for his or her behavior during the episode; thus, the spouse cannot legitimately express anger or hostility toward his or her afflicted partner, who creates problems only because of an *illness*. However, the spouse's anger and resentment are expressed *indirectly* in various ways. This indirect expression of anger adversely affects the marital relationship in many areas and often contributes to the development of further hypomanic or manic episodes.

Thus, a vicious cycle is established in which the spouse's denied or suppressed anger and resentment towards his or her afflicted partner contribute to marital problems and tension that increase the likelihood of further hypomanic episodes. These episodes consolidate an illness model and add to the spouse's problems in expressing anger and resentment *directly* to the afflicted person. Thus, the spouse's *indirect* expression of hostility increases, adding further to the likelihood of future hypomanic episodes.

There is another factor that powerfully reinforces the illness model in bipolar disorders: the use of lithium carbonate. This drug is undoubtedly helpful in reducing the intensity and frequency of manic and hypomanic episodes. However, it rarely eliminates them altogether, and many patients with bipolar disorder respond to the drug poorly or not at all. But because manic and hypomanic episodes are so profoundly upsetting and disrupting, and are not generally prevented by other medications, lithium carbonate is often prescribed for long periods even in cases where it is of marginal or doubtful benefit. As I pointed out in Chapter 5, the regular monitoring of lithium levels in the blood, requiring attendance at a medical clinic, powerfully reinforces the illness model.

Systematic studies of the families of patients with bipolar disorder have shown that the condition is present in patients' relatives more often than would be expected by chance. From such studies has emerged good evidence of a genetic or hereditary contribution to bipolar disorder. This has added yet more weight to the illness model.

Because of the above factors, bipolar disorder is almost universally treated as a biologically determined medical illness with a biochemical basis. As a result, environmental contributions to its development and maintenance have been virtually ignored. In their anxiety to protect bipolar patients and their spouses from needless anxiety and suffering, most psychiatrists emphasise that the condition is an illness for which the afflicted person and his or her spouse have no personal responsibility. Unfortunately, this well-meant reassurance discourages patients and spouses from examining possible environmental, intrapsychic, marital, and interpersonal contributions to the disorder. It also encourages dependence on the psychiatrist and the medical model.

However, the recent widespread, mainly successful use of lithium carbonate has produced a paradoxical effect: It has clearly exposed the fact that many patients with bipolar disorder have highly disturbed marriages that contribute to the persistence of the condition. For example, Mayo (1979) suggests: "Some therapists have assumed that if the illness can be cured, the marriage will be fine. Frequently the opposite is true. Treatment with lithium does indeed contain and control the illness, revealing in bas-relief a marriage that is faulty in its own right. More importantly it becomes clear that the marriage was 'sick' from its inception" (p. 424).

She adds: "Therapy includes helping the spouse as well as the patient to accept that much of the patient's behaviour stems from basic personality characteristics that might have contributed negatively to the marital relationship whether or not the patient had become ill. . . . Attention is focused on enabling the spouse to assume more responsibility for his/her own behaviour that may unwittingly trigger a train of events, which leads to exacerbation of symptoms in the patient" (p. 424).

Mayo concludes that an emphasis on individual therapy is unhelpful or deleterious for many patients with bipolar disorder, whereas couples therapy, although difficult, is often rewarding.

Mayo is not entirely alone in emphasizing the central importance of the marriage relationship in perpetuating bipolar disorder in many cases. Her views are strongly supported by Lesser (1983), who emphasized that marital conflict invariably *preceded* bipolar disorder, and recommended conjoint therapy, combined with lithium carbonate, as the treatment of choice. Although others (Hoover & Fitzgerald, 1981; Janowsky, Leff, & Epstein, 1970) have found a higher than normal incidence of marital conflict and unexpressed hostility in the marriages of patients with bipolar disorder, they have not reported a causal link between marital conflict and hypomanic episodes. However, linear causal relationships are rare in the marriages of patients with persisting psychological disorders. Nearly always, overt or denied marital conflict, personality abnormalities, and the patient's symptoms reinforce and perpetuate each other in a vicious cycle.

In spite of the higher than normal divorce rate of patients with bipolar disorder, a large minority of patients remain married to the same person until one or the other partner dies. Wadeson and Fitzgerald (1971) found "strong dependency needs in both patient and spouse and the wish for the other to be strong; domination by the patient, greater passivity in the spouse; greater feelings of the closeness to the other in the patient compared with the spouse."

Whatever the precise psychological basis for these marriages, their prolonged survival in the face of profound turmoil, conflict, and disruption is another example of the way in which sex-role stereotyping, personality abnormalities, and psychological symptoms interact to help preserve marriages against seemingly impossible odds.

CHAPTER SEVEN

Marriage and Anxiety Disorders

The Epidemiologic Catchment Area research program (Myers *et al.*, 1984) has yielded up-to-date and reliable data on the community prevalence of anxiety disorders. Using *DSM-III* criteria, Myers *et al.* reported a 6-month prevalence of about 7.5%. Alcohol and drug-dependence/abuse was the next most common disorder (about 6.5%) followed by affective disorders (about 6.0%). Thus, it appears that anxiety disorders may have overtaken depression as the most common psychiatric disorder in the community, although depression probably remains more common in clinical practice. Andrews *et al.* (1985) have calculated that no less than 3% of the general population suffers from chronic, disabling anxiety disorders, a figure that suggests nearly 7 million sufferers in the United States alone.

Anxiety disorders represent about one-third of the psychiatric cases seen by family physicians (Mann *et al.*, 1981). Because of the persisting nature of many anxiety disorders, they probably constitute at least one quarter of the nonpsychotic caseload of the average general psychiatrist.

The distribution of anxiety disorders by age and sex is broadly similar to that of depression. They are about twice as common in women as in men. Their peak prevalence occurs between the ages of 25–44 in women and 45–64 in men (Myers *et al.*, 1984).

From the above data it is clear that developing more effective treatments for anxiety disorders is one of the major challenges facing contemporary mental health workers. Unfortunately, the psychiatric literature in this area is confusing and often misleading. This is particularly true with regard to the relevance of marital and sex-role issues, some reasons for which have been discussed in previous chapters. An additional, potent reason relates to the lack of publications by skilled, eclectic clinicians, a great majority of whom are engaged primarily in private practice.

Success in the private practice of general psychiatry requires the development of highly sophisticated and effective therapeutic skills. Thus, the most skilled and successful clinicians are generally found in flourishing private practices. Unfortunately, psychiatrists who are successful in private practice have little incentive to publish in professional journals. Their reputations are generally based on local recognition of their excellence; as long as they continue to provide an outstanding service to their patients and colleagues, their clinical practice will flourish, sometimes to an embarrassing extent. Publishing in professional journals is largely irrelevant to the conduct of their careers, although on the comparatively rare occasions that they do publish clinical research, their reports are often as outstanding and insightful as their clinical work.

Thus, the health care professions have very restricted access to the attitudes, techniques, and perspectives of highly skilled and sophisticated clinical psychiatrists. This has had a stultifying effect on the development of more effective treatments for complex psychiatric conditions such as chronic anxiety disorders.

PHOBIC DISORDERS

Phobias account for at least two thirds of all anxiety disorders in the community (Myers *et al.*, 1984). Agoraphobia is by far the most common phobic disorder seen by psychiatrists, representing at least 60% of cases (Marks, 1969). About 85% of people seeking treatment for agoraphobia are women (Vose, 1981). However, the male–female ratio in the general community varies somewhat with age (Myers *et al.*, 1984): averaging data from three different communities, women comprised 77% of agoraphobia sufferers in the 25–44 age group, whereas they comprised only 58% between the ages 45–64.

In women, the prevalence of agoraphobia in the community peaks between the ages of 25–44 at about 6%, whereas in men it peaks in the 45–64 age group at about 1.8%.

Of women with agoraphobia who seek psychological or psychiatric treatment, about 80% are married (Vose, 1981). Thus, about *two thirds* of agoraphobia sufferers seen by psychiatrists or psychologists are married women. In this respect, agoraphobia is unique among phobic disorders.

There is no good evidence that marital factors are particularly important in generating or maintaining phobic disorders other than agoraphobia. Thus, the remainder of this section will be devoted to agoraphobia.

AGORAPHOBIA

Agoraphobia is a disorder that is notoriously persisting and difficult to treat. The mean age of onset is about 28 years (Burns & Thorpe, 1977a, 1977b; Doctor, 1982), and the average duration of symptoms prior to entering specialized treatment programmes is 8–10 years (Buglass *et al.*, 1977; Doctor, 1982; Hafner & Marks, 1976; Marks & Herst, 1970). During this time, a majority of patients fail to respond to a wide range of psychiatric and psychological treatments (Vose, 1981).

Simple versus Complex Agoraphobia

Chambless and Goldstein (1981) proposed that agoraphobia comprises two relatively distinct syndromes, which they termed "simple" and "complex" agoraphobia, the latter being the more common clinical syndrome. Simple agoraphobia is generally precipitated by specific traumatic events, often against a background of accumulating life stress. It usually occurs in people who do not have major personality abnormalities or marital problems, is rarely complicated by significant hypochondriasis and obsessive compulsive symptoms, and responds fairly well to behavior therapy.

Complex agoraphobia is generally precipitated by marital conflict. It is characterized by pronounced anticipatory anxiety and a wide range of additional psychological symptoms, and is nearly always associated with personality disorder, often of the dependent type. Generally, behavior therapy is either refused, ineffective, or followed by relapses associated with marital conflicts.

There is experimental support for Chambless and Goldstein's classification (Hafner, 1977, 1982a). Working entirely independently of Chambless and Goldstein, I also defined two relatively distinct types of agoraphobia. Although the level of agoraphobic symptoms was similar in both types of disorder, one type showed levels of general phobic and psychoneurotic symptoms that were much lower than in the other type. The former type, in which agoraphobic symptoms existed in relative isolation, is comparable with Chambless and Goldstein's simple agoraphobia. Although many patients in this group initially appeared to have personality abnormalities, of which excessive self-criticism and guilt were major features, these abnormalities were largely reversed after behavior therapy, to which the patients generally responded well. When the husbands of these patients showed personality abnormalities, which were characterized by excessive extrapunitiveness, these were relatively mild. If marital difficulties occurred after successful behavior therapy, these were rarely associated with persisting relapse of the patients' agoraphobia.

Patients in the other group had very high levels of general phobic and psychoneurotic symptoms. Severe hypochondriasis, obsessive compulsive symptoms, generalized anxiety, social phobias, and depression were common, as were major personality abnormalities characterized mainly by a strong tendency to blame and criticize other people. This abnormality did not change after treatment, and appeared to be a relatively enduring feature of the personality structure of these women. Although initial response to behavior therapy was often fairly good, several patients relapsed, usually because of marital difficulties that appeared to have been exacerbated by the patient's initial positive response to treatment. Overall, this group of patients had characteristics that coincided closely with those described by Chambless and Goldstein as complex agoraphobia.

The Overrepresentation of Simple Agoraphobia in Clinical Research

Data showing that simple agoraphobia is grossly overrepresented in systematic clinical research were outlined and discussed in Chapter 5. It is now relevant to consider some additional reasons for this.

In recent years, research has come to surpass clinical excellence as a means of gaining promotion and recognition for those employed by organizations concerned with mental health. Psychiatrists and clinical psychologists are strongly favored for senior posts in the public domain if they have published in major professional journals or have a research degree. The reputations of academic departments of psychiatry in hospitals and universities are determined largely by the quality and quantity of the publications that emerge from them.

Full-time research for a Ph.D. or, in Commonwealth countries, an M.D., must nearly always be completed within 2–3 years. Few research grants run for longer than this. Thus, modern researchers in psychiatry and psychology are under great pressure to design projects that are neat and tidy and can be completed fairly rapidly. Psychiatric patients do not in general lend themselves to neat and tidy research, particularly if they have complex and serious disorders. For example, it is widely recognized among clinical research workers that psychiatric patients normally found in abundance mysteriously disappear as soon as they are required for a research project. No one has researched this extraordinary yet ubiquitous phenomenon!

In the case of agoraphobia, nearly all research workers deliberately exclude complex cases. There are two main reasons for this. First, most agoraphobia research compares two or more types of treatment. For methodological reasons, these treatments must be clearly defined and are usually, therefore, uncomplicated unimodal or bimodal approaches. Comparing various types of behavior therapy is popular among clinical psychologists, and psychiatrists often compare drugs, sometimes combined with behavior therapies. People with complex agoraphobia are rarely suited to unimodal or bimodal treatments, and so are often excluded from such programs. Even if they are invited to participate, they usually refuse or drop out prematurely, making the research "untidy" or inconclusive. They are, of course, excluded from the research findings.

Second, scientific methodology requires the elimination of any factors that are not directly relevant to the research. Thus, the presence of problems and symptoms in addition to agoraphobia is considered scientifically undesirable. Once again, this leads to the exclusion of complex cases.

Although most systematic research on agoraphobia is based on simple cases, this is rarely acknowledged or understood. Therefore, it is widely and mistakenly assumed that treatments that are effective in simple agoraphobia are appropriate for agoraphobia in general. As a result, drug and behavioral treatments have become grossly overvalued. In contrast, the multimodal approach, of which a central aspect is attention to the marriage, is virtually ignored. This fundamental error is self-perpetuating: Since most people with simple agoraphobia are comparatively easy to treat, research workers are usually rewarded by treatment success as well as readily publishable findings. This increases the demand for cases of simple agoraphobia and helps to perpetuate the illusion that they are representative of agoraphobia in general.

Complex Agoraphobia

Complex cases represent the clinical reality of agoraphobia for a majority of skilled and experienced therapists, several of whom have written about the central role of marriage in perpetuating the disorder (Chambless & Goldstein, 1981; Fry, 1962; Goodstein & Swift, 1977; Holmes, 1982; Quadrio, 1983, 1984; Schwartz & Val, 1984; Webster, 1953).

Fodor (1974) has emphasized sex-role stereotyping in the genesis and maintenance of complex agoraphobia. She regards agoraphobic women as exhibiting an extreme stereotype of female behavior, to which they have been conditioned throughout childhood. These women tend to choose men whose view of themselves is based on an extreme male sex-role stereotype. Agoraphobic symptoms in the women develop as part of the failure of one or both marriage partners to modify their stereotypes. I have elaborated elsewhere (Hafner, 1984a, 1984b, 1985, in press) a similar viewpoint.

Predictably, there is an almost complete absence of research data on sex-role stereotyping in agoraphobia. Sex-role stereotyping per se is not a major issue in simple agoraphobia, which, as we have seen, is erroneously construed by researchers as the representative syndrome. Thus, any systematic research on stereotyping is unlikely to yield positive results. Furthermore, agoraphobia is subject to the strong bias against research into sex-role issues that was discussed in Chapters 2 and 5. Nonetheless, Benson and Brehony (1978) were able to demonstrate a strong relationship between self-reported agoraphobic symptoms and adherence to a sex-role stereotype in a population of college students. Unfortunately, there are major problems in generalizing from student or volunteer populations to clinical populations, so that these findings must be interpreted with caution.

At a clinical level, the real issues in treating complex agoraphobia in married women are usually concerned with sex-role stereotypes. The husbands of such women generally cling much more strongly to a stereotyped perspective of marriage than do their wives. Some psychological reasons for this were outlined in Chapter 3: Where identification with a male sex-role stereotype is a substitute for gender identity, pressure to relinquish the stereotype may evoke fears of total disintegration of the sense of self. We saw in Chapter 4 that such fears are not unfounded: In "Machismo Unmasked" the husband became psychotic when his wife recovered from agoraphobia. Her increased autonomy and assertiveness shattered his stereotyped view of marriage and invalidated his identification with the male sex-role stereotype.

There are many other reasons for the husbands of severely disabled agoraphobic women to cling to the male sex-role stereotype. Caring for a fearful, dependent, and housebound woman initially overextends even the most stereotyped perspective on marriage. Many husbands resent the limitations imposed on them by their wives' agoraphobia, even though they welcome their wives' dependency. This ambivalence is obscured by the idea that agoraphobia is an *illness*: Since adherence to marital vows, human decency, and moral obligation demand that husbands care for sick wives, there is no choice but to preserve the marital status quo. This also means preserving the stereotype. Thus, husbands become entrenched in a posture of denying feelings of weakness, frustration, uncertainty, and vulnerability. Required to shoulder their wives' problems and deny their own, they ignore their own personal development. Any questioning of their stereotyped attitudes and behavior is profoundly challenging as they approach their middle years, since it threatens to expose the sensitive, vulnerable, dependent, and emotional aspects of themselves that have been buried deep within them since early childhood.

It is therefore not surprising that the husbands of women with complex agoraphobia are generally reluctant to become involved in conjoint therapy with their wives. They have too much to lose. Special strategies are required to constructively involve such men in therapy. I will elaborate these in Chapter 9.

Simple Agoraphobia and Sex-Role Conflict

In Chapter 6, the case "Solitary Confinement" showed how idealization and stereotyping of maternal and marital roles contributed to profound and persisting depression in a woman (Catherine) who, before marriage and motherhood, was reasonably happy and contented with life. Catherine, in common with many depressed housewives, had never done well academically and, on leaving school, had no aspirations other than a mundane job to be replaced as soon as possible by marriage. Largely by chance, her natural talents were recognized, and she became a highly valued employee. Although she greatly enjoyed her work, on marriage she relinquished it with few misgivings. This was possible because her commitment to the idea of a career was only embryonic: Basically, Catherine still regarded work for women as simply an interlude between school and marriage. Thus, she initially accepted her "solitary confinement" in the home, with its inevitable consequence of depression.

In similar domestic circumstances, many women develop simple agoraphobia rather than depression. They differ from women like Catherine in two major respects: First, they tend to have a family history of anxiety disorders, suggesting a genetic loading; and second, their personal aspirations in adolescence and early adulthood extend *beyond* marriage and motherhood.

Nearly always, they are academically successful at school, or show promise and talent in music or artistic areas. They are unusually competitive, vigorous, and well-organized young women. Often, their family backgrounds are free of ostensibly pathogenic factors, and their premarital adjustment is good. In terms of object relations theory, they have negotiated the depressive position. Typically, their mothers are intelligent, overconscientious women who are committed to marriage and motherhood on a full-time basis. These mothers vicariously satisfy their needs to compete and to achieve by strongly encouraging, and identifying with, their daughters' competitiveness. Often, they devote most of their free time to encouraging and facilitating their daughters' academic and extracurricular activities. This generates a profound but unconscious conflict within their daughters. On the one hand, these girls are firmly encouraged to be ambitious, competitive, and successful: attributes that belong to the *male* sex-role stereotype. On the other hand, they strongly identify with their mothers, who epitomize a *female* sex-role stereotype. This profound conflict lies dormant within these women until it is exposed by the realities of marriage and motherhood. The sequence of events is typically as follows.

The mothers of preagoraphobic women rely very heavily on their daughters to provide meaning, purpose, and fulfillment in their lives. They have invested enormous time and energy in their daughters, and they want a continuing return on this investment: a return that is threatened when their ambitious, competitive daughters seek to leave home and lead independent lives. These mothers have an unusually strong influence on their daughters, since they have been the senior members of close, ambivalent partnerships with them for many years. In essence, the preagoraphobic daughter wishes to dissolve the partnership; her mother wishes to preserve it. An unspoken compromise is reached: the daughter tacitly offers *her own child* to replace the huge vacuum left by her departure into adulthood.

In order to keep her side of the bargain, the preagoraphobic daughter is pressured into marriage. Her childhood conditioning requires *either* a full-time commitment to a career *or* a full-time commitment to marriage and motherhood. Thus, on marriage, she postpones her personal aspirations, whether academic, artistic, or career-oriented. This decision is powerfully reinforced by her mother, who is thereby protected from the loss of her investment in her daughter: As a young mother, her daughter will remain within her sphere of influence and, together with child, will continue to provide her with meaning, purpose, and vicarious gratification. Furthermore, the mother is protected from the enormous envy that she might experience if her daughter achieved *genuine* independence from her and led her own life,

158

free of the self-sacrifice and constraints of traditional, stereotyped mother-hood.

The preagoraphobic woman is likely to marry a man who matches or exceeds her in ambition and competitiveness. He is unlikely to give her much practical or emotional support in raising their young children: Wedded to a sex-role stereotyped perspective, he will be preoccupied with work or career commitments and will have little time or energy to give to his wife and family. Doubtless, he will expect from his wife the same emotional and practical support and encouragement that she craves from him. Thus, the preagora-phobic woman is driven to seek practical help from her mother. This is readily forthcoming, but at the price of preserving the ambivalent, over-dependent relationship between mother and daughter.

Agoraphobia often develops as follows. The preagoraphobic woman is overprotective toward her children for two reasons: First, she is re-creating the overinvolved style of her own mother; second, she is struggling to disguise her hostility toward them. This deeply buried hostility originates in the fact that marriage and motherhood have deprived her of opportunities for the direct personal fulfillment that, until childbirth, was a central powerful theme in her life. The children are in reality innocent, but are the most visible source of everyday frustrations as well as constraints upon personal freedom. Their mother's buried hostility toward them emerges indirectly as an irrational fear that they may come to harm, and this reinforces her overprotectiveness.

This conflict contributes to panic attacks that occur when the mother is *alone outside the home*. These are often triggered by unconscious guilt and anxiety about leaving her children with others, and by fears for their safety and well-being. Seeing others going freely about their own business, unen-cumbered by children, contributes to the *background* tension and intrapsy-chic conflict out of which panics emerge. The panic attacks are acutely unpleasant and frightening, and generally lead to an *avoidance* of situations in which they occur. Thus, agoraphobia emerges.

Although very inconvenient and distressing, agoraphobia protects the young mother from two profound but partly unconscious conflicts in her life. First, it *forces* her to be dependent on her mother: Since there is no choice in this matter, her ambivalence about it is lessened or suppressed. Even so, Buglass et al. (1977) found that 20 out of 33 married agoraphobic women reported distressing ambivalence toward their mothers. *Only 2* of the 33 women in the control group reported similar feelings. This significant differ-ence was also found in the *premorbid* period.

Second, it *forces* her to relinquish her aspirations about activities beyond the home, and reduces the related intrapsychic conflict: She has no choice but to be confined to the domestic area. In relation to this, Burns and Thorpe (1977a, 1977b) surveyed 850 agoraphobic women and found that over 85% were not employed outside the home. Of these, *88% claimed that they would seek work outside the home were it not for their agoraphobia.*

Marks and Herst (1970) compared "discontented" agoraphobic wives who wished to work outside the home with "contented" ones who said they were happy to remain full-time housewives. The "discontented" wives were significantly more phobic, depressed, irritable, and exhausted than the "contented" ones. However: "Somewhat surprisingly, discontented housewives rated their premorbid personality as more sociable ($p < .001$), less anxious ($p < .001$) and more independent ($p < .001$) than did the contented housewives. Discontented housewives were also more extroverted at present ($p < .01$) as well as in the past" (p. 21).

Marks and Herst were surprised at their data because they did not acknowledge sex-role conflict as a central theme in agoraphobia. However, from the sex-roles perspective outlined above, their findings are largely predictable.

On balance, the discomfort and inconvenience of agoraphobia are less painful than grappling constantly with inner conflicts concerning the profound issues of autonomy and self-fulfillment versus dependence and vicarious gratification. Because simple agoraphobia reduces or eliminates profound intrapsychic conflict, it becomes *largely self-perpetuating* until the origins of this conflict are resolved.

Unimodal or bimodal treatments for simple agoraphobia work well mainly because the intrapsychic conflict that precipitated the agoraphobia is no longer present. By the time women with simple agoraphobia are referred for specialized treatment, their children have usually been at school for a few years and are becoming independent. Thus, there is no apparent obstacle to these women resuming their *personal* aspirations and, in addition, becoming more independent of their mothers. Often, however, their husbands are reluctant to relinquish their positions as sole income earners, or may envy or ridicule their wives' aspirations. In such circumstances, the struggle for genuine power sharing and equality of status within the marriage may be as great, or greater than, the struggle to overcome the agoraphobia. Therapists who ignore issues of power, autonomy, and control within the marriage are unlikely to be fully successful in their efforts to help their patients recover from simple agoraphobia.

AGORAPHOBIA IN MEN

Although the 6-month prevalence of agoraphobia in men aged 18–65 is over 1%, very little has been published about male agoraphobia. Presumably, this reflects the overwhelming preponderance of women among those who seek treatment for the condition.

Liotti and Guidano (1976) reported their experiences in treating 21 men with agoraphobia over a 2-year period. Fifteen of these men presented with a uniform syndrome, the main features of which were an intolerance of being alone; a hypochondriacal preoccupation with palpitations and shortness of breath linked with a fear of heart attack, which persisted despite frequent reassurance from their physicians; resistance to all forms of treatment, including behavior therapy; and the onset of symptoms shortly after marriage or after an apparently minor marital crisis.

I reported similar findings in a systematic comparison of 20 men and 20 women with agoraphobia (Hafner, 1981a, 1983b). Those men who responded well to behavior therapy had personality structures, marital relationships, and psychological symptoms that were significantly different from those of the poor responders. The former group suffered from a disorder that is broadly comparable to simple agoraphobia in women, although in men a fear of losing control of aggressive impulses replaces panic attacks as the most common reason for fear and avoidance of public places.

Many men with simple agoraphobia find it difficult to identify with a traditional, sex-role-stereotyped view of appropriate masculine behavior, both within marriage and in general. As a result, they tend to seek greater-than-usual involvement in domestic and child-care activities. This is generally resisted by their wives, who consider nonstereotyped behavior to be "unmanly," or an attempt to poach on their domestic "territory."

The good response to behavioral treatment of the men with simple agoraphobia in my 1983b study was partly attributable to a decrease in sex-role conflict in their marriages and lives in general. At the time of entry to the study, the mean age of these men was 36, and they had been disabled by agoraphobia for a mean of 9 years. During these years, their children had become much less dependent, and this had allowed both marriage partners greater flexibility with regard to sex roles.

Complex Agoraphobia in Men: Escape from Sex-Role Tyranny

The most common pattern of marital interaction in complex agoraphobia in men is that illustrated by the cases "The Reluctant Nurse–Wife" in Chapter 4, and "The Little Father" later in this chapter.

Almost all of the men with complex agoraphobia I have seen came from disturbed families that were usually dominated by their mothers. Nearly always, their father's contribution to family life was minimal, often because of alcohol problems. Over one quarter of the men had lost their fathers in childhood through death, separation, or divorce.

These men acquired a strong primary identification with their mothers and had little opportunity to develop a true sense of gender identity in the context of a father–son relationship. Thus, as in the case of the husbands of women with complex agoraphobia, they identified with the male sex-role stereotype as a substitute for true gender and personal identity.

Through marriage, they sought women onto whom they could transfer the powerful, ambivalent dependency that they experienced toward their mothers. However, they also expected their wives to complement the male sex-role stereotyped images that they had of themselves. As a result, they expected their wives to be both powerful and protective and dependent and submissive. Anxiety symptoms emerged out of marital conflict that was precipitated by these totally incompatible expectations. Often, the anxiety symptoms were compounded by unresolved grief over lost or absent fathers.

These observations are supported by those of Liotti and Guidano (1976): "Before the appearance of the husband's neurotic disturbance, aggressive interchanges between partners were rare, mainly because the wife seemed to have accepted a submissive position. During a period immediately preceding the appearance of the husband's symptoms there was a sharp rise in the frequency of marital quarrels. Most often this appeared to be precipitated by the wife's departure from the original contract, and in particular a movement away from marital submission . . . with the onset of the husband's neurotic fears the marital quarrels showed a reduction in intensity and reverted to a series of continuous, monotonous arguments about the inconsistency (according to the wife) or the consistency (according to the husband) of his phobia, *as well as about the consequent limitations of the husband's interpersonal and occupational activities*" (p. 162; italics added).

The wives of men with complex agoraphobia nearly always have a strong and dutiful commitment to a sex-role stereotyped idea of marriage. To complement their almost exclusive devotion to children and domesticity, they expect their husbands to devote themselves wholeheartedly to the roles of breadwinner and strong, wise, benign, emotionally controlled head of the family—modern day patriarchs who display traditional authoritarianism softened by contemporary democracy.

In reality, these husbands are rarely the superhuman creatures that their wives expect them to be. Indeed, they are often rather diffident, unassertive men who have married with the unconscious wish to be mothered. They find the roles of exclusive breadwinner and modern-day patriarch burdensome, constricting, and unfulfilling. In their fantasies, they seek escape and adventure. Objectively, their wives are often forceful, dominating women who fit the female sex-role stereotype as poorly as their husbands fit its opposite. But powerful sex-role conditioning and rigidly stereotyped role concepts trap both partners within their ill-fitting molds.

In these circumstances, if the husband becomes depressed or anxious for any reason, this represents a profound challenge to the wife's stereotyped perspective—a perspective from which men are not allowed to become weepy and anxious. However, panic attacks and the *bodily* symptoms of anxiety are acceptable, since they can be construed as an *illness* rather than as *weakness*, or worse still, as "feminine" behavior. Thus, when the husband displays any of the bodily concomitants of panic and severe anxiety, the wife responds to these with sympathy and nurturing behavior. To respond in such a way to a sick husband is entirely compatible with a sex-role-stereotyped perspective.

In sharp contrast, displays of weeping, fearfulness, emotional dependency, or tortured self-doubt by the husband are met with hostility and rejection, since they are signs of weakness and "femininity" rather than illness. This hostile rejection by the wife creates profound anger and resentment in the husband, since he craves to unburden himself to a sympathetic, understanding, and supportive mother figure. The anger is suppressed or buried, but emerges indirectly, often in the form of more panic and anxiety symptoms. The bodily concomitants of these are powerfully reinforced by the wife's protective, caring response to them.

Once the agoraphobia is consolidated, the basic marital dilemma is resolved or ameliorated: *Wives become powerful and protective in relation to their husbands' panic attacks and related symptoms*, but at the same time, husbands are able to *control and dominate* their wives by insisting that their lives revolve entirely around their panic attacks and related symptoms and disabilities. Of these, the profound fear of being alone or physically separated from their wives is the most significant, allowing many men with complex agoraphobia to achieve almost total control over their spouses.

This is not to suggest that the fear of being alone is not entirely genuine. The stress of their symptoms and the marital conflict cause these men to utilize primitive psychological defense mechanisms, of which splitting and projective identification are the most prominent. It will be recalled from Chapter 3 that the use of these and related primitive defensive maneuvers evokes a fear that the mother figure has been destroyed in her absence by the subject's aggressive impulses.

Men with complex agoraphobia habitually suppress, repress, or deny aggressive thoughts and impulses (Hafner, 1981a). Thus, their overwhelming fears that harm will befall their wives in their absence appear irrational to them, and are not easily discussed.

At a symbolic level, physical separation from their wives also evokes in these men a profound fear of losing their sense of personal identity. This unconscious fear is manifested in, and reinforced by, the nature of the symptoms that they experience when they are physically separated from their wives and/or unable to contact them immediately:

> Almost invariably, the onset of symptoms occurred suddenly while the patient was alone outside the home. . . . Separation from the spouse appeared to be the key precipitant. . . . [These men] found it very difficult to describe the most frightening, central aspects of the attack, but the terms most commonly used were "mental black out," "total confusion," "mental disintegration," and similar descriptions. The fear was of loss of consciousness, or total loss of voluntary control over mental and physical events. This constellation of mental events was invariably acutely and profoundly unpleasant. . . . The somatic accompaniments of those episodes were those of acute fear; choking sensations, difficulties in breathing and palpitations were particularly prominent. Common accompanying cognitions were a strong urge to rejoin the wife or parent as soon as possible. (Hafner, 1981a, p. 247).

This pattern of symptoms is strikingly similar to Melanie Klein's description of "the final recourse of an overwhelmingly threatened sense of self"—

namely, *ego disintegration* (see Chapter 3). It is clinical support for the theory that the use of primitive psychological defense mechanisms underlies the symptoms of men with complex agoraphobia.

Finally, if the anxiety and phobic symptoms are severe enough, they may prevent the husband from working. This consolidates his sick, dependent position and his wife's posture as a mother substitute. The husband has at last escaped from the tyranny of the male sex-role stereotype, only to replace it with the sick role and chronic invalidity.

PHOBIAS IN MEN AND ALCOHOL DEPENDENCY

Recent research (Smail, Stockwell, Canter, & Hodgson, 1984) has suggested that a substantial minority or even a small majority of men who seek treatment for alcohol problems are suffering from an underlying phobic disorder. The most common of these is probably agoraphobia, either alone or combined with social phobia.

As Murphy *et al.* (1984) showed, alcohol abuse/dependence in the community has an overall 6-month prevalence rate of about 6.5%. Rates are much higher in men than in women. The peak prevalence for men is about 12%, and occurs in the 25-44 age group. The peak prevalence for women of about 3.5% occurs in the 18-24 age group, falling to about 1.7% in the 25-44 age group.

If only one fifth (probably an underestimate) of men age 25-44 with major alcohol problems have underlying agoraphobia, this yields a hidden or disguised prevalence of about 2.5%. If to this rate is added the 1.5% prevalence of overt agoraphobia in men aged 25-44 (Myers *et al.*, 1984), then the true prevalence of agoraphobia in younger married men is probably around 4%. Thus, in reality, agoraphobia may be almost as much a problem for men as it is for women.

However, the male sex-role stereotype is largely incompatible with seeking professional help for emotional problems, although it powerfully reinforces heavy drinking. As a result, many men attempt to disguise or ameliorate their phobic symptoms with alcohol, a drug that appears highly effective for such purposes. Unfortunately, the habitual use of alcohol creates its own problems; these are then superimposed on the underlying phobic disorder and may exacerbate it. After a few years of alcohol dependency, the original phobic disorder may be so well disguised as to escape attention from all but the most skilled and thorough health care workers.

ANXIETY STATES

There is controversy about the *DSM-III* diagnostic group "anxiety states." Some authors argue that creating distinct categories for panic disorders and generalized anxiety disorders is artificial, and that the two conditions overlap greatly, not only with each other, but with somatoform disorders and agoraphobia. Clinical realities tend to support this viewpoint: I can recall seeing few patients who reported only those symptoms described in the *DSM-III* subcategories. However, the precise pattern of symptoms is not a critical issue with regard to marital interaction: Most married women with severe, complex, and persisting anxiety states have marriage relationships similar to those described in Chapter 5 under the heading "Marital Repercussions of Illness-Confirming Behavior." Most married men with such disorders have marriage relationships similar to those described in this chapter under the heading "Complex Agoraphobia in Men: Escape from Sex-Role Tyranny."

There are, of course, several other types of marital interaction in persisting anxiety states. Of these, a particularly common one is associated with unresolved grief in one or both marriage partners.

Anxiety States and Abnormal Grief

In traditional societies, elaborate mourning rituals and ceremonies surround the death of a member of the community, creating a framework within which the bereaved relatives and friends may experience and ventilate their painful emotions and work through the mourning process. Such rituals and ceremonies are now largely absent from English-speaking societies. In the absence of an appropriate framework, it is difficult or impossible to accomplish the tasks of mourning. Furthermore, many people are unaware of the central importance of completing the mourning process. Instead, they struggle to suppress or bury their painful feelings and try to carry on as usual. Invariably, the buried feelings emerge later on, usually in a disguised or modified form, of which panic attacks and anxiety symptoms are a common example. The precise mechanisms involved are as follows.

THE BIOLOGICAL BASIS OF GRIEF

The intensity of the human response to bereavement has its origins in humankind's early social evolution. It will be recalled from Chapter 2 that a central feature of our evolution was the development of small, cohesive hominid groups that competed with each other for territory. Considerable mobility was built into this way of life. Separation from the tribal group or from hunting or gathering subgroups meant almost certain death through starvation or at the hands of animal predators or rival hominid aggressors. This was particularly true of infants and children, of whom those most likely to be reunited with their adult group were the ones who were able to attract attention to their position. This was most likely to occur through noisy and prolonged vocalization. Thus, the capacity to create a sustained din in response to separation became an important survival characteristic of the human species. After many thousands of years of evolution, this response to separation became a fundamental human instinct. Although it is now largely redundant as a survival characteristic, it remains within all of us, whether children or adults, as an inescapable aspect of our response to loss and bereavement.

In physiological terms, loud, prolonged vocalization of a reflex or instinctual nature requires the maintenance of high levels of arousal. During high arousal, emotions are usually experienced with great intensity. Thus, the experience of intense emotions is an intrinsic part of the human response to bereavement. Traditional mourning rituals encourage loud and sustained vocalization and the expression of emotions. After a few days of this, arousal levels decline and with them the intensity of emotional experience and expression. It then becomes possible for the bereaved person to complete the emotional and cognitive aspects of the bereavement process over the next few weeks or months.

THE EMERGENCE OF ANXIETY SYMPTOMS AS A RESULT OF UNRESOLVED GRIEF

A central feature of the failure to mourn is suppression or repression of intense anger, fear, and related emotions. Because these emotions cannot be expressed and discharged, levels of arousal remain persistently high and the process of mourning becomes arrested. Subsequently, the bereaved person may successfully carry on with usual activities, but anxiety symptoms commonly emerge sooner or later.

Anxiety symptoms can manifest themselves in relation to almost any organ or system in the body. When they emerge in the context of unresolved grief, they are puzzling and worrying to the sufferer, who does not connect them with his or her bereavement, particularly if it occurred a considerable time previously. Sometimes, anxiety symptoms do not emerge until several years after the bereavement, usually on or around an anniversary of the death. Such *anniversary reactions* occur most commonly in the first 5 years, but not infrequently 10, 20, or 25 years later. I have known troublesome anxiety symptoms to emerge for the first time on the 50th anniversary of the death of a close relative.

In arrested grieving, although most aspects of the mourning process have been relegated to the unconscious, the bereaved person is nonetheless in a state of grief at a bodily level. In such circumstances, the psychophysiological mechanisms that underly the mourning process remain in a state of overresponsiveness. When anxiety symptoms emerge, they often become a *displaced* focus for the arrested mourning process: Symbolically, the loss of health comes to represent the lost relative, and the search for a cure or a medical explanation for the symptoms unconsciously represents a search for the lost relative (intermittent searching behavior is common after a bereavement, and may continue for months or even years). Feelings of fear, guilt, and despair are displaced onto the symptoms; feelings of anger are displaced onto doctors and others who fail to find a cure, or onto the spouse or other relatives, who are perceived as hostile and unsympathetic.

This sequence of events is a special case of the pattern of symptom development and maintenance described in Chapter 5 under the heading "Denial of Marital Conflict and Its Repercussions." The fruitless search for a cure or medical explanation for the symptoms continues as long as the grief remains unresolved. Not uncommonly, such patients go to their graves in a state of unresolved grief, usually after many years of displaced mourning. Only in death, which they most fear, are they finally reunited with the real objects of their grief.

MARITAL INTERACTION AND ABNORMAL GRIEF

My conjoint approach to the treatment of married people suffering from anxiety states has revealed a surprising phenomenon: When a married person presents with persisting anxiety symptoms, it is common to find that *both* partners in the marriage are in a state of abnormal grief. Nearly always, these grief problems originated *before* the marriage, usually in relation to the death of a parent. Unconsciously, these couples chose each other because both were suffering from abnormal grief. Again at an unconscious level, each partner hoped to get help from the other in working through and resolving their grief. Unfortunately, their subsequent marital interaction almost invariably perpetuates rather than resolves the problem.

Classically, one partner develops anxiety symptoms that persist in spite of a wide range of medications. These symptoms and their repercussions become a displaced focus for the grief of *both* partners. As a result, the symptoms are held firmly in place by marital interaction and resist all attempts at conventional medical treatment. Neither partner is able to acknowledge or work through his or her unresolved grief.

Even if the partner with anxiety symptoms is identified as being in a state of abnormal grief, psychological treatment for this is unlikely to be helpful unless both marriage partners are involved. The reasons for this are as follows. Getting in touch with buried feelings of grief is a profoundly challenging and painful task. Nonetheless, very few people with arrested mourning lack the courage to attempt grief work if they fully understand why it is necessary. Unfortunately, spouses often undermine patients' attempts at initiating grief work because this threatens to expose their own grief problems. Often, spouses ridicule the idea of grief work, insisting that it is irrelevant to events that belong in the past and should remain there. If the patient actually starts grief work, the spouse often interferes with the process by making it difficult for the patient to weep freely, which is fundamental to grief work. These problems can be resolved by involving the spouse in therapy and explaining the patient's need for support and encouragement in a profoundly challenging task. As a result of couples therapy, the spouse often becomes able to acknowledge his or her own grief problems, and to join the patient in resolving them.

OBSESSIVE COMPULSIVE DISORDERS

Although obsessive compulsive disorders are relatively uncommon, with a 6-month prevalence of about 1% in men and 1.5% in women (Murphy *et al.*, 1984), they have received a disproportionately large amount of attention in the psychiatric literature because they are bizarre and fascinating as well as disabling and persisting. In one of the most comprehensive books ever written on the subject, Rachman and Hodgson (1980) cite nearly 400 references to the professional and scientific literature that deal with obsessive compulsive disorders, but they devote less than 3 of over 400 pages of text to a discussion of the marital aspects of the condition. They suggest that "the spouses who continue to live with a severely obsessional husband or wife are inevitably the more patient and devoted ones. . . . In some notable cases the affected person, or patient, exercises inordinate power over the lives of family members, even to the point of tyranny" (p. 64).

Similar viewpoints are found in the psychoanalytic literature. For example, Rice (1974) describes a married woman with an obsessive compulsive disorder who received 7 years of psychoanalytic psychotherapy that resulted in a lessening of her anxiety and depression, although her obsessive compulsive symptoms became worse. Strikingly, they ceased immediately and permanently following the death of her husband, after which she continued in therapy for 9 months, leaving against the therapist's advice. Rice's exclusive preoccupation with the patient's personal psychopathology persisted throughout therapy, to the extent of his refusal to discuss her rage toward her husband: "I had the opportunity to see a display of her rage (without the assaultiveness) on only one occasion . . . because I did not permit such expression to occur again" (p. 56). There is no mention of the possibility that the patient's rage toward her husband may have been partly justified by his behavior toward her, and that this may have contributed to her symptoms. Instead, the patient's husband is *her* victim: "One potent way that she was able to express the negative side of her ambivalence to her husband was by including him in her rituals and making him suffer thereby."

Behaviorists and psychoanalysts alike perpetuate the idea of the long-suffering, almost superhumanly tolerant family or spouse caring for the demanding, ungrateful patient. Although this may be true in many instances, there is evidence that spouses or families sometimes have a vested interest in the continuing disability of the designated patient, and may unwittingly be contributing to the maintenance of symptoms. This is illustrated in Haley's (1963) account of a married woman with a classical obsessive compulsive disorder: "If her case were written up from the classic point of view, she would be described in terms of her history, her fantasies, her guilts and so on. If her husband were mentioned, it would probably be only a passing statement that he was understandably unhappy about her compulsion. . . . However, in this case her husband was brought into therapy and an examination of the interpersonal context of her hand washing revealed an intense and bitter struggle between the patient and her husband. . . . He demanded his own way, wanting his wife to do what he said and do it promptly. Although the wife objected to her husband's tyrannical ways, she was unable to oppose him on any issue—except her hand washing. . . . As a result of her hand washing she actually managed to refuse to do anything he suggested" (p. 14).

Haley points out that the wife's symptoms protected the husband from facing his own problems and other difficulties within the marriage; furthermore, as the wife improved, the husband became disturbed and behaved in ways that negated the improvement.

Where marital or family interaction reinforce the patient's obsessive compulsive symptoms, or where the symptoms are an alternative to overt marital or interpersonal conflict, treating the symptoms alone is likely to be fruitless. Behavioral, psychoanalytic, or drug therapy, when focused mainly or exclusively on the patient's symptoms or psychopathology, can serve to consolidate the symptoms as the main focus of dissatisfaction within the marriage. Subsequently, it may be impossible for therapists to enable the couple to examine the patient's symptoms from an interpersonal or marital perspective. The following cases illustrate such a series of events. These cases and some additional material were initially published elsewhere (Hafner, 1982b) and are reproduced with permission.

Case 1: Ingrid

Ingrid A, age 39 years, had started excessive domestic and personal cleaning while pregnant, 4 years prior to referral to the program. Her symptoms markedly increased after the death, 2 years before referral, of her mother-in-law, who lived in the same house. In the 18 months prior to referral, Ingrid's entire day was spent washing and scrubbing herself, her house, and her two young children. She had failed to benefit from 2 years of comprehensive psychiatric treatment including home-based behavior therapy. Although she improved somewhat during active therapy phases, she invariably relapsed.

Ingrid's husband was an emotionally cold, rigid, authoritarian man who demanded that his wife and children obey him instantly and without question. His father had died when he was a young child, and he had been brought up by his mother, who did not remarry. He showed no signs of bereavement when his mother, to whom he was very close, died 2 years prior to Ingrid's referral. His approach to Ingrid's symptoms was one of anger and control. He frequently criticized her for her rituals, and often physically restrained her from executing them, which she invariably resented. The couple had not shared sexual intercourse for over 2 years. Mr. A stated that only his sense of loyalty prevented him from leaving the marriage.

At the start of multimodal therapy, Ingrid blamed herself entirely for her symptoms and felt that her husband's behavior toward her was fully justified. She described her husband as "perfect." However, during a role-play session, she suddenly began screaming with rage at the therapist who represented her husband when he tried to pull her away from a wash basin during her compulsive hand washing. Subsequently she acknowledged for the first time considerable anger toward her husband, particularly concerning the way he reacted to her symptoms.

Once it was established that the interaction between Ingrid and her husband influenced the frequency of her rituals and hand washing, conjoint marital therapy was initiated. Attempts at altering marital interaction failed entirely, mainly because of Mr. A's unwillingness to change his attitudes and behavior toward Ingrid. When it was suggested to Mr. A that an unresolved bereavement reaction to his mother's death might be contributing to their marital difficulties, he angrily denied any personal problems, insisting that his wife's illness was the only problem within the marriage.

During a total of 8-months intensive multimodal therapy, Ingrid was virtually symptom-free while in the hospital, but invariably relapsed on returning home.

Case 2: Yvonne

Yvonne B, age 46 years, had an 8-year history of compulsive cleaning, checking, and obsessional ruminating. Her symptoms had begun shortly after the birth of her son, and centered around her fears that she might injure or harm him through neglect or impulsive assault. She repeated many domestic tasks over 50 times until they were performed "perfectly," or until exhaustion occurred. Although Yvonne had responded to intensive in-patient drug and behavior therapy on several occasions during her 6-year treatment history, she invariably relapsed on returning home.

Yvonne's husband was one of 12 siblings. He described his mother as a cold, strict, and authoritarian woman who had raised her children with negligible support from her mainly absent husband. During conjoint marital therapy, Mr. B admitted a total inability to express affection, and major problems in social and interpersonal adjustment. He said that he had no interest in sex with his wife, with whom he had not had intercourse for over 2 years, and which had been unsatisfactory for 8 years, ostensibly because of his premature ejaculation. His first priority was his work, which was nonetheless rather mundane and routine. He suffered from agoraphobia and at times could travel only with the couple's 22-year-old daughter, who attended several family therapy sessions.

During these sessions, Mr. B and his daughter managed to convey the distinct impression that they thought that Yvonne was crazy. Mr. B had the utmost difficulty recalling what Yvonne said, even if she repeated it. This made progress extremely difficult. It eventually became clear that Mr. B and his daughter were happier when Yvonne was in the hospital. They had no wish to alter their unusual, overinvolved relationship, even when it became clear that Yvonne's anxiety and cleaning rituals were exacerbated by a fear that the daughter was taking over her domestic role. When Yvonne was at home, there was constant argument between the women over domestic tasks, with Mr. B generally supporting the daughter. Yvonne felt unwanted and unloved, and this was reinforced by her husband's admission that he had often thought of leaving her, but felt morally obliged to remain in the marriage. These factors largely explained why Yvonne was almost free of symptoms in the hospital, but invariably relapsed at home.

Case 3: Lynette

Lynette C, age 33 years, had developed obsessive compulsive symptoms at the age of 19. They greatly worsened shortly after her marriage and prevented her from working outside the home, since she spent all day performing rituals and domestic tasks. Should she fail to complete her rituals or tasks, she experienced intense panic attacks.

Lynette met her husband when both were in a mental hospital, she being treated with drugs and behavior therapy for her obsessional symptoms, and he for depression. They married when she was 26 and he 29. Mr. C described himself as a very shy, sensitive person, easily embarrassed. He had lived with his parents until his marriage, and remained very attached to his mother, who looked after the couple's two young children.

During conjoint marital interviews it emerged that the couple had not had sexual intercourse together for over 3 years, ostensibly because Lynette viewed the act with disgust, although Mr. C had suffered from premature ejaculation. Mr. C blamed his wife for her symptoms and frequently criticized her inability to master them. He frequently humiliated her during conjoint sessions by ignoring, criticizing, or denigrating her. However, he said that attending to his wife's problems and symptoms stopped him from worrying about his own. Carrying out domestic tasks for her made him feel useful and needed. He stated explicitly that he would leave the marriage should Lynette become more assertive, competent, or independent. Lynette stated that since she felt unable to survive without her husband, she could not risk changing in ways that were unacceptable to him. She felt that conjoint marital sessions were inappropriate, since they made her husband angry, causing him, for example, to cease his twice-daily telephone calls to her, the absence of which caused her intense anxiety. Conjoint marital interviews were therefore stopped after four sessions. Although Lynette's symptoms had been virtually absent in the hospital, they returned within a week of her discharge.

Case 4: Cathy

Cathy D, 22 years old, had developed a severe obsessive compulsive disorder shortly after her marriage when she was 18. Her symptoms had been exacerbated by the birth of her 18-month-old son, who was the focal point of her rituals and obsessions, which were aimed at protecting him and herself from contamination by germs. She spent many hours disinfecting and cleaning the house, and insisted that her husband remove his shoes and clothing as soon as he entered their home.

Cathy's husband came from a disturbed family background characterized by extreme denial of feelings. He had remained very close to his mother, who looked after the couple's son when Cathy was in the hospital. During conjoint marital sessions, he tended to ignore or cut through what Cathy said, and often talked as if she were not present. It emerged that he usually watched television or went out while Cathy was disinfecting the house, although at other times he helped her with her rituals, since this was easier than confronting her. During conjoint interviews, he denied that there were any real problems, either with the obsessions or in other areas, even though it had been established previously that Cathy found sexual intercourse extremely unpleasant and avoided it if possible.

Mr. D apparently found it impossible to acknowledge any feelings of frustration, disappointment, or anger toward his wife or about his marriage: He simply denied the existence of any problems. However, it emerged that the couple had major fights over Cathy's symptoms: not infrequently, Mr. D would become exasperated by Cathy's cleaning rituals, and would physically prevent her from carrying them out. These physical struggles almost invariably led to Cathy screaming with rage at her husband and were often ended with an exchange of blows. Cathy blamed herself for these fights, and this added to her enormous sense of guilt.

During 5 months as an inpatient, Cathy was virtually symptom-free but invariably relapsed on returning home for weekend leave.

Case 5: Fiona

Fiona E, age 48 years, had for 20 years suffered from severe obsessive compulsive symptoms relating to fears of contamination by dogs' feces and urine, and, in particular, dogs' saliva, because of its undetectability. When her husband or children entered the house, she demanded that they step into a large cardboard box, remove their shoes and outer garments, and then change into decontaminated indoor clothing. She spent most of the day washing and rewashing clothes, carpets, and curtains to protect herself against contamination.

Mr. E, an accountant age 49 years, was socially phobic and abnormally obsessional. He avoided any social contact other than at his work in a small office. His work was his first priority, and his leisure time was almost entirely occupied with reading newspapers. One entire room of the house was stacked with piles of old newspapers, which he indexed and cross-indexed in relation to matters of interest.

During conjoint therapy, it emerged that Mr. and Mrs. E had never had a satisfactory sex life together, something that Mr. E attributed to Fiona's sexual naïveté and that Fiona attributed to her husband's premature ejaculation. Neither had ever been able to discuss their sexual problems. For many years, there had been virtually no verbal communication between the couple, although Mr. E spoke comparatively freely to their 20-year-old daughter, to whom he was very close. This daughter was virtually housebound by agoraphobic symptoms. It was clear that the daughter carried out domestic tasks more efficiently and effectively than Mrs. E, who felt useless and inadequate in the face of her daughter's domestic competence.

Mrs. E had no motivation to overcome her symptoms and could see no purpose in therapy. She felt that as long as the marital climate remained cold and frustrating, and as long as Mr. E remained socially phobic, there was little value in her attempting to change in any way. Mr. E saw no purpose in changing his own behavior and attitudes. However, he felt that if his wife's symptoms improved, this might provide him with an incentive to communicate with her more freely. Although Mrs. E was virtually free of symptoms in the hospital, she relapsed shortly after returning home.

A Caricature of the Female Sex-Role Stereotype

The symptoms of the five married women described above are fairly representative of those seen in severe obsessive compulsive disorder in married women. The patients' all-consuming preoccupation with washing, cleaning, and other domestic tasks is classical. When I first wrote up these cases some years ago, I was largely unaware of the contribution of sex-role stereotyping to the development and maintenance of their symptoms. Now, it has become much clearer.

In essence, these women represent a caricature of the female sex-role stereotype. They struggle endlessly to preserve an impeccably clean, perfectly ordered domestic environment. They have time for nothing else. Their childhood sex-role conditioning is often extremely powerful, and they come early to identify strongly but ambivalently with the female sex-role stereotype of dependency and domesticity. As married women they unconsciously hate their enforced domesticity and dependency on their husbands. They loathe boring, repetitive, domestic tasks, and are full of rage about their situation. But they are unable to challenge at a conscious level their ingrained stereotypes, and so remain trapped within them.

They cope by attacking with detergents, scrubbing brushes, mops, and vacuum cleaners the most immediate source of their rage: the home itself. Constant hard physical work followed by exhaustion diffuses their pent-up energy and aggression. As long as they keep busy, they are able to ward off feelings of anger, guilt, and despair. By constantly struggling to be perfect housewives, they are able to obscure from themselves their profound ambivalence to the role.

Marital Contributions to Symptom Maintenance

The single most powerful contributor to symptom maintenance is the wives' stereotyped view of marriage. However, without constant reinforcement by husbands and others, wives' sex-role conditioning would almost certainly extinguish. All five of the husbands described in the case histories believed that married women belonged in the home and that they should devote themselves exclusively to their children, husbands, and related domestic activities. These men also believed that their wives should be subservient to them and bow to their superior judgment.

In addition to the powerful but nonspecific stereotyping factor, there was some more specific marital contributors to the maintenance of these wives' symptoms. These contributors can be recognized clearly in obsessive compulsive disorder because the condition is so persistent and disabling. *However, they are often present in other psychiatric disorders of comparable severity and duration.*

SHIFTING THE FOCUS OF MARITAL DISSATISFACTION

In all five cases, shared sexual activity had been highly unsatisfactory from early in marriage. In Cases 2 and 3, the husbands admitted to premature ejaculation, but this problem was never discussed because the patient's symptoms and problems had become the main focus of dissatisfaction within the marriage. In the remaining cases, the shifting of marital conflict from sex to the patients' symptoms protected the husbands from their wives' assertions that they, the husbands, contributed to sexual problems and dissatisfaction within the marriage. Hence, the pressure on the husbands to acknowledge aspects of their own shortcomings and inadequacies within the marriage was removed.

ROLE CONFLICT AND TAKEOVER

In Cases 1–4, there was evidence of considerable role conflict early in marriage, usually between the patients and their mothers-in-law. The husbands' mothers sought to establish within their sons' marriages roles for themselves that were resented or unwanted by the patient. However, the patients' husbands were invariably unable to confront their mothers about these unwelcome intrusions into the marriage, usually because of their need to preserve close, strongly ambivalent relationships with them. This left the patients feeling constantly let down and disappointed by their husbands, who, in spite of their stated intentions of standing by and supporting their wives, seemed, when put to the test, to side with their mothers (and others) against the patient. In Cases 2 and 5, daughters were clearly competing with the patients for key domestic roles, and in both cases their fathers tacitly or overtly supported them in this.

The effect of these subtle, tacit, or overt attempts at eroding the patients' domestic roles was to leave the patients feeling anxious and insecure. This, in turn, exacerbated the obsessive compulsive symptoms, setting up a vicious cycle that ultimately left the patients with no domestic roles whatsoever, so that they felt entirely useless and inadequate in their domestic environment. *Ultimately, they were left only with their roles as patients.*

HUSBANDS' DENIAL OF PERSONAL PROBLEMS

In all five cases, husbands' personal problems were obscured by the patients' symptoms. In Case 1, the husband's angry preoccupation with his wife's symptoms and his constant attempts to dominate and control her seemed to help protect him from experiencing very painful, suppressed feelings of his own about his mother's death. Instead of feeling anger and anxiety as part of a bereavement reaction, he experienced these feelings in relation to his wife's symptoms. Although blaming his wife for these feelings protected him from the full pain of bereavement, it prevented him from working through his grief.

In Cases 2, 3, and 5, the husbands were markedly socially phobic and withdrawn. Early in marriage, this had led to marital conflict because, before the full development of their symptoms, the patients had tended to be more sociable and outgoing than their husbands. Once the symptoms were fully developed, the virtual absence of any social life was blamed on the patients' symptoms, and the husbands did not have to confront their own personal problems in relating to others socially. In Case 2, the husband had moderate agoraphobia in addition to social phobias. In Case 5 the husband was himself abnormally obsessional. In Case 3, the husband stated explicitly that focusing on his wife's problems protected him from worrying about his own, and that performing domestic tasks elevated his self-esteem.

Although there was clear evidence in Cases 1–4 of the husbands' abnormal, ambivalent dependence on their mothers, the patients' almost total dependence on their husbands helped the husbands to deny their own dependency problems. Furthermore, the patients' incapacitating symptoms justified a takeover of domestic roles by their mothers-in-law. This protected the patients' husbands from examining their own overinvolvement with their mothers, since their mothers' frequent presence was attributed to the patients' symptoms.

Although all five husbands had at times threatened to leave their wives, all stated that they had not done so because of a sense of duty and marital or moral obligation. They believed that their wives would be unable to survive without them, and their wives shared this belief, fearing that their husbands might leave them if the obsessive compulsive symptoms were not present to preserve the "compulsory" nature of the marriage. They were thus ambivalent about the symptomatic improvement that their husbands and others were exhorting them to achieve. The husbands felt secure in the knowledge that their wives could never leave them as long as they remained ill, and this protected the husbands from having to examine their own capacity to manage alone or to attract a different mate. It also allowed them to treat their wives in ways that might otherwise have caused them to leave. Furthermore, the husbands' self-esteem was enhanced by the idea that they were meeting difficult and demanding obligations within unsatisfactory marriages out of a sense of duty or moral obligation. This helped them discount any criticism from their wives or others regarding their behavior within the marriage.

OBSESSIVE COMPULSIVE DISORDERS IN MEN

Although obsessive compulsive disorder is probably only slightly more common in women than in men (Murphy *et al.*, 1984; Rachman & Hodgson, 1980), men and women differ greatly with regard to the precise nature of symptoms: *Nearly 90% of women, but little more than 10% of men, are compulsive cleaners of the home* (Rachman & Hodgson, 1980). In contrast, men are more likely to be compulsive checkers. This is striking evidence in support of the idea that obsessive compulsive disorders in women are often a caricature of the female sex-role stereotype. It has been suggested that obsessive compulsive disorder in men is a caricature of the male sex-role stereotype. It is, however, more accurate to suggest that obsessive compulsive disorder in men often represents a *failure* to achieve ideals based on a male sex-role stereotype. The following case illustrates this.

The Little Father

The term "little mother" is not uncommonly applied to girls who in childhood are required to take over key aspects of their mothers' role. "Little fathers" also exist, although I have rarely heard the term used. David, 35, had been a "little father."

DAVID

David was referred to me by a psychiatrist after he had failed to respond to a range of psychiatric treatments, including tricyclic antidepressants and electroconvulsive therapy, over the previous 2 years. His symptoms were comprised mainly of checking and counting rituals that he felt compelled to do in order to protect his wife and children from accidents or illness. He described an "internal command" to touch certain objects repeatedly. For example: "Yesterday I felt this strong urge to touch my son's bed 500 times. I tried to resist, but I got more and more anxious and fearful. I became dizzy, got pains in my chest and tingling in my fingers and face. I felt better as soon as I started the ritual, and when I'd finished, I was quite relaxed and satisfied."

The anxiety-reducing effects of the rituals rarely lasted more than 20–30 minutes. David felt compelled to repeat them throughout the day. His commonest ritual was to touch walls, up to 600 times, but a wide range of other objects was included in his touching rituals. If he lost count, or was interrupted, he had to start again. In addition, when he showered or bathed, he had to wash parts of his body a fixed number of times, ranging from 60–100. Checking was a major problem. Often he checked taps, doors, windows, and switches up to 30 times before he was able to convince himself that they were shut or turned off. If he performed simple tasks such as tidying a room, he felt compelled to constantly check and rearrange the position of objects. Even mowing the lawn was virtually impossible because of a compulsion to constantly retrace his steps. At times he would stare fixedly at particular objects for several minutes, to convince himself that they really existed. He had given up driving a car because of his compulsion to keep going back to check that he had not caused an accident: Local journeys had often taken an hour or more, or were never completed.

For the past 2 years, these symptoms had occupied virtually all his waking time, dominating his life and preventing him from undertaking any constructive activities. Although he had experienced some minor checking and touching rituals in adolescence, the symptoms did not become an inconvenience until about 2 years after his marriage to Linda when he was 23. They had started to become troublesome when he was about 27, and had been a major problem for the past 6–7 years.

David's childhood was very disturbed. He recalled almost continual verbal and physical conflict between his parents, and his father frequently beat his mother. Violence in the home was habitual. David recalled his mother repeatedly beating his older sister with a broom handle and, on one occasion, deliberately pouring boiling water over her. He himself was sometimes severely beaten by his mother, and he had needed to invent a variety of alternative explanations for the bruises when they were noticed by school friends or teachers.

David's father, Ben, worked long hours in a mundane, poorly paid job and was uninvolved in domestic matters. David recalled that in the evenings and on Sundays, Ben sat around the house looking tired and miserable: "I would go up and speak to him, but there would be no reply."

Ben died from bowel cancer when David was 15. He had deteriorated mentally and physically for about a year before his death, but David had felt powerless to do anything for him. After Ben's death, David felt a deep sense of guilt, wishing he had helped his father more.

David's need to be a "little father" originated mainly from his mother's inability to manage domestic and financial matters, which Ben left entirely to her. She constantly overspent the family budget and used David to get her out of problems with creditors. From the age of 6 or 7, David would have to stay home from school in order to help and protect her. She insisted that he not tell Ben about their problems, so that David was forced to deceive his father. She frequently turned to David for emotional support and understanding about her worries, expecting him, a 7-year-old child, to "father" her. Thus, David had no real childhood. Denied the chance of playing with other children after school and at weekends, he adopted from a very early age the role of a protective "father" to his mother. This role was powerfully reinforced when, as happened occasionally, he was able to protect his mother by placing himself physically between her and Ben when the couple were on the verge of a fistfight.

Sometimes, however, his mother's frustration and rage about her situation became unbearable, and she would vent her anger by savagely beating David. On these occasions he buried his hatred for his mother so deeply within him that it never surfaced in his conscious mind. Unable to blame his mother for these vicious attacks, he came to believe that he deserved them, although he did not know why.

In spite of his horrendous family life, David did fairly well at school. He dreamed of being a famous attorney. However, he had to start work in a local factory at 15 to help support his mother and sister, who was then 17 and unemployed. At 18 he started night school, and at 22 passed, on a second attempt, the preliminary examination required in his state to gain eligibility for a clerkship in an attorney's office. When he married Linda, he had been working as an attorney's clerk for about 6 months. He was recognized more for his reliability and perseverance than for his brilliance and promise.

LINDA

Linda was the only child of a couple who had a rigidly sex-role-stereotyped marriage. Her father, a successful corporate lawyer, had desperately wanted a son, but Linda's mother had been advised on medical grounds against further children. Linda's father initially disguised his disappointment with Linda by overindulging her and treating her as a boy. Linda's mother resented this and strongly encouraged displays of femininity in her daughter, and attempted also to undermine Linda's relationship with her father. Linda's mother appeared to have won this struggle for her daughter's allegiance: Linda developed from early childhood an intense interest in nurturing activities and proclaimed, almost as soon as she could talk, her wish to look after children when she grew up. This consuming interest in nurturing persisted in spite of her father's rejection and increasing hostility toward her. When she married David she had been working as a fully trained nursery nurse for a year. A shy and inhibited young woman, she lived at home and continued to be dominated by her grossly overprotective mother. Her powerful identification with the female sex-role-stereotype effectively obscured her substantial problems of gender and personal identity formation.

THE MARRIAGE

When David and Linda married, they both assumed that David would become a rich and famous attorney and that Linda would be his loyal and faithful handmaiden, devoting her life to his welfare and that of his children.

This arrangement worked very well for the first 2 years of their marriage, during which time a son and a daughter were born. However, the couple had fundamentally different views about child raising: Linda relied on shouting and smacking, whereas David abhorred this approach, since it reminded him of his own horrific childhood. When he objected to Linda about her approach to child raising, she became enraged. She made it abundantly clear that he was poaching on *her* territory, and told him to stick to *his* role of providing his family's material needs and, of course, becoming a rich and famous attorney. Characteristically, David completely suppressed his rage about Linda's inflexibility. Instead of directly expressing his anger and dissatisfaction, he withdrew almost entirely from family life and buried himself in his work. However, his rage toward Linda constantly threatened to surface and challenge his idealized image of her. It emerged *indirectly* as irrational fears for her safety, and he coped with these fears by using the compulsive rituals to ward them off.

The touching rituals began to interfere with David's work. This created an almost unmanageable anxiety within him, since by now the main source of his self-esteem was an unshakable belief that he would ultimately become a famous attorney. Thus, he worked even longer hours, studying for his bar exams whenever he had any free time. Predictably, he failed the exams.

David's obsessive compulsive symptoms worsened subtantially after this, and his increased touching, counting, and checking activities added to his inefficiency at work. After two more exam failures, David was asked to resign. At 31, his initially promising career appeared to be in ruins. He got a job as a clerk in the office of a less reputable attorney, but lasted only 5 months before he was dismissed on the grounds of inefficiency. He was unable to find another job as an attorney's clerk. Rather than accept alternative work, he remained unemployed, studying at home for his bar exams:

Incredibly, his confidence in ultimate success and fame remained unshaken. He attributed his failures to his obsessive compulsive symptoms, and was totally convinced that once they were "cured," he would successfully resume his old career.

Linda felt betrayed by the failure of David's career. It was, she felt, a violation of their marriage contract, which had been based on the idea of David's ultimate wealth and fame. David had concealed his obsessive compulsive symptoms from Linda for the first 6 years of their marriage. When their increasing severity had forced him to reveal them, he had underplayed their significance, so that Linda had not understood how disabling they were. After David stopped work, the full extent of his symptoms was revealed to Linda. She insisted that he seek medical help. Initial consultations confirmed the idea of an illness; this unleashed Linda's powerful nurturing drive. She devoted herself wholeheartedly to the care of her "sick" husband, transforming her anger and disappointment with David into constant supervision of him. Inevitably, she tried to stop him from carrying out his rituals, but with no success. This was highly frustrating for both of them and actually made David's symptoms worse.

Within a year of stopping work, David's rituals and obsessions were taking up virtually all of his waking hours. He could no longer study for his exams, but nonetheless clung to the idea that he would successfully resume his career when his illness was cured. Linda's life revolved around David and his illness, the two boys, and domestic matters. She was fairly content. Caring for a sick husband was an extension and consolidation of her idealized, stereotyped ideas about maternal and marital roles. Her self-sacrificing devotion to David allowed her to feel valued and worthwhile as a person, and helped to obscure any negative feelings she had about her stereotyped self-image.

For David, the situation was intolerable. He had only one aim in life: to resume his career. As a "little father," he had known nothing except being responsible for another person—his mother. His attempts in childhood to protect and care for his mother had, of course, been doomed: As a small child he could not in reality take care of his mother's emotional, practical, and economic needs. The idea of failing once again, in adulthood, to look after the most important woman in life, was utterly repugnant to him.

David had never learned how to play, or relax, or enjoy the company of other people. Any creative impulses had been ruthlessly suppressed in the service of work-oriented efforts and achievements. He regarded artistic, musical, or literary endeavors as essentially nonproductive, and had no interest in them. His only source of satisfaction, meaning, or purpose in life was work, and providing for his family. The obsessive compulsive symptoms stopped him from working. Yet the harder he and Linda fought them, the worse they became.

When I interviewed David for the first time, he repeatedly praised Linda for her devotion to him and emphasized what a good marriage they had. During my first conjoint interview with the couple, Linda explained that a previous therapist had suggested marital therapy, to which they had rather reluctantly agreed. Half-way through the second conjoint session, Linda had stormed out. She felt that the therapist was blaming *her* for some of David's symptoms and problems. This had enraged Linda beyond measure, since she believed the opposite to be true, namely, that she was devoting her life to helping and caring for David, who had a medical illness for which neither of them were to blame.

Although I did not offer it, both David and Linda were adamant in their rejection of a couple's approach to therapy. They insisted that treatment should focus exclusively on David's symptoms. In view of the severity of David's condition, I arranged for him to be admitted to a psychiatric unit as an in-patient. His treatment was composed mainly of behavior therapy. Two experienced and highly skilled nurses were allocated to his care, so that one of them could be with him throughout the day. In essence, the nurses sought to prevent him from carrying out his rituals, and taught him to cope in other ways with his anxiety and fears about the safety of his wife and children. Treatment was extremely arduous: It was 3 weeks before he could spend a morning or afternoon free of rituals and obsessions. After reaching this stage, he no longer required the constant supervision of a nurse, although he required occasional help in resisting rituals.

After 9 weeks in the hospital, David was almost entirely free of rituals, and his irrational fears about the safety of his family were greatly reduced. Both David and Linda were delighted with his improvement, and he was discharged from the hospital full of enthusiasm about a return to work.

Within 10 days of returning home, David relapsed completely. He was readmitted to the hospital and within 3 weeks was once again almost free of symptoms. On returning home, he relapsed completely within 2 weeks, and was again brought back into hospital. On this occasion, close attention was paid to precisely what had occurred at home, and the following picture emerged.

When David was severely "ill," his obsessive compulsive symptoms occupied virtually all his waking time. In addition to providing a focus for Linda's care-giving activities, this precluded David from any involvement with his children or domestic matters. On recovery, he was anxious to make up for his lack of involvement. However, his attempts at this were strongly resisted by Linda, who had always regarded the domestic area as her own exclusive territory. Furthermore, a subtle shift had occurred in Linda's attitude to David: Because of his "illness," she no longer regarded him as a good influence on the boys, and she sought to minimize his contact with them. If David persisted in his attempts at domestic role sharing and parenting, Linda became enraged. Unable to express any anger directly toward her, David was forced to bury his hostility within himself. As a result, his obsessive compulsive symptoms reemerged. This sharply reduced marital tension and conflict, which further reinforced the symptoms. The reemergence of symptoms allowed Linda to resume her nurturing behavior toward David. By this stage, he received care and affection from Linda only when his symptoms elicited it, so that the symptoms were powerfully reinforced by Linda's attention.

In such circumstances, it was almost inevitable that David relapsed at home. However, the couple were unaware of the mechanisms involved, and it was impossible to get them to examine the marital contribution to David's symptoms. Instead, they became increasingly frustrated about the failure of treatment, although only Linda was able to express this directly. The couple readily acknowledged that David relapsed whenever he came home, but both firmly denied that their marital interaction and attitudes contributed to this. From their perspective, it was the absence of hospital treatment that caused David's relapse. In reality, however, David received almost no treatment in the hospital after his fourth admission. His improvement was attributable to being away from Linda: Even visits from her were usually followed by a worsening in his condition.

After 6 months of repeated admissions, a skilled and experienced therapist started to treat David at home. She used behavioral techniques similar to those that had helped David on his first admission to the hospital under my care. This approach was highly successful as long as the therapist was present, but David invariably relapsed within 1 or 2 days after her visits. Again, the couple attributed David's relapses to the absence of suitable treatment.

David was on the threshold of becoming a long-term patient in a mental hospital when fate intervened after nearly 18 months of largely fruitless therapeutic efforts, including antidepressant medications. Linda was admitted to the hospital for a hysterectomy. There were technical complications, and she remained in the hospital for a month. Linda had expected David to collapse totally while she was in the hospital. To the astonishment of both of them, he flourished, becoming symptom-free within 2 weeks. He formed a mutually supportive relationship with a female neighbor, which Linda tried to end when she returned from the hospital. This created marital conflict of an entirely new kind, and forced the couple to acknowledge for the first time major marital problems over and above those related to David's symptoms. Attempts at conjoint marital therapy failed because of the couple's rage toward each other. David moved in with the neighbor, who was separated from her husband. His obsessive compulsive symptoms remained virtually absent.

I followed David up for a further 18 months. He remained substantially free of symptoms, and planned to marry his new partner when his divorce from Linda was finalized. He had resumed work in a local attorney's office, but had a much more realistic attitude to his career prospects. His ambition was to pass his bar exams and to function competently, but not brilliantly, in employment or partnership with a group of local attorneys. Linda had initially coped badly with the separation, but was now adjusting. She had retained custody of the boys, but David had sufficient access to allow him a parental role that he believed was far superior to what he had been permitted when he and Linda were together.

COMMENTS

One effect of David's obsessive compulsive disorder was to prevent him from achieving his ambition to become a rich and famous attorney—an ambition that was clearly based on a male sex-role stereotype, and that was patently unrealistic to all except David and Linda. Thus, David's symptoms initially had a protective effect: The couple were able to blame David's career setbacks on his "illness," thereby preserving their fantasy of David's ultimate success and wealth once he had been "cured."

Later on, as the prospect of David's real success became very remote, Linda clung more rigidly than David to the original fantasy. To her, the idea of being married to an unsuccessful or mediocre attorney was totally repugnant. She preferred to be married to a brilliant but sick man whose failure was thrust upon him by ill fortune. Here it will be recalled that Linda's father was a highly successful corporate lawyer: This may well have contributed to her total inability to accept mediocrity in her husband. Probably more important was her need to obtain vicarious gratification through David's achievements.

Linda's attitudes and expectations put David in an impossible situation: She demanded that he be either ill or brilliant. In reality, he was neither. Only by escaping from the marriage was he able to accept the likelihood of his mediocrity as an attorney. He then no longer needed the obsessive compulsive symptoms to protect him from a profound sense of failure and from his unconscious rage toward Linda. He was able to start life afresh as a fairly ordinary man with fairly ordinary expectations, and perhaps with as much chance of happiness and contentment as the fairly ordinary people around him.

CHAPTER EIGHT

Marriage and Psychosis

In the absence of brain damage, the commonest psychosis is schizophrenic disorder, formerly called "schizophrenia," a term still widely used. Before a *DSM-III* diagnosis of schizophrenic disorder can be made, the main features of the condition must have been present continuously for at least 6 months. This requirement was only recently introduced, and in the past, many conditions of much shorter duration were diagnosed as schizophrenia. Hence, in reviewing the literature on marriage and psychosis, it is often impossible to determine whether a particular paper refers to schizophrenic disorder as it would now be recognized, or to some different but related condition. Thus, for the purposes of this chapter, I do not always make a rigid distinction between schizophrenic disorder and related conditions of briefer duration. Even one brief psychotic episode can have a devastating effect on a marriage.

SEX DIFFERENCES

In Marital Status

There is a consensus in the professional literature that men with schizophrenic disorder are much less likely to marry than women with the same affliction. This view has received solid support in a recent study by Loranger (1984) of 100 men and 100 women with a *DSM-III* diagnosis of schizophrenic disorder. Only 10% of the men, as compared with 50% of the women, had married. These figures are lower than those generally reported, and this probably reflects the very strict diagnostic criteria employed in Loranger's study. If those with psychotic conditions closely related to schizophrenic disorder are also taken into account, then a reasonable estimate would be that about 25% of men and about 70% of women have married (Gibbons, Horn, Powell, & Gibbons, 1984).

Whatever the precise figures, it is clear that marriage rates among men with schizophrenic disorders are greatly below normal, whereas marriage rates among women so afflicted are only slightly below normal. Many factors contribute to this gender difference, of which the most important is probably the earlier age of onset of schizophrenic disorder in men.

In Age of Onset

Loranger's (1984) study showed also that the onset of schizophrenic disorder occurred on average some 5 years earlier in men than in women. About 90% of men, compared with about 60% of women, became schizophrenic before the age of 30. Similar findings were reported by Gold (1984), who suggested that schizophrenia occurs in later life (specifically, after age 45) far more often than is recognized in *DSM-III*. Rabins, Pauker, and Thomas (1984) found a female/male ratio of 11:1 in patients who developed a schizophrenic disorder after the age of 44. They suggested that future versions of *DSM-III* should be modified to include the category "late-onset schizophrenia." Thus, late-onset schizophrenia appears to be overwhelmingly a disorder of women, most of whom are or have been married and have borne children. In contrast, schizophrenia as a whole affects men and women equally (Loranger, 1984).

The earlier onset of schizophrenic disorder in men means that they are much more likely than women to be psychologically and socially impaired before they reach the usual age of marriage. As Gold (1984) has suggested, a given degree of psychosocial handicap will reduce the likelihood of marriage more in men than in women:

> In the modern technological age of the U.S. culture the male is usually expected to be the more assertive in meeting, courting, marrying, and supporting the female. With equal impairment in both sexes, this would generally handicap the male to a disproportionate degree, compared to the generally more passive role of the female during the courtship process. Thus, female schizophrenics would be more likely to be married than male schizophrenics (p. 231).

Such a viewpoint is eminently compatible with Murstein's theories of mate selection, outlined in Chapter 3.

The finding of a substantial difference between men and women with regard to age of onset leads to speculation as to whether the *symptoms* of schizophrenia show gender-related differences. To date, there has been very little systematic research in this area, although a recent study by Rudden, Sweeney, Frances, and Gilmore (1983) found gender-related differences in the *content of delusions*.

Women reported significantly more heterosexual erotic delusions (with themes mainly of erotomania or sexual harassment or jealousy) than men, whereas men reported significantly more homosexual erotic delusions, with themes often centered around aggression by a hostile male figure. Interpersonal and family conflicts were significantly more common as precipitants of psychotic episodes in women than in men, and women reported significantly more symptoms of depression.

Rudden *et al.* point out that "the paranoid disorders in particular seem to be described according to a male prototype, one that neglects important clinical findings in women" (p. 1578). They conclude: "Women, unlike men, do not have to stop identifying with their mother in order to form a stable gender identity. This could account for the fact that issues of masculine identity and concerns with homosexuality predominate for men, while sexual role issues seem to be more problematic for women" (p. 1578). Their findings regarding gender-related differences in the content of delusions are strikingly consistent with those of Lucas, Sainsbury, and Collins (1962), who found, in addition, that the grandiose delusions of men with schizophrenia contained significantly more themes related to power and authority, whereas those of women tended to include themes related to wealth and social status. Interestingly, Loranger (1984) suggested that sex-role issues may contribute to the earlier onset of schizophrenic disorder in men: "It could be that the adolescent and early adult years are more stressful for male patients than female patients. There may be greater cultural pressures on young men to achieve social and financial independence. Whether or not this is true, it still remains uncertain whether mastery of these developmental tasks is relevant to the development of schizophrenia. The hypothesis is difficult to test" (p. 160).

Difficult to test it may be, but it nonetheless deserves a great deal more systematic attention than it has received to date. Indeed, the few well-designed studies of sex-role issues in schizophrenic disorder suggest that sex-role conflict and stereotyping are as important in this area as they are in depression and anxiety disorders.

RESEARCH ON SEX-ROLE ISSUES IN SCHIZOPHRENIC DISORDER

In a recent review, Al-Issa (1982) noted several reports demonstrating a *reversal* of sex-role and gender identity in schizophrenic disorder. For example, a Puerto Rican community study found that married women with schizophrenia tended to be aggressive and defiant toward their husbands, whereas married men withdrew and became dependent on their wives: "The behavior of the male is incompatible with normal *machismo*, which emphasizes strength of character, dominance and independance. The behavior of the female schizophrenic is inconsistent with cultural expectations of humble, differential and conforming behavior" (p. 159).

In North America and Britain, married women with schizophrenic disorder are more likely to be admitted and readmitted to the hospital if they show "masculine" characteristics such as low anxiety and high ego strength, if they perform poorly in a traditional domestic role, if they drink excessively, or if they are sexually promiscuous.

Al-Issa (1982) points out that such behaviors indicating reversal of gender identity and sex role may increase the likelihood of hospital admission, so that these characteristics may be overrepresented in chronically hospitalized populations. However, LaTorre and Piper (1979) found no relationship between gender identity and length of hospitalization in a population of 44 patients selected on the basis of Research Diagnostic Criteria for schizophrenia. In fact, these patients showed significant confusion and abnormalities only on measures of socially desirable sex roles and sex-role preference.

LaTorre and Piper concluded that opposite sex-role preference and ignorance of appropriate sex-role behaviors *interact* as major contributors to the development and maintenance of schizophrenic disorder. Although the research evidence for this is by no means conclusive, LaTorre's (1976) sex-role theory of schizophrenia is the only one that adequately explains the gender-related early-onset pattern that characterizes the disorder. It merits more serious consideration than it has received to date.

MARRIAGE AND MEN WITH SCHIZOPHRENIA

Since so few men with schizophrenic disorder marry, it might be expected that their marriages would show a number of unusual features. That this is true with regard to choice of marriage partner has been convincingly demonstrated by Planansky and Johnston (1967).

These two researchers studied the wives of 96 men who had been recently admitted to a mental hospital with a diagnosis of schizophrenia. The womens' responses to a detailed questionnaire were compared with those of a group of women married to men who did not suffer from schizophrenia. The following similarities and differences emerged.

The average age at marriage was similar in both groups (22 for the wives and 25 for the husbands). The couples in both groups were very similar on average educational level, length of courtship, and current ratings of marital happiness. However, the wives of the men with schizophrenia rated themselves as *very much more active in pursuit of their husbands* during courtship than the wives of the normal men. When asked to rate those attributes of their husbands-to-be that had most attracted them during courtship, further differences emerged. Twice as important overall to the wives of the men with schizophrenia were the following attributes (the precise figures for the schizophrenic and normal groups are given in parentheses): romantic (45 vs. 25); quiet (44 vs. 21); sensitive (41 vs. 21); shy (26 vs. 5); "I took pity on him" (17 vs. 2); "he made me feel needed" (43 vs. 27); sexy (19 vs. 8); good-looking (59 vs. 42).

In contrast, the wives of the normal men rated the following attributes as significantly more important: decisive and capable (33 vs. 20); masculine (57 vs. 32); popular (35 vs. 19); good common sense (54 vs. 29).

These differences were clearly reflected in the courtship activities of the two groups: sporting, social, and outdoor activities had been indulged in far more frequently by the normal group, whereas the schizophrenic group had spent almost twice as much time together at home or dating alone.

Interestingly, the wives of the men with schizophrenia seem to have been aware of the faults of their husbands-to-be during the courtship period. They rated the following negative traits in their husbands far more often than did the wives of the normal men: blue (12 vs. 0); suspicious (30 vs. 8); jealous (52 vs. 32); moody (36 vs. 14); easily angered (36 vs. 22); drinking (31 vs. 15); few friends (26 vs. 4).

Planansky and Johnston interviewed many of the wives of the schizophrenic men, or studied reports of interviews by others. They found that the *passivity* inherent in schizophrenia was generally construed as desirable during courtship. Typically, wives would say of the courtship period, "he was so good to everyone," and describe their husbands-to-be as "quiet, unassuming, docile, nice guy, easy to get along with, never complained." Some women were attracted by their courtship partner's interest in deep philosophical themes, so strikingly different from the interests of other men, and which they assumed reflected intellectual superiority. Several wives expressed a desire to change their husbands; for example: "I married him because I felt I could help him—he looked and talked with such indifference and hatred for the human race." A few women from very disturbed backgrounds reported that in comparison with their own relatives, their husbands-to-be appeared well adjusted; others from similar backgrounds admitted that they married their husbands because they appeared to be the best of a poor lot, and an inadequate husband was better than none.

Planansky and Johnston concluded that the wives of the men with schizophrenia "might feel emotionally uncomfortable with a typically masculine, firm, active companion." This discomfort was presumably so strong that they chose husbands of an entirely opposite disposition, even though this required them to disregard some obvious negative attributes in these men.

In terms of the model outlined in Chapter 3, these women identified so strongly with the nurturing and care-giving aspects of the female sex-role stereotype that they used these as the basis for their close personal relationships with men. Given a passive, dependent man to look after, they felt useful and fulfilled. However, Planansky and Johnston's clinical observations suggest a variety of other types of premarital adjustment in these wives.

Only a small minority of the men in the study had schizophrenia *before* they married. It is possible that marital interaction contributed to the onset and maintenance of their psychotic symptoms. Equally, it is possible that for some men, marriage exerted a protective effect, delaying the onset of schizophrenia or ameliorating its symptoms. However, Loranger's data (1984) suggest that marriage does not have an overall protective effect on men prone to schizophrenic disorder: The married men developed their symptoms an average of 6.3 years earlier than married women, a gender difference in age of onset that was greater than that for the unmarried patients.

Hostility in the Marriages of Men with Schizophrenia

There is good evidence that certain types of marital interaction contribute to the development and maintenance of schizophrenic disorder in men. In a now, famous study, Brown, Birley, and Wing (1972) assessed the amount of hostility and criticism expressed by key relatives toward a total of 101 patients with schizophrenia. Of these patients, 47 were married and living with their spouses.

As judged during a structured interview by an experienced mental health worker, nearly half the spouses made frequent critical and hostile remarks about the patient. During the 9 months after this interview, the relapse rate in this group was almost 60%. Nearly all patients who relapsed were readmitted to a hospital. In marked contrast, the relapse rate was less than 20% in the patients whose spouses were not notably critical or hostile toward them. If the spouse was rated as both low in hostility and warm and caring, the relapse rate was even lower. Although the relapse rate was high in unmarried patients whose key relatives were described as emotionally overinvolved with them, emotional overinvolvement was rarely a problem in patients' spouses, and did not influence the relapse rate in married patients.

Of the married men with schizophrenia, 44% relapsed, whereas this occurred in only 17% of the married women. This suggests that marriage has a "protective" effect on married women with schizophrenic disorder, but not on married men.

Many psychiatrists were initially reluctant to accept the findings of Brown and colleagues because they conflicted with the idea that schizophrenia is a medical illness. The fact that relatives' behavior toward the patient was by far the most powerful influence on the course of the disorder suggested strongly that psychosocial factors were much more relevant than was generally believed.

Four years later, Vaughn and Leff (1976) repeated and extended the work of Brown and his colleagues. Their results were almost identical. Given such overwhelming evidence for the importance of psychosocial factors in schizophrenia, the attitudes of psychiatrists and other mental health workers began to change. Recently, systematic efforts have been made to devise ways of reducing the hostility of key relatives toward patients with schizophrenia, and of improving the general quality of family interaction (Falloon, Boyd, & McGill, 1984). Most of this work has focused on young, unmarried patients living with their parents, since intervention in this group is likely to yield the greatest long-term benefits. Early results have been very encouraging. Falloon, Boyd, McGill, Razani, Moss, and Gilderman (1982) compared family therapy with individual therapy in a group of 36 patients with clear-cut schizophrenia. During the 9 months after therapy, only one of the 18 patients from the family therapy group relapsed, whereas relapse occurred in 8 of the patients treated with individual therapy. These differences in relapse rates were reflected in the greatly superior overall adjustment of the family-treated patients 9 months after therapy.

It is not clear whether the family-oriented therapy techniques of Falloon and others are as suitable for treating married patients as they are for treating single patients in close contact with their parents. The earlier finding by Brown *et al.* (1972) that emotional overinvolvement is common in the key relatives of unmarried patients, but rare in patients' spouses, suggests that different techniques may be required for treating married patients and their partners. Some clues about techniques that are likely to be helpful in the therapy of married men with schizophrenia can be found in the professional literature.

Intervening in the Marriages of Men with Schizophrenia

In a fascinating study, Kern (1967) described how he successfully conducted conjoint marital therapy in the case of Mr. B, a 36-year-old man with paranoid schizophrenia.

Mr. B's father had died suddenly from a heart attack when Mr. B was 5 years old. This had left him with a strong and enduring need for a father substitute, and he had married Mrs. B primarily to obtain a father-in-law, whom Mrs. B described as "a shadowy figure who rarely communicated with other members of the family and was apparently incapable of significant display of affection." Subsequently, Mr. B revered, emulated, and totally identified with his father-in-law, whose sudden death—from a heart attack like Mr. B's natural father—had initiated the development of his paranoid schizophrenia.

Mr. B's main symptom was a conviction that he was doomed to die shortly in the same way as his father-in-law. He stopped working, and had developed an intense hatred for his mother-in-law, whom he believed had caused her husband's death. He believed also that his own mother had caused the death of his father. Furthermore, he thought that his wife was planning to kill him.

After treatment in the hospital for 6 weeks, he started "many months" of weekly outpatient sessions of individual psychoanalytically oriented psychotherapy. This, however, appeared to make him worse, in that he became more and more preoccupied about his wife and her supposed designs on his life. He began to issue veiled threats to kill her, and/or to commit suicide. At this stage, Mrs. B was assessed with a view to involving her in conjoint therapy.

Mrs. B had married Mr. B when she was 16 and he 26. Her main motive was to escape from her highly disturbed family, within which she had since early childhood experienced constant and painful feelings of loneliness and alienation. Her whole aim in life was to marry, have children, and be looked after by a caring husband. She had vowed that she would do anything to "hold my man," rather than experience again the painful isolation of her childhood. She admitted, however, that she was full of rage about her husband's treatment of her, but that she was terrified of expressing it openly to him, in case he abandoned her and their three children.

During conjoint therapy, Mr. B said that although his wife denied her plans to kill him and her hatred of him, he could see it in her eyes. In reality, Mrs. B frequently glared at her husband with a look of intense hatred, while at the same time totally denying any anger and accusing him of being "crazy" for suggesting it. It thus became very clear that Mrs. B's unexpressed rage was reinforcing Mr. B's delusional beliefs, and that these beliefs were reinforcing his ill-treatment of her, which, in turn, reinforced her rage toward him. In this way, marital interaction was perpetuating Mr. B's paranoid schizophrenia.

Conjoint therapy occupied 52 sessions over 12 months. In essence, treatment allowed the couple to become more understanding of each other's problems, and more communicative about their true feelings. Mrs. B became able to express her anger and frustration directly to her husband; as she did so, her hostile glares decreased in frequency and intensity. Gradually, the couple came to view each other in a more positive and realistic manner. Mr. B stopped being psychotic, saying: "I used to think I was rotting away just because my father-in-law died. I got Annie [his wife] and my mother all mixed up. You wouldn't think it was possible to believe that I was my dad and Annie was my mother. . . . I must have been really nuts. . . . I haven't thought this clear for years, maybe never" (p. 289).

At the end of therapy, there was much less friction in the marriage, and the couple felt confident that they could work together at managing future problems. Kern followed up Mr. B for 3½ years, during which time he remained free of psychotic symptoms. The marriage endured.

Kern's report was based on intensive study of a single case: Caution is required before his findings and techniques can be generalized to similar cases. Nonetheless, his clinical observations are compatible with Brown and his colleagues' findings about high levels of spouses' hostility contributing to the relapse of patients with schizophrenia: If this hostility was expressed to the patient *indirectly*, it could serve to perpetuate the disorder in ways similar to those described by Kern.

Although Kern's perspective remained essentially psychoanalytic throughout, he was able to acknowledge that prolonged psychoanalytically oriented individual psychotherapy made Mr. B worse. This deterioration can be explained from a sex-role/object relations perspective. Mr. B clearly identified totally with his father-in-law as a replacement for his dead father and as the epitomy of an idealized male sex-role stereotype. It is highly likely that he came to identify in a similar way with Dr. Kern, a relatively powerful, successful, male figure. This would have increased or consolidated Mr. B's need to deal with his unacceptable "female" gender identity—based on a persisting primary identification with his mother—by projective identification within his marriage. Since his wife, through splitting and projective identification, had come to represent the persecuting "bad object" containing his split-off "feminine" attributes and characteristics, it is not surprising that Mr. B's hostile feelings towards his wife increased to a dangerous intensity.

Fortunately, Dr. Kern had the wisdom to initiate couples therapy, which was ultimately successful after 52 sessions. Had therapy focused directly on sex-role issues, it may well have required fewer sessions. However, the challenge of psychotherapy in such cases is often very great, and the time and effort required should never be underestimated.

Sex-Role Conflict as a Source of Marital Hostility

The wife described by Kern clearly identified totally with the female sex-role stereotype. This identification was matched by her stereotyped expectations of her husband. Many of the wives described by Planansky and Johnston (1967) seemed to be quite different: although they appear to have identified strongly with the nurturing, care-giving aspects of the female sex-role stereotype, their expectations of their husbands were in many ways radically different from the male sex-role stereotype. This could give rise to marital hostility in the following way.

The women in Planansky and Johnston's study actively selected their husbands for their dependent, shy, sensitive, and docile disposition, which they clearly found attractive. They presumably believed that at a personal level, marriage to such men would be harmonious, equitable, and fulfilling. However, they clearly expected their husbands to be adequate providers for them and their children: Here, it is of interest that the wives of the men with schizophrenia had an average of three children, compared with an average of two for the wives of the normal men. Unfortunately, the traits for which they selected their husbands at a personal level were largely incompatible with occupational, financial, or social success.

Thus, through marriage, the husbands of these women were placed in an impossible position: On the one hand, their wives expected them to be sensitive, docile, dependent, and easygoing; on the other hand, they expected them to be assertive, vigorous, competitive, and hardworking breadwinners. Exposure to such mutually incompatible expectations must have generated profound conflict in these already vulnerable men, and may well have contributed to the onset or maintenance of their psychotic symptoms. Once schizophrenia was established, their role as breadwinner became progressively impaired, and their inadequacy as providers became a major focus for their wives' hostility. In many instances, wives were forced reluctantly into role reversal, since their earning capacity became superior to that of their husbands. Although this was, in fact, the logical outcome of the original mate selection process, it was resented and resisted by both partners as an aberration and continued to provide a focus for wives' hostility and criticism of their husbands.

Although role reversal appears to be the likely outcome of many marriages contracted by men prone to schizophrenic disorder, it is generally resisted by both partners. Therapy that encourages a more flexible view of sex roles may well reduce marital and intrapsychic tension and conflict. This is likely to lower the wife's hostility to the patient, and hence the likelihood of relapse. Role sharing may be particularly appropriate within such marriages. Working legitimately outside the home would create opportunities for the wives to express the forceful, assertive, "masculine" aspects of their personalities; and a legitimate domestic role would enable their husbands to express the sensitive, caring, "feminine" aspects of themselves. In this way, both partners would escape the destructive tyranny of rigid adherence to traditional sex-role assumptions and expectations.

Clearly, modification of attitudes to sex roles is most likely to be successful in younger couples. In older couples, who may have preserved rigid attitudes to sex roles for many years, attempts to modify these attitudes are unlikely to be of value, and may be harmful. This is illustrated by the case of a 55-year-old man with schizophrenia described by Leff, Kuipers, Berkovitz, Eberlein-Vries, and Sturgeon (1982): "His wife was critical of him and showed little warmth. She attended the group regularly and we held several conjoint marital sessions, but at follow-up her critical attitudes were unaltered and the marital relationship appeared to be unchanged. However, the patient had taken on a job as a security guard and because of the shifts he worked was in low contact (with his wife) for 5 out of every 6 weeks. He remained free of symptoms throughout the 9 months" (p. 131).

In this case, a return to work allowed the patient to avoid prolonged contact with his hostile, critical wife. This, combined with the positive effects of reestablishing a work role, contributed to his freedom from symptoms throughout the follow-up period. Attempts during therapy to encourage role sharing in this couple would almost certainly have been inappropriate.

Even in younger couples, it may be extremely difficult to modify attitudes to sex roles. Leff *et al.* (1982) provide an example of this in their report of a 42-year-old married man whose schizophrenic symptoms had stopped him from working for 18 months: "His wife was very intolerant of his handicaps and extremely critical of his inability to play a man's role in the family. She used the group to vent a great deal of anger. Family sessions were held, sometimes including the children, but our attempts to persuade patient and wife to spend less time together were unsuccessful. . . . At follow-up her criticism had considerably abated, although not below the crucial level, and they remained in high contact. Nevertheless he remained free of psychotic symptoms, although he continued to exhibit a significant degree of depression" (p. 131).

Reports such as these are a reminder of our need for new theories concerning strategies for intervening in the marriages of people with schizophrenia. The development of more effective techniques in this area is one of the many challenges facing contemporary psychiatry.

MARRIAGE AND WOMEN WITH SCHIZOPHRENIA

As we have seen, Loranger (1984) and Gold (1984) outlined evidence that the onset of schizophrenic disorder in married women occurs on average at least 6 years later than it does in married men. Unfortunately, Loranger does not provide separate data for married and unmarried patients. However, for the women overall, the peak period of onset was between 24 and 29 years of age, and 60% of the women had their first psychotic episode between 20 and 34 years of age. The average age of onset for the women overall was 27.

For married women, the years between 24 and 29 generally coincide with maximum sex-role conflict and marital strain: Children are young and demanding; husbands are committed to work rather than domestic matters; and there are many other conflicts and problems that even the best adjusted couples have difficulty in acknowledging and resolving. Some of these were illustrated in earlier chapters. Together with the work of Rudden *et al.* (1983) already cited, the following evidence strongly suggests that acute psychosis in married women is commonly precipitated by marital stress.

Psychosis and Marital Stress

The important work of Faergeman (1963) shows that acute psychotic episodes in married women are very often preceded by marital conflict. Faergeman carefully documented the stresses that occurred immediately before acute psychotic episodes in 170 patients, many of whom subsequently developed schizophrenia. Of these patients, 117 were women, of whom a majority were married. The case histories of many of the married women reveal profound marital difficulties, usually relating to sex roles or the expression of sexuality. These problems often surfaced, or were acutely exacerbated, shortly before a psychotic episode. The following examples demonstrate this.

FAERGEMAN'S CASE 22

The 34-year-old wife of a shipbuilder. "The patient had been depressed for some time because of marital conflicts [suspected infidelity on the part of the husband]. . . . She developed convictions of being followed, was anxious and contemplated suicide. . . ."

FAERGEMAN'S CASE 32

The 37-year-old wife of a fireman. Her admission to the hospital followed a divorce notice from her husband, who *later gave up plans for a divorce because of her illness* (my italics). "The patient . . . became increasingly withdrawn and peculiar to the point that she now functioned mechanically like a robot in a household, barely maintaining contact with her husband and son, sleeping in a corner of the room and scarcely ever changing her clothes."

FAERGEMAN'S CASE 37

A 30-year-old married female teacher. "In the eighth year of her marriage she discovered that her husband was unfaithful to her. . . . She had 'funny thoughts' and was afraid of becoming insane. She was hospitalized for almost a year and recovered completely. Five years later an attachment she formed with a fellow teacher was dissolved. This time auditory and visual hallucinations were added to the previous symptoms and the picture became increasingly schizophrenic."

FAERGEMAN'S CASE 85

The 30-year-old wife of a tailor. "She claimed that her difficulties began the year before when she caught her husband kissing the maid. She was very unhappy about him and felt he did not love her enough. She felt that she needed a great deal of love."

FAERGEMAN'S CASE 118

The 35-year-old wife of a policeman. "When she discovered that for years her husband had had a girl friend she . . . became visually hallucinated. She saw black devils under the bed and hanging on the walls; they took the shape of her husband and made fun of her. . . ." Subsequently "her husband had become a model of bourgeois virtues and the childless marriage ever since had been a happy one."

Problems of sexuality and related sex-role issues may be equally important in unmarried women. In a *large majority* of Faergeman's descriptions of single or divorced women, it is clear that the psychotic episode was preceded by acute conflicts and difficulties in their relationships with men. For example:

FAERGEMAN'S CASE 87

A 36-year-old unmarried office worker. "In order to support herself and her small daughter she had found a job in an office and at the same time accepted financial help from a friend of her father's. This man insisted that, in return, she became [sic] his mistress. This she did, but it disturbed her a great deal, particularly after she had fallen in love with a young man with whom she also began an affair. The stress of the situation caused a turbid state with hallucinations (there were men lying in the beds next to hers, yelling at her, the nurses tortured her, etc.)."

The Impact of Psychosis on Marriage

A single psychotic episode may enrich or impoverish a marriage. This is well illustrated by the work of Dupont, Ryder, and Grunebaum (1971), who studied the marital interaction of 44 couples in which one spouse had been diagnosed as psychotic. To the authors' surprise, they found that 70% of the couples reported that the impact of the psychotic episode on the marriage had been positive as well as negative. One-third of the couples said that the positive effects outweighed the negative effects. The positive effects were composed mainly of a greater closeness, understanding, and co-operation between marriage partners who *before* the psychotic episode had been living in emotional isolation: "Many felt disappointed that their marriages had failed to live up to a romantic model, but rather than facing this disappointment and the anger to which it gave rise, they became increasingly distant from one another. . . . Generally, the nonpsychotic spouse acknowledged that *his failure to communicate his feelings, or to try to appreciate the feelings of the other* [italics added], had played a crucial role in his spouse's psychosis" (p. 736).

Couples who viewed the psychosis as having a mainly positive effect on the marriage had an overall psychological adjustment that was greatly superior to that of the couples who reported a mainly negative impact. Patients in the positive impact group showed less than half the overall psychological disturbance of those in the negative impact group, and spouses in the positive impact group showed *less than one-sixth* of the disturbance of those in the negative impact group. These findings were broadly confirmed by Fowler and Tsuang (1975), who studied the spouses of 15 men and 34 women with schizophrenia. Twelve of the patients' husbands, and 7 of their wives, had a formal psychiatric disorder in their own right. The two commonest diagnoses were personality disorder and alcoholism.

Not surprisingly, marital happiness was much lower in the negative impact couples, who saw the psychotic episode as the *exclusive problem of the patient*: "These couples were convinced that the illness had originated in the individual's childhood or even in his heredity. Thus the illness was considered mysterious and unmodifiable. These couples felt helpless and angry" (p. 737).

With regard to the marriages of the female patients, about one-third improved after the psychotic episode, and about one-quarter deteriorated further. In at least one-third of cases, the psychotic episode was followed shortly by separation or divorce. That divorce is unusually common in women with schizophrenia was confirmed in a recent large-scale British study by Gibbons et al. (1984). They found that 70% of the women had been married at some time, but only 40% were still married at the time of the study. The respective figures for the men with schizophrenia were 27% and 13%.

The research finding of an unusually high separation or divorce rate in women with schizophrenia is not surprising. Clinical observations suggest that where divorce occurs after a psychotic episode, it is rarely the first episode, and usually the marriage has already deteriorated significantly. Thus, the psychotic episode is the precipitant of a separation or divorce that would probably have occurred anyway, albeit somewhat later.

In the case of those women whose marriages improve after their psychotic episode, any preexisting impetus toward separation or divorce is likely to be reduced, and with it the husband's criticism and hostility toward his wife. We know from the work of Leff et al. (1982) that high levels of hostility in the spouse are strongly associated with the patient's subsequent relapse, and that a reduction in the spouse's hostility reduces the likelihood of relapse. Thus, in marriages that are improved by the impact of a psychotic episode, the likelihood of further episodes is reduced or eliminated. Indeed, the psychotic episode might be regarded as self-limiting, since it reduced or eliminated the marital problems that precipitated it.

Much more difficult to understand is the persistence, often for many years, of marriages in which the wife has repeated psychotic episodes or develops a chronic schizophrenic disorder. In my view, psychiatric treatment and the medical model are often important in preserving these marriages.

The Impact of Psychiatric Treatment

The way in which psychiatrists and other mental health workers handle a married woman's first or second psychotic episode is often critical in determining subsequent marital interaction and hence the prognosis. The following case illustrates this.

THE ASTRONOMER'S WIFE

Barbara developed her first psychotic episode at the age of 35, when her only child, a son, was just 2 years old. She was admitted on a compulsory basis to a mental hospital in a highly disturbed state, believing that someone was out to kill her because she knew of a huge conspiracy concerning computer fraud (interestingly, when fully recovered she said of computers "they are powerful things, exciting, terrible monsters, they extend the mind, complement it"). Barbara also believed that attempts were being made to control her brain through the radio. She talked constantly of "love, fidelity, and truth" between her husband and herself. She claimed repeatedly that the nursing staff were going to give her orgasms, which she denied having experienced previously.

Barbara's family background was characterized by a strong, ambivalent relationship with her father. He had always urged her to be competitive, ambitious, and hardworking, and to pursue a career, which she had done with some success. However, at the same time he expected her to put *his* needs before her own. For example, when she was in her late 20s, she had planned to accept a challenging job abroad, but abandoned the idea when her father became ill and insisted that she nurse him.

Barbara placed great value on intellectual activities and had a consuming interest in world affairs. She would talk animatedly for hours with her only close friend, a woman the same age, about global politics and general philosophical matters.

She married Lyndon when she was 32 and he 31, feeling relieved that she had been rescued from spinsterhood by a personable, pleasant, hardworking man.

Lyndon came from an unremarkable working-class family, and was very anxious to improve his social and economic status. When he married Barbara, he was used to working long hours. In his free time he devoted himself to astronomy, for which he had a consuming passion. After their marriage, Lyndon built a small observatory in the backyard of their home, from which he observed the skies whenever the weather allowed it. If not at work or in his observatory, he read or attended meetings about astronomy and related matters.

Barbara had relinquished her career in favor of full-time motherhood, which she found unexpectedly demanding and frustrating. She craved stimulating adult companionship during her long hours at home alone with her son. Her best friend continued to work full-time, which greatly restricted the frequency of their meetings. Lyndon spent very little time with her, was emotionally cold, and entirely failed to respond to her requests for conversation. Indeed, he often ignored her remarks and questions. His passion for astronomy continued unabated.

Barbara's first psychotic episode had been precipitated by the departure to another state of her best friend, which had left her with no one that she felt she could really talk to. Her unconscious rage and despair about her situation had become uncontainable, and had emerged in the content of her psychotic episode.

Her psychosis resolved after a few days in hospital. On her return, Lyndon emotionally withdrew even further from Barbara. Secretly, he often thought of her as "that mad woman"; the little eccentricities that before her psychosis had been endearing were now profoundly irritating to him. The psychiatrist at the hospital had emphasized that Barbara's psychotic episode was a medical illness that could be ameliorated by drugs, and he had suggested the likelihood of a biochemical origin. Thus, the couple became convinced that Barbara's psychosis was part of a mysterious illness for which neither had personal responsibility.

Three months later, Barbara had a more severe and prolonged psychotic episode. On this occasion the main theme of her delusions was a worldwide conspiracy in which the people on the side of good had telepathic powers that they used to combat the forces of evil. It was after this episode that I was asked to see Barbara for the first time.

At that stage of my career, I was largely unaware of the importance of marital factors in psychosis, and I saw Barbara on an individual basis, attempting to elucidate her underlying psychopathology. Although she mentioned that Lyndon had by now almost totally withdrawn from her, she at no time related her psychotic episodes to her domestic situation, so that I was not led to this as a focus of therapy.

Late one Sunday afternoon, Lyndon rang me at home, insisting that I come round immediately because Barbara was once again "going crazy." When I arrived, she was indeed on the threshold of a psychotic episode, highly agitated and with many paranoid thoughts. I spent the next 2 hours attempting to reassure her and trying to persuade her to take antipsychotic medication. During this time, her anger about her situation flowed freely, and the real origins of her psychosis dawned upon Lyndon and me for the first time. It became abundantly clear that Barbara regarded Lyndon's emotional and physical withdrawal, and his cold rejection of her, as the main cause of her breaks with reality. During her psychotic episodes she experienced the sense of personal significance, involvement, and communication with others that she craved. But she could express her *real* feelings only when in a prepsychotic state. Finally, Barbara agreed to take some antipsychotic medication; within 30 minutes she began to improve, and the next morning, after a sound night's sleep, she had largely recovered.

From that day on, Lyndon's attitudes and behavior toward Barbara changed dramatically. He greatly reduced the amount of time he spent stargazing and studying astronomy. He became much warmer toward her, and did his best to be caring and concerned. He became more involved with their son and with domestic matters. The marriage improved greatly. I followed up Barbara for nearly 6 years, during which time she remained entirely free of psychotic episodes and was generally in robust physical and mental health.

COMMENT

I am sure that if Lyndon had called an ambulance that Sunday afternoon, instead of insisting that I came round, Barbara would have been admitted for the third time to the local mental hospital. This would have reinforced the couple's belief that Barbara suffered from a mysterious illness beyond the control or responsibility of either of them. In the face of Barbara's "madness," Lyndon's hostility and withdrawal would have increased, making further psychotic episodes almost inevitable. In all likelihood, the marriage would have ended within a few years, by which time Barbara would perhaps have developed a formal schizophrenic disorder.

As it was, my presence contained Barbara in a prepsychotic state long enough for the truth to emerge in such a forceful way that it could not be ignored. Since Lyndon was basically a fairly well adjusted man, free of major psychopathology, he was able to accept that he had been at fault, and subsequently did his very best to make up for this. As a result, the marriage improved and the marital and domestic stresses on Barbara were ameliorated, allowing her to remain in good health.

Why Do Men Stay Married to Psychotic Women?

Living with a woman who has a persisting schizophrenic disorder or a closely related condition would seem to be an extremely difficult task with few rewards. Yet at least 40% of women with schizophrenia have enduring marriages. There are a number of reports that help to explain why so many husbands are willing to remain indefinitely married to women with schizophrenia.

In a paper called "Willing Victims: The Husbands of Paranoid Women," Dupont and Grunebaum (1968) suggest: "These women had chosen husbands who were passive, socially isolated, and unable to directly express angry or sexual feelings; they were likely to be active participants in the bizarre behaviour of their wives" (p. 151).

Dupont and Grunebaum's findings are based on a detailed study of 9 couples in which the wife suffered from definite paranoid delusions, but without hallucinations or significant psychological deterioration.

The backgrounds of the husbands were found to be strikingly uniform. All were brought up by a powerful, dominating mother in the virtual absence of a father, usually because of very long working hours, but in two cases through death and in one case through desertion. These men idealized their mothers as loving and strong-willed, and denied or repressed any negative thoughts and feelings about them. They appear to have identified strongly with the male sex-role stereotype, and were deeply committed to the idea of complete self-sufficiency and to the role of breadwinner. However, they entirely lacked the assertiveness and open competitiveness inherent in the male sex-role stereotype, and were incapable of *directly* expressing angry feelings. As a result, they tended to be unsuccessful in their business undertakings.

The average age at marriage of the wives was 29, and of the husbands, 37. Before marriage, both partners had few friends and a very limited social life, and little sexual experience. The wives had notably stable and successful employment histories, usually in work that required a very conscientious and reliable attitude. Wives' descriptions of their husbands during courtship focused on their reliability and lack of anger and meanness.

After marriage, all the women stopped work to become full-time house-wives and, except in the case of one childless couple, dedicated and conscie tious mothers. However, the couples remained socially isolated. For example, none reported social relationships with the parents of their childrens' friends. Although the wives tended to be critical of their husbands, these men none-theless preserved towards them the same idealized, stereotyped attitudes that they held toward their mothers. Before the first psychotic episode, which occurred on average 10 years after marriage, these marriages seemed emo-tionally empty, and devoid of any shared interests or activities.

In nearly all cases, two types of change in the marriage immediately preceded the wife's psychosis. First, the husband became even less available to his wife, usually because of increased commitment to work or other nondomestic activities. Second, the couple ceased sexual intercourse to-gether, usually because of the wife's reluctance.

Once the psychosis developed, "six of the nine wives became brutally hostile to their husbands, accusing them of being sexually unfaithful and generally irresponsible. In five of these cases the husband was the central 'persecutor' in his wife's delusional system. . . . All nine husbands denied that they had ever had an extramarital sexual affair" (p. 154).

Invariably, husbands agreed to their wives' demands, even when these were quite evidently based on delusions. The authors suggest that this rein-forced the wives' delusional systems until finally they were admitted to a mental hospital during an acute psychotic episode.

In spite of the psychosis, all 9 wives preserved high standards of domestic and child care, although some refused to perform certain domestic services for their husbands. The idea that husbands were "willing victims" came from the observation that they often provoked outbursts of rage in their wives after the onset of the psychosis. However, they invariably denied provoking these outbursts, and instead adopted a posture of innocent martyrdom.

Most of what is described by Dupont and Grunebaum can be explained in terms of the couples' rigid adherence to a sex-role-stereotyped view of marriage and family life. The husbands seem desperate to preserve their stereotyped view of themselves as hardworking, self-sacrificing breadwinners with loyal and devoted wives who live for and through them and their children. They cling to this stereotype because both their personal and gender identity is based upon it in ways which were described in Chapter 3.

To preserve the stereotype, in which their wives are equated with an idealized mother, they are forced to deny that in their childhood their mothers were in reality often overcritical of them, excessively controlling and dominating, and sometimes abusive. These husbands are also forced to deny that their wives have an assertive, competitive, forceful, and independent aspect that for many years before marriage found expression through their successful employment outside the home. In adapting to a stereotype of full-time marriage and motherhood, the wives, too, are forced to deny their own directly competitive, assertive, and independent aspects.

The wives' psychoses help to preserve the couples' stereotypes. The wives become aggressive and competitive, at least to husbands, but only because they are *ill*. They have an independent, exciting, and challenging life of their own, but only in their psychotic fantasies. The illness model of psychosis allows the husbands both to accept their wives' behavior and to preserve intact their stereotyped attitudes. The idea of caring for a sick wife actually reinforces the breadwinner/protector aspect of the male sex-role stereotype. Once the wife has been admitted to a mental hospital, the couples' social isolation becomes almost complete. Thus, there is no external pressure on the marriage partners to modify their stereotypes.

The wives' psychoses hinder their employment outside the home, preserving the husbands' relatively powerful positions as sole breadwinners. Effectively confined to the home by their psychoses, wives strive to perform optimally as mothers and household managers. Doubtless, husbands' *indirect* expression of anger reinforces their wives' symptoms in ways similar to those outlined in Kern's case described earlier. Wives' *direct* hostility to husbands sustains the latter's repressed anger, and also allows them to adopt a posture of martyred self-sacrifice, a posture no doubt adopted by their mothers as they struggled to bring up their sons virtually single-handed. Thus, martyrdom helps these husbands to preserve their unconscious primary identification with their mothers without challenging their conscious identification with the male sex-role stereotype. Ultimately, this is the main reason for the persistence of these marriages: The unconscious gratification that the husbands obtain from their wives' behavior outweighs the problems it causes.

Husbands Who Encourage Their Wives' Psychoses

The husbands described by Dupont and Grunebaum did not *directly* encourage their wives' psychoses: Their inability to confront their wives, and their willingness to collude in their delusions, *indirectly* encouraged their wives' symptoms. That some husbands directly and actively reinforce their wives' psychotic behavior was suggested to me by the following case.

THE VANISHING DETECTIVE

Martha, age 48, had been admitted, acutely psychotic, to her local mental hospital on at least 15 occasions during the 9 years that followed her first psychotic episode. She had been diagnosed as a "chronic schizophrenic," and was well-known to the regular staff. I was asked to visit her at home by her family physician; he had become concerned about the mental and physical health of both Martha and her husband George, who was a 51-year-old laborer for the local council.

When I arrived, Martha was expecting me. George had not yet returned from work, and Martha had forgotten to inform him of my proposed visit. Martha and I chatted about how she was coping in general, and about her delusions, which centered around the idea that she was a victim of police harassment and, in particular, of relentless persecution by a certain detective. There was a knock on the door, and Martha went to open it, returning distressed and saying that it was "the detective," who had vanished as usual. The knock was repeated, and this time I went with Martha to the door. There was no one there. Martha and I walked around the house, and found George hiding behind an angle in the wall. Caught in the act, George was forced to admit that he had been "the detective" for a number of years, systematically reinforcing Martha's delusional system and contributing to her psychotic episodes. He had displayed extraordinary ingenuity and imagination in sustaining the idea of a persecuting detective: unexplained noises in the night, objects moved or mislaid, mysterious footprints, windows apparently opened from the outside, and so on.

I was able to elucidate George's reasons for being "the detective" during several subsequent conjoint and individual sessions. At the conscious level, George thought of himself as simply having fun. Unconsciously, he seemed to have the following motives.

Having a "crazy" wife actually made him feel better about himself. Not only did he have a menial job, but he was in poor health: Arthritis made it increasingly difficult for him to work enjoyably and effectively. Focusing on Martha's "craziness," and playing games that added to it, protected him from feeling depressed about his own situation. When he did feel depressed or exhausted, he could blame it on the strains of living with Martha.

Martha's delusions entertained George, and he found her psychotic episodes both disturbing and exciting in the context of his otherwise drab, isolated life. Since she had been labeled mentally ill, George was in some ways more tolerant of her. Instead of complaining constantly about her erratic attention to domestic matters, he took over several of Martha's domestic tasks himself. Although this allowed him to feel more useful and worthwhile as a person, it increased Martha's sense of frustration, uselessness, and inadequacy, which was added to by George's tendency to ridicule her about her delusions.

Predictably, Martha was profoundly angry and distressed when the truth about "the detective" emerged. Gradually, however, she became less enraged, and her delusions faded. George became severely depressed as Martha got better, since her "craziness" no longer protected him from facing up to his own difficulties. Fortunately, he was willing to talk about his problems and accept medication for his depression. When his depression lifted, his arthritis became less painful and troublesome. As a result, he was able to enjoy his work more, and he resumed some of his previous interests. The couple made several changes in their relationship. They began to communicate more directly and freely with each other, and a clearly defined domestic division of labor was agreed upon. Martha became more involved in activities outside the home. I followed up Martha and George for 3½ years, during which time Martha remained substantially free of psychotic symptoms and George remained in reasonable health.

COMMENT

It is impossible to determine how many husbands actively reinforce their wives' psychotic symptoms. Unless caught in the act, like George, their behavior is most unlikely to be detected. However, from a therapeutic perspective, it is not essential to determine whether husbands' reinforce their wives' symptoms deliberately or unwittingly. It is important only to acknowledge that treatment is unlikely to be successful unless the husband is actively and constructively involved in it.

Martha's case is reminiscent of "The Poltergeist Mystery" in Chapter 4. In that case, however, the wife developed severe anxiety symptoms in relation to her husband's trickery and deceit. This is a reminder that husbands' behavior toward wives is only a *contributing factor* to wives' psychiatric disorders. Although a husband's behavior may be a powerful factor in precipitating or perpetuating his wife's disorder, the precise nature of the symptoms is determined mainly by the wife's heredity, constitution, upbringing, and experience of life prior to marriage.

CONCLUSIONS

Conflict over sex-role stereotypes is a valid explanation for the gender difference in the age at onset of schizophrenic disorder. Men, in general, are confronted with conflicts about being unambitious, submissive, co-operative, sensitive, caring, and understanding versus being ambitious, aggressive, competitive, dominating, and insensitive. In young men prone to schizophrenia, this conflict over sex-role stereotypes may be of such intensity that it is beyond resolution. In such circumstances, schizophrenic disorder is an adaptive response: While the behavioral symptoms consolidate a posture of dependency, passivity, and compliance, the delusions allow a sense of achievement, power, recognition, and significance. Because men in general are required to confront conflicts about sex-role stereotypes in adolescence and early adulthood, men prone to schizophrenic disorder develop the condition at a relatively young age. Those few who marry bring the same conflicts into their marital relationship, so that the disorder emerges within marriage and is often perpetuated by it.

For women, sex-role conflict generally becomes acute only *after marriage and childbirth*. At this time, they often feel compelled to undertake a total and exclusive commitment to domestic life. Profound conflict is created by subsequent loss of independence and demands for self-sacrifice in the service of children and husband versus their desire for personal, competitive, independent, and active involvement in the outside world. The emergence of psychosis resolves this conflict: In their delusions, psychotic women are centrally involved in a busy, complex, competitive and somewhat hazardous world; but in reality the psychosis chains them securely to the domestic. Even if they are reduced to automatons, as in Faergeman's Case 32 described earlier, they struggle to perform their domestic duties effectively.

Thus, schizophrenic disorders may be as adaptive for women as they are for men. The fact that sexual themes occur so very commonly in the psychoses of women probably reflects prevailing social attitudes toward female sexuality. Women have less freedom than men to express and gratify directly their sexual thoughts, feelings, and impulses; hence the need for their indirect expression and gratification in the form of delusions and hallucinations. Gender differences in social attitudes to sexuality are gradually lessening, and this should ultimately be reflected in a decrease in the overrepresentation of sexual themes in the psychoses of women.

If survival is taken as an index of the value of schizophrenic disorder as an adaptation to profound intrapsychic conflict, then the disorder is more adaptive for women: Roy (1982) reported that about 10% of patients with chronic schizophrenia commit suicide, and that 80% of these are men.

Future Directions

Thanks to the pioneering efforts of Brown, Leff, Vaughn, Falloon, and others, it is now clear that the likelihood of relapse in schizophrenic disorder can be greatly reduced, and often eliminated altogether, by appropriate intervention in patients' marital or family relationships. Our knowledge about optimal therapeutic techniques and strategies is in its infancy. In the next and final chapter, I outline some therapeutic innovations that have proved helpful not only in the treatment of schizophrenic disorder, but in a wide range of other disorders in married people.

CHAPTER NINE

Spouse-Aided Therapy and Beyond

Chapter 1 outlined the evolution of marriage from an essentially economic to a primarily psychological institution. As long as the basis of marriage was rooted in economics, married couples were required to work together in order to achieve obvious goals such as improving their living standards beyond subsistence level and maximizing the likelihood of the physical survival of their offspring.

Although marriage in the industrialized world has, in reality, become an institution concerned primarily with psychological well-being rather than physical survival, this is not generally acknowledged. Thus, little encouragement has been given to the idea that married couples should work systematically together at goals that concern their *psychological* development and well-being. Indeed, when couples find the courage to seek help for the psychological aspects of their relationship, they are likely to be stigmatized by their peer group and others in their social network.

Social stigmatization of those who openly acknowledge the need for professional help with their marriage has negative repercussions. Couples often postpone seeking counseling or therapy until marital conflict is of long-standing duration or has become almost unbearable. By this time, marital stress may have precipitated psychological symptoms in one or both partners.

Failure to acknowledge or seek help for marital problems is most likely to occur in those who cling to a stereotyped or idealized view of marriage. It was shown in Chapter 3 that such people, or their marriage partners, are at increased risk for the development of psychological symptoms. Although sex-role conflict and stereotyping are important in the process of symptom formation and maintenance, their pathogenicity is greatly amplified in the context of poor object relations and related personality abnormalities. In such circumstances, the idea of a psychiatric illness or disorder requiring *individual* treatment is likely to emerge. Precisely how this may occur is outlined in chapters 4 and 5.

Evidence has been outlined in previous chapters that individual treatment for married patients with severe psychological disorders may have negative repercussions. In a proportion of cases, such treatment helps to maintain the patient's symptoms as a displaced focus of marital conflict or dissatisfaction. The following section discusses additional data on the effects of individual therapy for married patients.

INDIVIDUAL THERAPY FOR MARRIED PATIENTS

Some advantages to psychiatrists of preserving a basic allegiance to the medical model were outlined in Chapter 5. Treating the patient on an individual basis is inherent in the medical model, with its emphasis on medical diagnosis and drug treatments for illnesses that are regarded as essentially biochemical in origin. In psychiatry and allied disciplines, this emphasis on individual treatment is further reinforced by prevailing theories of mental illness and related therapeutic techniques. Practitioners of psychodynamic psychotherapy, with its emphasis on intrapsychic processes and transference issues, often actively avoid involving patients' relatives in therapy, since this is believed to dilute the power of the transference. Practitioners of behavior therapy, with its emphasis on learning theory derived largely from the study of individual animals in a laboratory setting, are also encouraged by their training to focus on the patient alone.

As a result of these powerful infuences toward individual therapy, many people with psychological symptoms are offered treatments that tend to disregard their current social network and relationships as a focus of active therapy. For unmarried young adults, this generally presents no problems. Unless they are still living with pathogenic families, such people are usually free of the types of relationship that perpetuate psychological symptoms. Individual psychodynamic psychotherapy is likely to release them from unconscious conflicts that might otherwise adversely infuence their choice of marriage partner. Individual behavior therapy is likely to free them of learned maladaptive behaviors that might inappropriately restrict their choice of mate. Furthermore, they are free to make changes in their life-style and attitudes without having to negotiate such changes with spouses or parents. Thus, individual psychotherapy, if properly conducted, is likely to be a liberating experience substantially free of negative social repercussions.

For married patients, this is much less likely to be the case. Any changes in their attitudes and behavior that derive from individual psychotherapy will inevitably have a direct effect on the spouse. Where these changes are seen by the spouse as desirable, they will doubtless be encouraged and facilitated. But if they are seen as undesirable, they will be resisted. This may lead to marital conflict, which creates new problems and perhaps new symptoms.

Negative Marital Repercussions of Individual Therapy

Hurvitz (1967) has discussed at length the problems that may result from treating married women with individual psychotherapy. The wife's identification with the therapist, usually male, causes her to adopt some of his attributes and values. Since the therapist is likely to be upper middle class, these attributes and values will probably clash with those of the patient's husband, unless he, too, is from the higher social echelons.

Married women in psychotherapy often develop strong sexual feelings toward the therapist, usually as part of the transference. The husband may note that his wife is likely to want intercourse after she has seen her therapist, but that at other times she is less willing to respond to his sexual advances, and that she tends to be detached during lovemaking. This leads the husband to feel sexually uncomfortable and inadequate with his wife. As a result "he taunts her about her feelings for the therapist while he fears to express his anxiety about some intimacy between them."

Furthermore: "The heightened sexual feelings which are aroused in the therapy, which the wife cannot express with the therapist, and which she does not want to express with her husband, may be demonstrated extramaritally" (p. 40). If this occurs, it inevitably causes fresh problems in the marriage.

According to Hurvitz, additional problems are created as the wife becomes psychologically knowledgeable and learns psychological jargon from her therapist. She uses this jargon in confrontations with her husband, and he rapidly learns to respond in kind. Thus, the couple acquire more sophisticated weaponry for their marital disputes, the net result of which is an escalation of their mutual hostility and criticism. This sharply reduces their capacity for shared problem-solving activities, a capacity that is decreased further by the husband's feeling that his wife does not need him to resolve her problems. Concurrently, the husband may come to believe that the therapist and his wife are allied against him, so that he becomes hostile to the therapist as well as to the process of therapy. Ultimately, "the husband is forced into ever more extreme behaviour to constrain his wife. . . . Every gain that she makes in therapy, which her husband regards as a threat to him, is met with such resistance and manipulation by him that the gain is negated. The old problems and complaints remain while new ones are created" (p. 41).

Because individual psychotherapy produced some initial improvement in the wife's symptoms, she and the therapist assume that more of the same will overcome symptoms and problems that in reality have emerged *as a consequence of* individual therapy. This sets up a vicious cycle in which individual therapy becomes interminable unless the patient's spouse is invited to directly participate. However, his anger toward the therapist makes it unlikely that he will constructively respond to such an invitation.

Hurvitz suggests that the above difficulties are inherent in the application of individual psychotherapy to married women, which therefore nearly always has long-term negative effects on the marriage. To prevent this, he recommends that the patient's spouse should always be involved in therapy from the outset.

Gurman and Kniskern (1978) reviewed the evidence for deterioration in patients during and after marital and family therapy. In the course of this comprehensive and thoughtful review, they also examined evidence for negative effects of individual psychotherapy: "That negative change may be produced in patients in various individual and group psychotherapies is now generally accepted by clinicians and researchers, despite persistent attempts, based on the questionable motives of a few, to discredit the available evidence" (p. 3).

Gurman and Kniskern found that the average deterioration rate after marital therapy was 11.6% when therapy was conducted on an individual basis, compared with only 5.6% when therapy was carried out conjointly. They suggested that these empirical data are substantial enough to outweigh theoretical arguments in support of individual therapy for marital problems.

Positive Marital Repercussions of Individual Therapy

A report by Fisher and Mendell (1958) suggests that Hurvitz's findings about the marital repercussions of individual therapy may be unduly pessimistic. These authors found that positive repercussions ocurred at least as often as negative ones. However, in the couples who showed the most improvement, the patient received both group and individual psychotherapy, so that Fisher and Mendell's findings cannot be directly compared with those of Hurvitz. Fisher and Mendell suggest that increased assertiveness and autonomy in the patient is the key to constructive changes in other family members: "The patient's increased independence may relieve them at least partially of feelings of obligation which have bound them to the patient in a certain way. Thus, there is a freeing of the whole family structure which sets the stage for the development of new modes of interaction" (p. 139).

Clinicians' Reluctance to Acknowledge Negative Marital Effects

Fox (1968) emphasized the lack of systematic data concerning the marital repercussions of individual psychotherapy and suggested that therapists' reluctance to examine the issue was a major reason for this. He posed the question: "Is it ethical to treat any person and ignore his spouse when there is a possibility that the spouse may be adversely effected [sic] by the treatment?" He added: "What is needed is the development of techniques which will enable patients to change in such a way that it is not at someone else's expense" (p. 15).

Fox's suggestion that practitioners of individual psychotherapy are reluctant to examine its marital repercussions is endorsed by a survey conducted by Hadley and Strupp (1976). These two researchers wrote to 150 expert clinicians, theoreticians, and researchers in the field of psychotherapy, asking them to respond to the following questions:

1. Is there a problem of negative effects of psychotherapy?
2. If so, what constitutes a negative effect. . . ?
3. What factors are prominently associated with or are responsible for negative effects?

There was a broad concensus among the respondents that, if it is possible for psychotherapy to produce beneficial effects, then it must also be capable of producing negative effects. There was almost unanimous agreement that, in routine clinical practice, negative effects are a real problem. However, the overwhelming concern of the respondents was the patient alone. Although a few referred to the general interpersonal effects of individual psychotherapy, none referred specifically to its marital repercussions. This is striking confirmation of the lack of desire among contemporary practitioners of individual psychotherapy to systematically investigate its effects on the patient's marriage.

This lack of desire may, of course, reflect an absence of married patients from their clinical practice. However, clinical and research reports suggest that at least one-third of all patients offered individual psychotherapy are married. Although this proportion may vary somewhat from therapist to therapist, there are few practitioners of individual psychotherapy who do not have a significant proportion of married patients in their caseload. If these practitioners are, in fact, generally disregarding the negative marital repercussions of their therapy, then this is clearly an unsatisfactory state of affairs.

Research on Marital Repercussions

Kohl (1962) described 39 mainly depressed married patients who were characterized by an insistence that their marriages were ideal and that psychiatric treatment should focus on their symptoms alone. These views were shared by the patients' spouses. However, as the patients recovered, their previously well spouses showed a variety of pathological reactions that often undermined the effects of treatment and exposed marital problems that were previously denied or obscured by the patients' symptoms.

Interestingly, Kohl noted that in those cases in which the patient had previously failed to respond to individual psychotherapy that had totally excluded the spouse, the latter had often viewed the therapist with resentment and suspicion. This observation supports Hurvitz's (1967) findings reported previously.

Of the spouses, 21 reacted to the patient's improvement with depression and severe anxiety. Another 4 made unsuccessful suicide attempts. Other common reactions to the patient's improvement included threats of divorce, recurrence of alcohol dependence after prolonged abstinence, and overt hostility toward the therapist and the process of therapy. All reactions represented the spouse's resistance to the patient's recovery: If this resistance was not dealt with by actively involving the spouse in therapy, then either the spouse became ill, or the patient's treatment was unsuccessful.

Struggles for power and control were the commonest themes observed within these marriages. The "well" spouse was able to dominate the "ill" partner as long as he or she remained ill: Recovery from illness threatened the dominance of the well spouse and precipitated within him or her one or more of the pathological reactions described.

Kohl suggests that if a couple denies marital problems at the start of treatment, the spouse should be included in the process of therapy as early as possible. This will not only increase the chances of the patient's recovery, but will also minimize the likelihood of negative repercussions within the marriage.

Marital Repercussions of Behavior Therapy for Agoraphobia

Although Kohl suggests that marital dynamics of the kind he describes are fairly common in psychiatric practice, he gives no prevalence data. Similarly, while several other authors have written anecdotal accounts of the negative effects of individual therapy on marriages and spouses, none have indicated how common such phenomena may be. Fortunately, my research with Isaac Marks into the behavioral treatment of agoraphobia (Hafner, 1984a; Hafner & Marks, 1976) yielded some guidelines about this.

Most patients were treated in groups of 4-6, all of whom had agoraphobia. This was a highly effective treatment, since group members supported and encouraged each other in the profoundly challenging task of overcoming phobias that were often very severe and long-standing. Furthermore, most patients responded to the chance of socializing together, thereby increasing their self-confidence and reducing their fear of human contact. Often, they kept in touch and gave each other support and encouragement after therapy had formally ended.

Over 60% of the patients were married women. Not all husbands responded positively to the dramatic changes that therapy induced in their wives. Far from being pleased with wives who had suddenly become much more confident, sociable, and able to lead independent lives, about one-third of husbands reacted by developing psychological symptoms of their own. As in the spouses described by Kohl, the commonest symptoms in husbands were anxiety and depression. Fortunately, almost all husbands who developed psychological symptoms recovered within a few months. Within a year, most had adapted to the changes in their wives, and many were themselves enjoying greater autonomy and personal fulfillment.

Like Kohl, I believe that the husbands developed psychological symptoms because of a sudden change in the balance of power within their marriages. Before treatment, the wives were generally unable to reenter the work force because of their agoraphobia, which also greatly restricted their social and recreational activities. In effect, they were confined by their symptoms to lives of total domesticity, and were almost entirely dependent on their husbands both emotionally and economically. Naturally, husbands had adapted to their powerful, dominant positions within marriage. However, their wives' agoraphobia had placed restrictions on the husbands' own social and leisure activities, and on their ability to respond to promotion opportunities at work. For example, many wives would not permit their husbands to travel out of the state because they felt unable to manage without them. Thus the husbands were unusually reliant on their roles as breadwinners, fathers, and caretakers of their wives to preserve their self-esteem.

Confronted suddenly with wives who after treatment no longer needed caretakers, and who generally planned to achieve a measure of economic independence through a return to the work force, it is not surprising that about one-third of the husbands developed psychological symptoms of their own. In several cases, wives responded to their husbands' symptoms by halting or reversing their progress in overcoming residual agoraphobic symptoms. In this way, the pretreatment marital status quo was partially restored, and the couple had time to adjust to the changes in their marriage. Fortunately, most wives who partially relapsed because of their husbands' problems were able to resume progress later on.

Are negative effects on a proportion of husbands inevitable as wives recover from agoraphobia, or can they be avoided? It may be that the pace and extent of wives' improvement is the critical factor in determining whether or not husands become symptomatic. Slow, steady, improvement in wives may allow husbands to adapt to marital changes without developing problems of their own. Equally, gradual improvement in wives may give husbands more time to create strategies aimed at preserving the pretherapy balance of power within the marriage. One such strategy might be to undermine wives' improvement, and there is little doubt that a proportion of husbands do, in fact, achieve this either deliberately or unconsciously (Lazarus, 1966). Some husbands doubtless try and stop their wives from initiating or pursuing appropriate treatment. Given that women with severe agoraphobia are virtually powerless within their marriages, such attempts are likely to be successful.

Obtaining accurate data about this sensitive area is extremely difficult. Ultimately, the question of the power balance within marriage and negative effects on husbands will be answered only through further research. Fortunately, this area is currently the subject of considerable interest. For example, Barlow, O'Brien, and Last (1984) and Barlow and Beck (1984) randomly allocated 28 married agoraphobic patients to individual or conjoint behavioral treatment. Conjoint treatment produced significantly better results than individual therapy, which was associated with a *deterioration* in several personal and interpersonal measures after 6 weeks of treatment.

The benefits of conjoint therapy were most pronounced in patients with initially bad marriages. The presence in Barlow *et al.*'s study of patients with demonstrably bad marriages probably explains why the results differ from those of a similar but smaller study by Cobb, Mathews, Childs-Clarke, and Blowers (1984), who found that conjoint behavioral therapy was *not* superior to individual therapy. In this study, the patients' pretherapy scores on a questionnaire measuring marital dissatisfaction averaged only 1.12 out of a maximum possible score of 8. This mean score is almost identical to that found by Milton and Hafner (1979) in a group of maritally *satisfied* patients with mainly simple agoraphobia, and it coincides with the normal population mean (Milton and Hafner used an earlier version of Cobb *et al.*'s marital questionnaire, dividing the total score by the number of scales to produce a *mean* score, so that for direct comparison Cobb *et al.*'s marital data must be divided by a factor of 10). Thus, Cobb *et al.*'s patients were predominantly happily married and suffering from *simple* agoraphobia, which (see Chapters 5 and 7) is much less likely to be linked with negative posttreatment marital repercussions than the more common *complex* agoraphobia.

Individual Therapy for Depressed Married Women

Indirect evidence of negative marital effects after individual psychotherapy for depressed married women comes from the work of Rounsaville *et al.* (1979a, 1979b). These researchers found that a majority of 150 women receiving psychiatric treatment for depression complained of marital problems. Of these women, 38 were randomly allocated to an average of 29 hours individual psychotherapy. The focus of therapy was on the patients' current interpersonal situations rather than on an exploration of unconscious processes, and its goal was to facilitate the patients' *mastery of current social roles*. However, therapy was no more effective in reducing marital conflict than brief monthly assessment interviews by a physician. Only 27% of the women reported any improvement in their marriages after psychotherapy. The depression of women who had no marital disputes, or who were able to resolve them during therapy, improved marginally. In contrast, the depression of women whose marital disputes failed to improve or worsened during therapy generally became more severe. Overall, the 38 women rated themselves as *more* depressed after individual psychotherapy than before. This surprising result was substantiated by an increase of about 50% in the assessor's ratings of depressive symptoms after therapy.

The authors do not discuss why individual therapy worsened the depression of many women. However, in attempting to help patients master their current social roles, therapists may have inadvertently increased levels of sex-role strain and conflict. This would, in turn, have raised the level of marital tension and conflict, increasing the patients' depression and setting up a vicious cycle similar to that described by Hurvitz (1967).

Rounsaville *et al.* conclude that although conjoint marital therapy may be the best way of dealing with marital disputes, "it is frequently not feasible to treat more than one partner of a couple. For this reason, the present investigators have attempted to develop more precise techniques for dealing with the marital disputes of depressed patients" (p. 509).

These attempts resulted in a new approach termed "Interpersonal Psychotherapy," which assumes that depression "occurs in an interpersonal context and that clarifying and *renegotiating* [italics added] the context associated with the onset of symptoms is important to recovery" (Weissman, Klerman, Prusoff, Sholomskas, & Padian, 1981, p. 51).

Thus, Weissman and colleagues appear to have moved away from individual therapy aimed at facilitating a *mastery* of social roles toward an approach that facilitates their *renegotiation*. However, renegotiation of social roles—and sex roles in particular—is unlikely to be successful without the involvement and co-operation of the spouse, and this may explain the rather limited effectiveness of Interpersonal Therapy (Weissman *et al.*, 1981). For example, 1 year after a course of Interpersonal Therapy, patients scored a mean of 0.6 on a self report measure of overall symptoms (SCL–90), whereas a control group who received "non-scheduled treatment" scored a mean of only 0.5. Furthermore, there were no significant outcome differences on any symptom measure, and patients receiving Interpersonal Therapy scored *worse* on a global measure of marital adjustment 1 year after treatment than did the control group.

Results such as these underline the need for systematic involvement of the spouse in the therapy of married people suffering from depression, particularly if it is of a persisting nature.

SPOUSE-AIDED THERAPY

Although overvaluation of the medical model and rigid adherence to psychodynamic and behavioral treatment approaches are major reasons for the frequent misapplication of individual therapy to married patients, there are other reasons for this. Probably the most important of these is the absence of suitable alternate treatment strategies.

The Limitations of Conjoint Marital Therapy

Extraordinary as it may seem, conjoint marital therapy has only recently become generally accepted as the treatment of choice for marital problems. As late as the 1960s, therapists expressed grave doubts about the wisdom of giving therapy to both partners together. Such doubts, which now appear absurd, were based largely on an overvaluation of psychodynamic theories and techniques. It is therefore something of an achievement that conjoint therapy is now almost universally regarded as the optimal approach to treating marital problems.

As we have seen, however, many married patients with psychological symptoms or psychiatric disorders insist that their marriages are ideal. They and their spouses are firmly against any attempts to examine or modify their marriage relationship. Instead, they strongly prefer a direct attack upon the patients' symptoms.

Even if marital problems are acknowledged, they are nearly always attributed to the patients' psychiatric disorder. Thus, once again, both partners believe that a direct attack on the patients' symptoms is the only logical approach.

Many therapists accept this plea for symptomatic treatment. However, when the symptoms are in reality a product of or an alternative to marital conflict, then to treat them in isolation is often unhelpful. Indeed, it may consolidate the symptoms as a displaced focus of marital conflict and dissatisfaction.

For those therapists who reject the couple's plea for symptomatic treatment alone, marital therapy appears to be a logical alternative or supplement to symptom-oriented therapy. Surprisingly often, couples will accept conjoint marital therapy, even though they view it as inappropriate. After a few sessions, the patient sometimes begins to understand the need for a direct examination of marital interaction. Nearly always, however, the spouse is reluctant to accept this, and struggles to preserve the idea that the patient's symptoms are the cause of all the marital problems (Cochrane, 1973). The more chronic or severe the symptoms, the more likely is this to occur. As a result, conjoint marital therapy is rarely effective in the treatment of severe, long-standing psychiatric disorders. If therapists nonetheless attempt to persevere with it, the spouse, the patient, or both simply cease to attend.

Theoretical Basis of Spouse-Aided Therapy

An awareness of the limitations of conjoint marital therapy in treating married patients with severe, long-standing psychological disorders led me to develop an alternative conjoint approach that I called "Spouse-aided Therapy" (Hafner, 1981b), although "Marriage Resource Therapy" is an equally appropriate term. My primary aim was to encourage both patients and spouses to become constructively involved in the patients' therapy. This required concurrent attention to the patient's symptoms per se, to marital interaction, and to both the spouse's and the patient's individual contributions to symptom maintenance. In developing such a therapy, the following problems had to be addressed.

THE SPOUSE'S HOSTILITY TO THE THERAPIST

Many married patients with severe, long-standing psychological disorders have been exposed to a range of individual treatments without experiencing significant or lasting benefit. The repeated failure of individual therapies naturally evokes frustration and often hostility in the spouse toward therapists who have failed to help. Furthermore, exclusion of the spouse from the patient's individual psychotherapy may arouse the spouse's hostility in ways described by Hurvitz (1967), discussed earlier in this chapter.

Not uncommonly, a patient deliberately misrepresents the therapist in discussions about therapy with his or her spouse. For example, a patient may report a neutral discussion with the therapist about separation or divorce as "My therapist thinks we should get a divorce." Naturally, this often enrages the spouse and greatly decreases the likelihood of his or her constructive involvement in therapy. This suits those patients who wish to preserve an exclusive relationship with the therapist.

There are many possible reasons for a patient's desire to prevent his or her spouse from seeing the therapist or from becoming involved in conjoint therapy. If the patient has misrepresented the therapist to the spouse, or misrepresented the spouse to the therapist, then this is likely to emerge if therapist and spouse meet. The more extensive the misrepresentations, the more does the patient seek to prevent such a meeting. Many patients develop sexual or idealized fantasies about the therapist that can be preserved only in the context of individual therapy. Such patients may strongly resist the idea of sharing their therapist with their spouse.

Thus, it often appears to patients in individual psychotherapy that it is in their interests to encourage hostile feelings in their spouse toward the therapist. The therapist will inevitably be made aware of this hostility and may react by developing hostile feelings to the patient's spouse. Invariably, patients transmit these feelings back to their spouses, thereby facilitating a vicious cycle of escalating hostility between therapist and spouse. Some patients are brilliant at this and can initiate the process after only one therapy session. Of course, such activities are in reality against their best interests, particularly if they lead to a therapeutic stalemate.

Some spouses will accept an invitation to become involved in conjoint therapy even though they are full of rage toward the therapist. Unless their rage is recognized by the therapist and confronted directly, it will be expressed indirectly and is likely to sabotage therapy. Turning the therapist into "a failure" is often enormously gratifying for angry spouses, particularly if they themselves have experienced a sense of failure in the context of the patients' previous, unsuccessful individual psychotherapy.

Not uncommonly, spouses may feel intensely angry, rivalrous, or jealous toward the therapist even if the couple has had no previous experience of psychiatric or psychological treatment. Such feelings usually relate to the spouse's use of primitive defensive maneuvers such as splitting and projective identification. Once again, unless these are recognized and dealt with during therapy, they will emerge as conscious or unconscious attempts at sabotage.

THE PATIENT'S AMBIVALENCE TO THE THERAPIST

If the patient has had extensive psychiatric or psychological treatment that has been unhelpful, it is very likely that he or she will be strongly ambivalent toward the therapist. On the one hand, the patient hopes that at last a cure will be forthcoming; on the other hand, feelings of hope are tempered by the reality of previous treatment failures. Indeed, the expectation of failure may outweigh the feeling of hope, but the patient nonetheless continues to search for help out of desperation or a lack of viable alternatives.

Patients' ambivalence may have a deeper origin. Those who have been raised in rejecting or otherwise pathogenic families commonly regard their parents as having failed them. This is true insofar as their parents failed to create for them a nurturing environment that facilitated their steady growth toward autonomy, competence, and positive self-regard. However, the real problem for such patients is not that their parents failed in their duty toward them, but that *as adults* they continue to blame their parents for their problems and difficulties. In many, this tendency to blame their parents generalizes to the therapist, or indeed to anyone who they feel should be trying to help them. As adults, they often end up refusing to take responsibility for their problems, blaming instead a hostile world full of unsympathetic, rejecting, and unhelpful people. Consciously or unconsciously, the therapist is viewed in the same light.

Such patients have a powerful need to turn the therapist into a "failed parent." They can achieve this by failing to respond to therapy. At one level this is enormously gratifying, since it confirms their belief that the world is full of people whose duty it is to help them, but who repeatedly fail in that duty out of ignorance, incompetence, or malice. They can then continue to blame other people for their problems and difficulties, and their own sense of failure and incompetence is lessened by the failure of an "expert." The more experienced and highly qualified the therapist, the more gratifying for the patient is his or her lack of success: Compared with the massive failure of a therapist with years of higher education and sophisticated professional training, the patient's failure to respond or to achieve is of little significance.

Some patients are brilliant at playing "the failed parent game." For example, they work their way up academic and professional hierarchies until they "defeat" a professor or head of department. Having achieved this pinnacle of success, they then sometimes recover spontaneously or through some nonprofessional agency; alternatively, they move to a new district and start again, perhaps to become "professional patients." Tragically, they remain unaware that they are the real failures, expending their creative energies in spurious rivalry rather than in more constructive endeavors.

The medical model may reinforce and consolidate the activities of such patients. Labeling their problems and symptoms an illness officially sanctions the idea that they are not responsible for them. Thus, during therapy, the medical model should be redefined in a way that allows the patients to begin to take some personal responsibility for their symptoms.

The Process of Spouse-Aided Therapy

OBTAINING THE PATIENT'S PERMISSION TO INVOLVE THE SPOUSE

It is, of course, essential to obtain the patient's permission before inviting the spouse to become involved in therapy. Sometimes permission is withheld, and there are several reasons for this. About one-third of married patients with severe, long-standing psychological disorders feel so dependent on their spouses that they dare not risk alienating them and being abandoned. Many are fearful that their spouses may become offended during therapy, or that they, the patients, will be required to express resentment and grievances about their spouses that they have long suppressed. It is usually possible to reassure such patients by explaining that the spouse's role is essentially *to help the therapist treat the patient*, and that great care will be taken during therapy not to offend or gratuitously upset the spouse. However, reassurance is not always possible, and fear of abandonment by a provoked or alienated spouse is one of the commonest reasons for patients refusing permission for their partner to be involved in therapy.

Another common reason is the wish to preserve personal secrets that might emerge during conjoint therapy. Often these concern previous or current clandestine extramarital liaisons. Whatever the precise reason for refusal—and patients are not always willing to reveal it—no pressure to agree to conjoint therapy should be placed on a reluctant patient. If conjoint therapy is unacceptable or impossible, and it is clear that individual therapy is likely to be useless or even harmful, then honesty demands that the patient is gently informed of this. Other options can then be explored, such as the possibility of accepting the status quo rather than continuing a fruitless search for a "cure."

Once permission has been obtained, the invitation to the spouse should be issued *personally*. If it is left to the patient to issue the invitation, all manner of possibilities arise for error or distortion. For example, what was intended as a polite invitation may emerge as: "The therapist says my problems are all your fault and he wants to see you about it." A personal telephone call is often best; a personal letter can be mislaid or even intercepted by an ambivalent patient, and I know of two husbands who were so hostile toward me after assessment interviews with their wives that they tore my letter to shreds without opening it! Although these men had not met me, their wives had misrepresented to them the content of the assessment interviews in ways that had fueled their husband's displaced hostility.

It is vital to point out to the spouse that spouse-aided therapy is *not* a marriage therapy, but an opportunity for him or her to become involved in the patient's therapy as an agent of change, cotherapist, or collaborator. It is emphasized that the *patient's symptoms* will be the initial treatment focus. This protects the spouse from feeling that the marriage relationship will be spuriously scrutinized or challenged.

THE PRELIMINARY INTERVIEW WITH THE SPOUSE

The first individual interview with the spouse is crucial because it creates the opportunity to initiate a mutually honest and open relationship. The most important obstacle to this is the "hidden agenda" of the spouse's contribution to the patient's continuing symptoms. Unless this is discussed, the therapist becomes duplicitous, since the focus of therapy has already been defined as the patient's symptoms.

I deal with this issue by congratulating the spouse on his or her previous attempts to help the patient to cope with severe, persisting, and disabling symptoms. I then seek the spouse's views on why the condition has persisted in spite of all his or her efforts to help. At this stage, most spouses admit to feelings of frustration, uncertainty, inadequacy, or helplessness regarding the patient's symptoms. I respond to this by suggesting that the spouse is probably not alone in feeling that way: After all, the patient has failed to respond to a wide range of drugs and other interventions by medical and other experts, who presumably share some of the spouse's feelings. The repeated failure of highly trained professionals is a clear indication of the enormous challenge the disorder presents to the health care professions. If the well-intentioned and expert efforts of doctors and other health care professionals have failed to help, then the spouse should certainly not be blamed for the failure of his or her own more amateur efforts. Even if it emerges that some of these efforts may have inadvertantly contributed to the patient's continuing symptoms, self-blame is inappropriate. In the absence of systematic guidance, the spouse cannot be blamed for trying any methods that appeared to hold some promise.

In the ensuing discussion, I invite the spouse's views on the origins and nature of the patient's symptoms, and any other comments or questions. Out of this generally emerges an agreement that the spouse needs to learn new, optimal strategies for helping the patient.

It is often useful to point out in this first interview that the marriage must be unusually strong, since it has withstood the challenge of several years of the patient's illness. This is not only true, but usually reflects the spouse's own views, and almost certainly those of the patient. Because the strength of the marriage has been acknowledged, the couple is less likely to become defensive when aspects of marital interaction emerge later in therapy as relevant topics for discussion.

Before ending the interview, it is essential to assess the spouse's personal adjustment and to give him or her the opportunity of discussing any personal problems and what help may be required in relation to these. Any potential obstacles to spouse-aided therapy, such as lack of commitment to the marriage or clandestine extramarital liaisons, must, if possible, be elicited at this stage.

ESTABLISHING TREATMENT GOALS

After the individual interviews of patient and spouse are completed, and if no obstacles to spouse-aided therapy have emerged, both partners are invited to a session aimed at establishing initial treatment goals that are *directly related to the patient's symptoms*. Both partners must be actively involved in establishing treatment goals. Active involvement of the spouse in choosing treatment goals requires him or her to take some direct responsibility for the treatment process. Thus, when conscious or unconscious attempts at sabotage emerge later, the spouse is compelled to acknowledge that the sabotage is directed at his or her own efforts as well as those of the resented or envied therapist.

It is equally vital for the patient to accept some direct, personal responsibility for the treatment process. Only in this way will the patient become able to stop blaming others for his or her problems and begin to accept the challenge of using personal and marital resources to overcome them.

Establishing valid treatment goals concerning the patient's symptoms requires broad agreement between patient, spouse, and therapist about their nature and severity. This topic may require a considerable proportion or perhaps all of the first session. This is time well spent, since it enables the spouse to learn more about the patient's real problems and difficulties. Most spouses are broadly familiar with the patient's symptoms per se, but usually have misconceptions about their origins. For example, many spouses regard the words "psychological" or "psychiatric" as implying that the symptoms are "imaginary," or subject to control or influence through the exercise of "will power." Spouses use this idea to justify their criticism of the patients' symptom-related behavior, and particularly their inability to "pull themselves together." Spouses often genuinely believe that criticism and vigorous exhortation will enhance the patients' motivation to improve through the exercise of "will power." Unfortunately, such attitudes and communications have an effect opposite to that intended: They simply add to patients' anger, hostility, frustration, despair, and, where present, self-blame and guilt. As a result, the patients' symptoms are indirectly perpetuated.

By the end of the first conjoint session, spouses generally have a clearer understanding of the precise nature of patients' symptoms and problems, and the beginnings of an understanding of the ways in which they may have unwittingly perpetuated them. Treatment goals can then be discussed and agreed upon, usually in the second session. *If agreement on treatment goals does not occur, or if either partner or both are unable to suggest at least one appropriate treatment goal, then spouse-aided therapy cannot proceed.* Alternative therapy arrangements should then be discussed, and arranged if this is appropriate or feasible.

IMPLEMENTING TREATMENT GOALS

Implementing treatment goals is the crux of spouse-aided therapy. Problems in carrying out treatment goals are inevitable. Examining the reasons for failure or difficulty requires a direct examination of marital interaction. It also requires detailed analysis and discussion of the contributions, both positive and negative, of husband and wife to problem-solving activities. Thus the couple must acknowledge that attention to marital interaction has become a valid aspect of the initial agreement, which was, of course, to work together at improving the patient's problems and symptoms.

Paradoxically, *success* with treatment goals may also compel couples toward an examination of their marital interaction and the spouses' contribution to symptom maintenance. This is well illustrated by the case of a young woman with severe agoraphobia. She and her husband collaborated quite well on initial treatment goals, which were aimed at helping the patient to overcome her fears of traveling and crowded places. After she achieved these goals, she planned to return to work. However, her husband was strongly against this, and the patient relapsed in the context of related arguments. Fortunately, the husband was willing to acknowledge that his objections to his wife working were irrational, based as they were on ungrounded fears that she might leave him if she became too independent. He became mildly depressed as he examined some of his personal problems, and was very unsettled for a time after his wife resumed work. However, the couple soon adjusted to the new balance of economic power within the marriage, and both agreed that their relationship had benefited from it.

By the time spouses' attitudes and behavior are clearly revealed as factors that directly or indirectly perpetuate patients' symptoms and related problems, the therapist and the spouse should have developed a good working relationship. Thus, the therapist is able to confront the spouse about the need to change unhelpful attitudes and behavior, and to help in this where necessary. The same is true of unhelpful attitudes and behavior in the patient. If such confrontations are undertaken before the development of a good working relationship, they may be disregarded or might alienate patient, spouse, or both from therapy.

Implementing treatment goals also exposes deeper levels of resistance to the therapist, and resentment and envy of his or her apparently superior personal adjustment. These themes must often be worked at repeatedly. Once again, the fact that the couple is actively involved in the therapy process makes it possible for the therapist to hand back to either partner or both the major responsibility for overcoming problems when unreasonable attempts are made to blame the therapist for failures. It is, of course, essential for the therapist to acknowledge fallibility, and to discuss the errors of judgement that he or she inevitably makes from time to time as therapy unfolds. Indeed, acknowledging fallibility is often instrumental in encouraging patients' genuine commitment to active participation in therapy. Because it destroys the idea that the therapist has all the answers, it requires patients and spouses to start looking for some constructive solutions of their own.

Couples inevitably acquire a more realistic picture of themselves, their partners, and their marriages in the course of their efforts at shared problem solving. If these efforts are mainly successful, they acquire more trust and confidence in themselves and in each other, and this often enables them to be open and honest in ways that are new to their relationship. This newfound intimacy can be both unsettling and rewarding, and the therapist may need to help couples adjust to this fresh aspect of their marriage. Once it is established, however, most couples feel confident that they will be able to continue working together at future problems without the therapist's help.

SPECIFIC TECHNIQUES IN SPOUSE-AIDED THERAPY

There are no new techniques in spouse-aided therapy. It should be regarded as a novel framework within which strategies and techniques of proven validity and effectiveness from other therapies may be applied. Competence in spouse-aided therapy requires a sound training and experience in mental health care and counseling. Therapists should be familiar with fundamental concepts such as transference and countertransference, and know how to deal competently with their manifestations and repercussions. Once the basic principles of spouse-aided therapy have been understood, it is possible to use it as a framework for the application of a whole range of specific strategies and techniques. Role play, role reversal, systematic desensitization, autogenic training, relaxation therapy, assertiveness training, and grief work are but a few of these.

Sometimes, the spouse responds to such techniques as readily, or more readily, than the patient. This is particularly true in the area of grief work: Often, spouses have a smaller burden of unresolved grief than the patient; if the spouse can start to grieve, this may encourage the patient to attempt it also.

SPOUSE-AIDED AND INDIVIDUAL THERAPY COMPARED

After a successful pilot study of spouse-aided therapy conducted mainly by psychiatrically trained nurses and social workers (Hafner, Hatton, & Larkin, 1981), the Commonwealth Department of Health funded a systematic randomized comparison of spouse-aided and individual therapy in the treatment of 53 married patients with a wide range of severe, long-standing psychological disorders (Badenoch, Fisher, Hafner, & Swift, 1984; Hafner, Badenoch, Fisher, & Swift, 1983).

Design of the Study

Entry criteria were: age 18–64, married, and a *primary* complaint of a psychiatric disorder of at least 6 months continuous duration.

Of 63 patients who met these criteria, 53 entered the study. The mean age of the study population was 40.3 years (range 20–62), the mean duration of marriage was 16.6 years (range 1–41) and the mean duration of illness was 7.2 years (range 9 months to 25 years). Of the patients, 30 were women.

Patients' *DSM-III* diagnoses were: depressive neurosis (dysthymic disorder)—14; major depressive episode—3; cyclothymic disorder—2; panic disorder—3; generalized anxiety disorder—2; agoraphobia with panic attacks—8; somatization disorders—5; psychogenic pain disorder—4; conversion disorder—1; hypochondriasis—3; obsessive compulsive disorder—2; schizoid personality disorder—1; mixed personality disorder—1; schizophrenic disorder, paranoid type—2; alcohol dependence—2.

Patients' mean score before therapy on a self-report measure of overall psychiatric symptoms was 48, which is almost double the normal population mean of 25, and above the mean score of 44 recorded by a group of 60 psychiatric *inpatients* used as a comparison group.

Thus, the patients represented a chronically and severely disabled population. As a group, they had received a great deal of previous medical, psychological, and psychiatric treatment for their disorders. In such a population, any enduring response to treatment is worthwhile.

Patients were randomly allocated to spouse-aided or individual therapy. Identical techniques (cognitive, behavioral, and psychodynamic) were used in both treatments: *The primary difference was the presence or absence of the patient's spouse.*

Results

The mean number of treatment hours was 9.6 for patients who received individual therapy and 9.3 for patients who received spouse-aided therapy.

On the overall symptom measure, only spouse-aided therapy was followed by statistically significant improvement, an improvement that was even greater at the 3-month follow-up (Hafner *et al.*, 1983).

On the *depression* scale of the symptom measure, patients treated individually, *and* their spouses, reported *more* symptoms at the 3-month follow-up than before therapy. These differences in treatment outcome were statistically significant for both patients ($p < .001$) and spouses ($p < .01$).

On the *marital questionnaire* (Hafner *et al.*, 1983), spouse-aided therapy was followed by significant and substantial improvements in patients' mean scores, and by nonsignificant but sustained improvements in spouses' mean scores. After individual therapy, patients' mean scores were unchanged and those of spouses *deteriorated*. These differences between individual and spouse-aided therapy were statistically significant ($p < .001$).

On specific measures of target and personal problems, improvements after spouse-aided therapy were significantly greater at the 3-month follow-up than those that occurred after individual therapy. Only after spouse-aided therapy did *spouses* report a significant and substantial improvement (almost 50%) in target and personal problems.

Measures of sexual activity and attitudes showed that, after individual therapy, patients and spouses reported a sustained *decrease* in frequency and enjoyment of sexual intercourse. In contrast, both partners reported sustained *increases* after spouse-aided therapy. Once again, these treatment outcome differences were statistically significant.

Outcome in Relation to Diagnosis

To determine if treatment outcome was influenced by *DSM-III* diagnosis, a majority of patients was divided into three broad diagnostic groups: depressive disorders—17; anxiety disorders—13; somatoform disorders—13. Within each diagnostic group, patients were subdivided according to the treatment they received. Diagnostic and treatment groups were then compared on all main measures. There were no significant differences between the three diagnostic groups on any measure before or after treatment, and there were no significant interactions between diagnostic category and type of treatment.

These findings suggest that both the benefits of spouse-aided therapy and the negative marital effects of individual therapy transcend psychiatric diagnosis.

Causes of Marital Deterioration during Individual Therapy

Discussion of the marriage relationship took up more time during individual therapy than it did during spouse-aided therapy: Consideration of the spouse's problems was extensive during spouse-aided therapy, which substantially reduced the time available for direct attention to the marriage.

However, the efforts made by patients to improve their marriage during individual therapy generally had the opposite effect. This was because spouses usually reacted negatively when patients confronted them about aspects of their behavior and attitudes that seemed incompatible with patients' symptomatic improvement and increased general well-being.

The data show that after 6 hours of individual therapy, spouses reported an *increase* in marital satisfaction to a mean score of 123, compared with a pretherapy mean of 132 and a posttherapy mean of 139 (higher scores indicate greater marital dissatisfaction). Clearly, the increase in spouses' marital dissatisfaction occurred primarily in relation to the final 3–4 hours of the patient's therapy. Apparently, it was not until patients had received a mean of 6 hours therapy that they became insightful, knowledgeable, and confident enough to confront their spouses.

Thus, although individual therapy often exposed marital conflicts, it usually failed to create a framework within which they could be discussed and resolved. The failure of couples' attempts to improve their relationship probably explains why both partners reported more depressive symptoms 3 months after individual therapy than beforehand.

Although by no means conclusive, these findings suggest that individual therapy may sometimes help to perpetuate severe chronic psychiatric disorder in married patients. Improvement in patients' anxiety and somatic symptoms immediately after individual therapy was often associated with raised marital dissatisfaction in spouses and a later increase in depression in both partners. Such a sequence of events may contribute to the demoralization commonly experienced by patients with severe, persisting psychiatric disorder and hence reduce the likelihood of sustained improvement or recovery.

THE FINDINGS OF COMPARABLE STUDIES

Pilkonis, Imber, Lewis, and Rubinsky (1984) assigned 64 patients (44 were assigned randomly) to an average of 27 sessions of individual, group, or conjoint therapy. Of these, 52 were married or cohabitating. The mean age of the initial sample was 32; nearly half reported psychiatric symptoms for less than 2 years, and the overall level of psychiatric disturbance was described as moderate.

Clearly the population treated by Pilkonis *et al.* was much younger and less seriously disabled than that treated by Hafner *et al.* (1983).

Although Pilkonis *et al.* mentioned no negative effect of individual therapy, they found that conjoint therapy was significantly superior to individual therapy in *chronically ill patients*, who were generally older. Furthermore, conjoint therapy was followed by significantly greater improvement in *older spouses*. These findings support those of Hafner *et al.* (1983) in suggesting the superiority of conjoint over individual therapy for the treatment of persisting psychiatric disorders in older married patients (that is, those populations with a mean age in excess of 40).

There are no other published studies systematically comparing individual and conjoint therapy in married patients. However, Greene, Lustig and

Lee (1976) reported their experience in the conjoint marital therapy of 100 couples in which one spouse had a primary affective disorder (PAD). They described the patients as "a striking group of individuals . . . whose behaviour was depressed or hyperactive, sometimes hostile and/or destructive, but whose marriages rarely ended in divorce" (p. 827).

Systematic questionnaire measurements revealed that "the overwhelming proportion of dyads (61%) shows an extroverted person married to a controlling one. This strongly suggests that the person with a primary affective disorder consciously and/or unconsciously selects an overcontrolling partner to help cope with the severity of his/her mood swings, whereas the overcontrolled, usually obsessive-compulsive, personality seeks the spontaneity of emotional expression of the PAD personality" (p. 828).

Although Greene et al. emphasize assortative mating in these couples, and claim to base their therapy on systems theory, they appear nonetheless to cling strongly to an illness model of affective disorder: "The identified patient and the marriage should be viewed as deserving the same long-term commitment as with diabetes mellitus" (p. 830).

Furthermore, the non-PAD spouse is trained as a long-term *manager* of the patient and marital system. No mention is made of the *spouse's contribution* to the patient's persisting disorder, or of the need to examine and modify this. The problem is seen to lie entirely in the patient's *illness*.

Such a treatment approach seems likely to help perpetuate the patient's symptoms, and this may explain Greene et al.'s pessimism: "The more experience we had with this type of marriage, the more we came to emphasise preventive work. Our current practice in premarital counselling is usually to advise against marriage when there is a history of primary affective disorder. It has been our experience that only 60% of the couples follow this suggestion."

Clearly, the power of mutual attraction based on couples' matching or interlocking problems of personal adjustment is generally greater than the power of professional advice against marriage. In any event, this advice assumes that those couples who seek professional help are representative of the general population of couples within which one partner suffers from a diathesis to affective disorder. This may not be so. Furthermore, many such couples may find their personal lives and marriages enriched by a shared struggle to manage and understand the dynamics of their relationship. This was certainly true of many couples interviewed 1 year after successful spouse-aided therapy.

Combining Individual and Spouse-Aided Therapy

Not all couples respond adequately to spouse-aided therapy (Badenoch et al., 1983). For example, if both partners have a strong, habitual tendency to be hostile and competitive and to blame, criticize, and mistrust each other, then fierce marital disputes are likely. Once a psychiatric disorder develops in one partner, his or her hostility and criticism tend to become inwardly directed, and the marital disputes become less frequent and intense. However, as the patient's symptoms improve during spouse-aided therapy, his or her hostility is increasingly directed outward. As a result, the frequency and intensity of marital disputes increase, and shared problem-solving activities become impossible. In consequence, some couples may decide that they are incompatible, and initiate separation or divorce. Spouse-aided therapy contributes to this outcome because it is so effective in generating rapid changes in the patient's attitudes and behavior: The marital system cannot adapt to the sudden redirection of the patient's hostility. Separation or divorce is not, of course, always undesirable, but it may occur prematurely or unnecessarily as a consequence of spouse-aided therapy. Thus, in highly competitive, hostile, and overcritical couples, spouse-aided therapy alone is probably ill-advised, and should be preceded or supplemented by individual therapy for one or both partners.

Many husbands within highly stereotyped marriages rely heavily on repression and denial to cope with hostile feelings about their wives' symptoms and problems. Thus, their ability to be warm and empathic with their wives is greatly limited. However, shared concern about their wives' "illness" creates a pseudointimacy that partially obscures the lack of real warmth and intimacy within the marriage. As the wives' symptoms improve, they may become more aware of their husbands' inability to meet their emotional needs. This inability is heightened during spouse-aided therapy, because the husbands are being asked to reappraise their stereotyped view of marriage. They commonly react to this profound challenge by increasing their defensive reliance on repression and denial. As a result, once wives have improved sufficiently, they may decide to leave the marriage out of a premature conviction that their husbands will never be able to meet their needs for warmth, emotional support, and companionship. Once again, spouse-aided therapy alone is inappropriate for such couples, and should be preceded or supplemented by individual therapy for both partners.

FUTURE DIRECTIONS

Personal Responsibility for Mental Health

In spite of recent advances in drug treatment, vast numbers of people suffer from persisting mental disorders that do not yield to modern medicine. The care of those suffering from severe, long-standing mental disorders is a huge drain on the health budget of all Western nations. In the case of married people, spouse-aided therapy is one way of handing back to them some of the responsibility for their own mental health. Most people have an extraordinary range of coping abilities. Potentially, the marriages of those with persisting mental disorders represent a vast, largely untapped coping resource for the increased mental well-being of not only the patients, but their spouses also. Given the opportunity, most married couples will recognize and use these resources. Spouse-aided therapy is one way of releasing this huge potential for self-help and personal growth toward better mental health. Widely applied, spouse-aided therapy or similar marriage resource approaches to mental disorder have the potential to substantially reduce the cost of mental health care. At the same time, such approaches will foster the idea that, ultimately, people are mainly responsible for their own mental health and well-being. If they accept this responsibility and its challenge, they will rarely fail to value themselves more as people, and to grow in genuine respect and care for their marriage partners and others close to them.

Preventive Approaches

It was shown in Chapter 3 that most young adolescents in contemporary America have highly unrealistic expectations of marriage. They often believe that it will in some magical way solve all their problems of personal adjustment and purpose in life. For some, this dream comes true. These are probably unusually well adjusted, flexible people who aim to put at least as much into their marriages as they take out. Most people, however, enter marriage with many unresolved adjustment problems. If they are fortunate in their choice of partner, marriage will provide a supportive framework within which they can work at their personal problems and emerge with more robust psychological health. For others, psychological symptoms will emerge from marital interaction in ways that have been described in this book.

It seems likely that suitable education would increase the chances of young people finding suitable marriage partners and, more important, working with them at their problems of personal adjustment and fulfillment. Sadly, very few schools in North America, Britain, and Australia have properly designed, systematic courses in marriage preparation. If such courses were widely introduced, they would probably have a significant impact on the whole range of problems facing modern marriage.

However, no amount of education about marriage per se will alter the powerful social pressures on young people to compete with each other for material possessions and socioeconomic status. In the absence of major social change, these competitive pressures will continue to add to the problems of modern marriage. As I suggested in Chapter 2, a highly competitive society based on patriarchy and related sex-role stereotypes has powerfully facilitated the development of modern industrial nations. Now, however, the idea of patriarchy and related stereotypes is creating more social problems than it alleviates. Many men and women are, of course, happy with the stereotype of marriage and motherhood. But increasing numbers of people seek a more flexible approach to sex roles, with a greater degree of role sharing and role reversal. The continuing social emphasis on traditional sex roles makes it difficult for most people to make such changes in their lives, even if they regard them as logical and reasonable.

At a practical level, much could be done to ease the profound sex-role conflict experienced by men and women who wish to devote equal energy and enthusiasm to parenthood and their jobs or careers, but who are prevented from doing so by lack of suitable child-care facilities and inflexible working hours. From the age of 2 most children are ready for well organized child-care facilities. Indeed, many would greatly benefit from the chance to socialize with their peers in stimulating, caring environments supervised by trained people with a genuine commitment to children and their welfare. Universal access to such facilities would be the single most important contribution to alleviating sex-role conflict and the stress and psychological symptoms that it creates. If the facilities were there, and if their routine use was socially accepted, many parents who now feel trapped in domestic roles for the sake of their offspring would be free to take their full place in the adult world without feeling anxious and guilty about neglecting their children. The positive impact of this on their mental health, and that of their children, would be immeasurable.

References

Ackerman, N. W. (1958). *The psychodynamics of family life.* New York: Basic Books.

Adams, B. N. (1979). Mate selection in the United States: A theoretical summarization. In W. R. Burr, R. Hill, F. Nye, and I. Reiss (Eds.), *Contemporary theories about the family.* New York: Free Press.

Akhter, S., & Byrne, J. P. (1983). The concept of splitting and its clinical relevance. *American Journal of Psychiatry, 140,* 1013–1015.

Al-Issa, I. (1982). Gender and schizophrenia. In I. Al-Issa (Ed.), *Gender and psychopathology.* New York: Academic Press.

Andrews, G., Brodaty, H., Christensen, H., Hadzi-Pavlovic, D., Harvey, P. R., Mattick, R. P., Tennant, C. C., Eisen, P., Hafner, R. J., & Tiller, J. (1985). Treatment outlines for the management of anxiety states. The quality assurance project. *Australian and New Zealand Journal of Psychiatry, 19,* 138–151.

Andrews, G., Brodaty, H., Christensen, H., Hadzi-Pavlovic, D., Harvey, P. R., Mattick, R. P., Tennant, C. C., Hafner, R. J., Meares, R., & Pilowsky, I. (in press). Treatment outlines for the management of hypochondriasis and somatization. The quality assurance project. *Australian and New Zealand Journal of Psychiatry.*

Ashton, H. (1984). Benzodiazepine withdrawal: An unfinished story. *British Medical Journal, 288,* 1135–1140.

Badenoch, A., Fisher, J., Hafner, J., & Swift, H. (1984). Predicting the outcome of spouse-aided therapy for persisting psychiatric disorders. *American Journal of Family Therapy, 12,* 59–71.

Barlow, D. H. (1981). On the relation of clinical research to clinical practice: Current issues, new directions. *Journal of Consulting and Clinical Psychology, 49,* 147–155.

Barlow, D. H., & Beck, J. G. (1984). Psychosocial treatment of anxiety disorders: Current status, future directions. In J. B. Williams & R. L. Spitzer (Eds.), *Psychotherapy research: Where are we and where should we go?* New York: Guilford.

Barlow, D. H., O'Brien, G. T., & Last, C. G. (1984). Couples treatment of agoraphobia. *Behavior Therapy, 15,* 41–58.

Barnes, G. E., & Prosen, H. (1984). Depression in general practice attenders. *Canadian Journal of Psychiatry, 29,* 2–10.

Barrett, J. E. (1984). Naturalistic changes after two years in neurotic disorders (RDC categories). *Comprehensive Psychiatry, 25,* 404–418.

Beaber, R. J., & Rodney, W. M. (1984). Underdiagnosis of hypochondriasis in family practice. *Psychosomatics, 25,* 39–46.

Bebbington, P. E., Sturt, E., Tennant, C., & Hurry, J. (1984). Misfortune and resilience: A community study of women. *Psychological Medicine, 14,* 347–363.

REFERENCES

Bem, S. L. (1974). The measurement of psychological androgyny. *Journal of Consulting and Clinical Psychology, 42*, 155–162.

Benson, B. A., & Brehony, K. A. (1978). *Sex role stereotypes and self-reports of fear and anxiety.* Paper presented at the meeting of the Psychonomic Society, San Antonio, TX.

Berg, I., Butler, A., Houston, J., & McGuire, R. (1984). Mental distress in mothers of young children in Harrogate. *Psychological Medicine, 14*, 391–399.

Berman, E., & Lief, H. (1975). Marital therapy from a psychiatric perspective. *American Journal of Psychiatry, 132*, 583–592.

Bird, H. W., Martin, P. A., & Schuham, A. (1983). The marriage of the "collapsible" man of prominence. *American Journal of Psychiatry, 140*, 291–295.

Birtchnell, J., & Kennard, J. (1983). Marriage and mental illness. *British Journal of Psychiatry, 142*, 193–198.

Bothwell, S., & Weissman, M. M. (1977). Social impairments four years after an acute depressive episode. *American Journal of Orthopsychiatry, 47*, 231–273.

Bowen, R. C., & Kohout, J. (1979). The relationship between agoraphobia and primary affective disorders. *Canadian Journal of Psychiatry, 24*, 317–322.

Briscoe, M. (1982). *Sex differences in psychological well being. Psychological Medicine Supplement 1.* Cambridge, U.K.: Cambridge University Press.

Broverman, I. H., Broverman, D., Clarkson, F., Rosenkrantz, D., & Vogel, S. (1972). Sex-role stereotypes: A current appraisal. *Journal of Social Issues, 28*, 59–78.

Brown, G. W., Birley, J. L. T., & Wing, J. K. (1972). Influence of family life on the course of schizophrenic disorders: A replication. *British Journal of Psychiatry, 121*, 241–258.

Brown, G. W., & Harris, T. (1978) *The social origins of depression.* London: Tavistock.

Buglass, D., Clarke, J., Henderson, A. S., Kreitman, N., & Presley, A. S. (1977). A study of agoraphobic housewives. *Psychological Medicine, 7*, 73–86.

Burns, L. E., & Thorpe, G. L. (1977a). The epidemiology of fears and phobias. *Journal of International Medical Research, 5* (Suppl. 5), 1–7.

Burns, L. E., & Thorpe, G. L. (1977b). Fears and clinical phobias: Epidemiological aspects and the National Survey of Agoraphobics. *Journal of International Medical Research, 5,* (Suppl. 1), 132–139.

Catalan, J., Gath, D., Edmonds, G., & Ennis, J. (1984). The effects of non-prescribing of anxiolytics in general practice: 1. Controlled evaluation of psychiatric and social outcome. *British Journal of Psychiatry, 144*, 593–602.

Chambless, D. L., & Goldstein, A. J. (1981). Clinical treatment of agoraphobia. In M. Mavissakalian & D. H. Barlow (Eds.), *Phobia: Psychological and pharmacological treatment.* New York: Guilford.

Chapman, J., & Park, S. (1984). Marital therapy and feminism. *Australian Journal of Family Therapy, 5*, 259–265.

Clancy, J., Noyes, R., Hoenk, P. R., & Slyman, D. J. (1978). Secondary depression in anxiety neurosis. *Journal of Nervous and Mental Disease, 166*, 846–850.

Cobb, J. P., Mathews, A. M., Childs-Clarke, A., & Blowers, C. M. (1984). The spouse as cotherapist in the treatment of agoraphobia. *British Journal of Psychiatry, 144*, 282–287.

Cochrane, N. (1973). Some reflections on the unsuccessful treatment of a group of married couples. *British Journal of Psychiatry, 123*, 395–401.

Cross, J. (1984). The status of women in Australian family therapy. *Australian Journal of Family Therapy, 5*, 101–109.

D'Arcy, C. (1982). Prevalence and correlates of nonpsychotic psychiatric symptoms in a general population. *Canadian Journal of Psychiatry, 27*, 316–324.

Davidson, L. R. (1981). Pressures and pretense: Living with gender stereotypes. *Sex Roles, 7*, 331–347.

Dean, D., Surtees, P., & Sashidaran, S. (1983). Comparison of research diagnostic systems in an Edinburgh community sample. *British Journal of Psychiatry, 142*, 247–256.

Dicks, H. V. (1963). Object relations theory and marital studies. *British Journal of Medical Psychology, 36,* 125–129.

Doctor, R. (1982). Major results of a large-scale pretreatment survey of agoraphobics. In R. L. Dupont (Ed.) *Phobia: A comprehensive summary of modern treatments.* New York: Brunner/Mazel.

Dunn, G. (1983). Longitudinal records of anxiety and depression in general practice: The second national morbidity survey. *Psychological Medicine, 13,* 897–906.

Dupont, R. L., & Grunebaum, H. (1968). Willing victims: The husbands of paranoid women. *American Journal of Psychiatry, 125,* 151–159.

Dupont, R. L., Ryder, R. G., & Grunebaum, H. U. (1971). An unexpected result of psychosis in marriage. *American Journal of Psychiatry, 128,* 735–739.

Edwards, S., & Kumar, V. (1984). A survey of prescribing of psychotropic drugs in a Birmingham psychiatric hospital. *British Journal of Psychiatry, 145,* 502–507.

Eisenstein, V. (Ed.). (1956). *Neurotic interaction in marriage.* London: Tavistock.

Elpern, S., & Karp, S. A. (1984). Sex-role orientation and depressive symptomatology. *Sex Roles, 10,* 987–992.

Erikson, E. H. (1968). *Identity, youth, and crisis.* New York: Norton.

Faergemen, P. M. (1963). *Psychogenic psychoses.* London: Butterworths.

Falloon, I. R. (Ed.). (in press). *Handbook of behavioral family therapy.* New York: Guilford.

Falloon, I. R., Boyd, J. G., & McGill, C. W. (1984). *Family care of schizophrenia: A problem-solving approach to the treatment of mental illness.* New York: Guilford.

Falloon, I. R., Boyd, J. G., McGill, C. W., Razani, J., Moss, H. B., & Gilderman, A. M. (1982). Family management in the prevention of exacerbations of schizophrenia. *New England Journal of Medicine, 306,* 1437–1440.

Fisher, S., & Mendel, D. (1958). The spread of psychotherapeutic effects from the patient to his family group. *Psychiatry, 21,* 133–140.

Fodor, I. G. (1974). The phobic syndrome in women: Implications for treatment. In V. Franks & V. Burtle (Eds.). *Women in therapy.* New York: Brunner/Mazel.

Fowler, R. C., & Tsuang, M. T. (1975). Spouses of schizophrenics: A blind comparative study. *Comprehensive Psychiatry, 16,* 339–341.

Fox, R. E. (1968). The effect of psychotherapy on the spouse. *Family Process, 7,* 7–16.

Frank, G. (1975). *Psychiatric diagnosis: A review of research.* New York: Pergamon.

Franks, V., & Rothblum, E. D. (Eds.). (1983). *The stereotyping of women.* New York: Springer.

Fry, W. F. (1962). The marital context of an anxiety syndrome. *Family Process, 1,* 245–252.

Garanki, H., Zitrin, C. M., & Klein, D. M. (1984). Treatment of panic disorder with imipramine alone. *Archives of General Psychiatry, 141,* 446–448.

Gibbons, J. S., Horn, S. H., Powell, J. M., & Gibbons, J. L. (1984). Schizophrenic patients and their families: A survey in a psychiatric service based on a D.G.H. unit. *British Journal of Psychiatry, 144,* 70–77.

Gold, D. D. (1984). Late age of onset schizophrenia: Present but unaccounted for. *Comprehensive Psychiatry, 25,* 225–237.

Goldberg, D. (1984). The recognition of psychiatric illness by non-psychiatrists. *Australian and New Zealand Journal of Psychiatry, 18,* 128–133.

Goldberg, D., & Huxley, P. (1980). *Mental illness in the community.* New York: Tavistock.

Goldberg, S. (1977). *The inevitability of patriarchy.* London: Temple Smith.

Goldman, J. D., & Goldman, R. J. (1983). Children's perceptions of their parents and their roles: A cross-national study in Australia, England, North America and Sweden. *Sex Roles, 9,* 791–812.

Goldman, N., & Ravid, R. (1980). Community surveys: Sex differences in mental illness. In M. Guttentag, S. Salasin, & D. Belle (Eds.), *The mental health of women.* New York: Academic Press.

REFERENCES

Goldstein, A. J., & Chambless, D. L. (1981). Denial of marital conflict in agoraphobia. In A. S. Gurman (Ed.), *Questions and answers in the practice of family therapy*. New York: Brunner/Mazel.

Goodstein, R., & Swift, K. (1977). Psychotherapy with phobic patients: The marriage relationship as the source of symptoms and the focus of treatment. *American Journal of Psychotherapy, 31*, 285–292.

Gordon, M. (1973). *The American family in social-historical perspective*. New York: St. Martin's Press.

Greene, B. L., Lustig, N., & Lee, R. R. (1976). Marital therapy when one spouse has a primary affective disorder. *American Journal of Psychiatry, 133*, 827–830.

Grove, W., Andreasen, N., McDonald-Scott, P., Keller, M., & Shapiro, R. (1981). Reliability studies of psychiatric diagnosis. *Archives of General Psychiatry, 38*, 408–413.

Guntrip, H. (1969). *Personality structure and human interaction*. New York: International Universities Press.

Gurman, A. S., & Kniskern, D. P. (1978). Deterioration in marital and family therapy: Empirical, clinical and conceptual issues. *Family Process, 17*, 3–20.

Hadley, S. W., & Strupp, H. H. (1976). Contemporary views on negative effects in psychotherapy. *Archives of General Psychiatry, 33*, 1291–1302.

Hafner, R. J. (1977). The husbands of agoraphobic women and their influence on treatment outcome. *British Journal of Psychiatry, 129*, 378–383.

Hafner, R. J. (1981a). Agoraphobia in men. *Australian and New Zealand Journal of Psychiatry, 15*, 243–249.

Hafner, R. J. (1981b). Spouse-aided therapy in psychiatry: An introduction. *Australian and New Zealand Journal of Psychiatry, 15*, 329–337.

Hafner, R. J. (1982a). The marital context of the agoraphobic syndrome. In A. Goldstein & D. Chambless (Eds.). *Agoraphobia: Multiple perspectives on theory and treatment*. New York: Wiley.

Hafner, R. J. (1982b). Marital interaction in persisting obsessive compulsive disorders. *Australian and New Zealand Journal of Psychiatry, 16*, 171–178.

Hafner, R. J. (1983a). Marital systems of agoraphobic women: Contributions of husbands' denial and projection. *Journal of Family Therapy, 5*, 379–396.

Hafner, R. J. (1983b). Behaviour therapy for agoraphobic men. *Behaviour Research and Therapy, 21*, 51–56.

Hafner, R. J. (1984a). The marital repercussions of behavior therapy for agoraphobia. *Psychotherapy, 251*, 530–542.

Hafner, R. J. (1984b). Predicting the effects on husbands of behaviour therapy for wives' agoraphobia. *Behaviour Research and Therapy, 22*, 217–226.

Hafner, R. J. (1985). Marital therapy for agoraphobia. In N. Jacobson & A. Gurman (Eds.), *Clinical handbook of marital therapy*. New York: Guilford.

Hafner, R. J. (in press). Behavioral family interventions with anxiety disorders. In I. R. Falloon (Ed.), *Handbook of behavioral family therapy*. New York: Guilford.

Hafner, R. J., Badenoch, A., Fisher, J., & Swift, H. (1983). Spouse-aided therapy in persisting psychiatric disorders: A systematic evaluation. *Family Process, 22*, 385–399.

Hafner, R. J., Hatton, P., & Larkin, F. (1981). Spouse-aided therapy and psychiatric nursing: A preliminary report. *Australian Journal of Family Therapy, 2*, 143–155.

Hafner, R. J., Lieberman, S., & Crisp, A. H. (1977). A survey of consultant psychiatrists' attitudes to their work, with particular reference to psychotherapy. *British Journal of Psychiatry, 131*, 415–419.

Hafner, R. J., & Marks, I. M. (1976). The exposure in vivo of agoraphobics: Contributions of diazepam, group exposure and anxiety evocation. *Psychological Medicine, 6*, 71–88.

Hafner, R. J., & Ross, M. W. (1983). Predicting the outcome of behaviour therapy for agoraphobia. *Behaviour Research and Therapy, 21*, 375–382.

Hagnell, O., Lanke, J., Rorsman, B., & Ojesjo, L. (1982). Are we entering an age of melancholy? Depressive illnesses in a prospective study over 25 years. *Psychological Medicine, 12,* 279–289.

Haley, J. (1963) *Strategies of psychotherapy.* New York: Grune & Stratton.

Hallam, R. S. (1978). Agoraphobia: A critical review of the concept. *British Journal of Psychiatry, 133,* 314–319.

Hare-Mustin, R. T. (1982). Women in psychotherapy. *Current Psychiatric Therapies, 21,* 117–128.

Hare-Mustin, R. T., Bennett, S. K., & Broderick, P. C. (1983). Attitude toward motherhood: Gender, generational and religious comparisons. *Sex Roles, 9,* 643–661.

Harrison, F. (1977). *The dark angel: Aspects of victorian sexuality.* London: Sheldon Press.

Heins, T. J. (1978). Marital interaction in depression. *Australian and New Zealand Journal of Psychiatry, 12,* 269–275.

Henderson, S., Byrne, D. G., & Duncan-Jones, P. (1981). *Neurosis and the social environment.* Sydney: Academic Press.

Holden, N. (1984). Prescribing psychotic drugs. *British Journal of Psychiatry, 145,* 93–94.

Holmes, J. (1982). Phobia and counterphobia: Family aspects of agoraphobia. *Journal of Family Therapy, 4,* 133–152.

Hoover, C. F., & Fitzgerald, R. G. (1981). Marital conflict of manic depressive patients. *Archives of General Psychiatry, 38,* 65–67.

Horwitz, A. H. (1982). Sex-role expectations, power, and psychological distress. *Sex Roles, 8,* 607–623.

Hurvitz, N. (1967). Marital problems following psychotherapy with one spouse. *Journal of Consulting and Clinical Psychology, 31,* 38–47.

Ickes, W., & Barnes, R. D. (1978). Boys and girls together—and alienated: On enacting stereotyped sex roles in mixed-sex dyads. *Journal of Personality and Social Psychology, 36,* 669–683.

James, K., & McIntyre, D. (1983). The reproduction of families: The social role of family therapy? *Journal of Marital and Family Therapy, 9,* 119–129.

Jannoun, L., Munby, M., Catalan, J., & Gelder, M. (1980). A home-based treatment programme for agoraphobia: Replication and controlled evaluation. *Behavior Therapy, 11,* 294–305.

Janowsky, D. S., Leff, M. J., & Epstein, R. S. (1970). Playing the manic game. *Archives of General Psychiatry, 22,* 252–261.

Kay, F. G. (1972). *The family in transition.* Newton Abbot, U.K.: David & Charles, Ltd.

Kedward, H. (1969). The outcome of neurotic illness in the community. *Social Psychiatry, 4,* 1–4.

Kern, J. W. (1967). Conjoint marital therapy: An interim measure in the treatment of psychosis. *Psychiatry, 30,* 283–293.

Kohl, R. N. (1962). Pathologic reactions of marital partners to improvements of patients. *American Journal of Psychiatry, 118,* 1036–1041.

Krause, N. (1983). Conflicting sex role expectations, housework dissatisfaction, and depressive symptoms among full-time housewives. *Sex Roles, 9,* 1115–1125.

Laslett, P. (1977). *Family life and illicit love in earlier generations.* New York: Cambridge University Press.

LaTorre, R. A. (1976). The psychological assessment of gender identity and gender role in schizophrenia. *Schizophrenia Bulletin, 2,* 266–285.

LaTorre, R. A., & Piper, W. E. (1979). Gender identity and gender role in schizophrenia. *Journal of Abnormal Psychology, 88,* 68–72.

Lazarus, A. A. (1966). Broad spectrum behaviour therapy and the treatment of agoraphobia. *Behaviour Research and Therapy, 4,* 95–97.

Lazarus, A. A. (1976). *Multimodal behaviour therapy.* New York: Springer.

Lederer, W. J., & Jackson, D. D. (1968). *The mirages of marriage.* New York: W. W. Norton.

REFERENCES

Leff, J., Kuipers, L., Berkovitz, R., Eberlein-Vries, R., & Sturgeon, D. (1982). A controlled trial of social intervention in the families of schizophrenic patients. *British Journal of Psychiatry, 141,* 121-134.

Lesser, A. L. (1983). Hypomania and marital conflict. *Canadian Journal of Psychiatry, 28,* 362-366.

Levi-Strauss, C. (1966). *The savage mind.* London: Weidenfeld & Nicolson.

Lindsell, H. (Ed.). (1971). *Revised standard edition of the Holy Bible.* Kentwood, MI: Zondervan.

Liotti, G., & Guidano, V. (1976). Behavioural analysis of marital interaction in male agoraphobic patients. *Behaviour Research and Therapy, 14,* 161-162.

Lombardo, J. P., & Lavine, L. O. (1981). Sex-role stereotyping and patterns of self-disclosure. *Sex Roles, 7,* 403-411.

Loranger, A. W. (1984). Sex differences at age of onset of schizophrenia. *Archives of General Psychiatry, 41,* 157-161.

Lorenz, K. (1966). *On aggression.* London: Methuen.

Lucas, C. J., Sainsbury, R., & Collins, G. (1962). A social and clinical study of delusions in schizophrenia. *Journal of Mental Science, 108,* 747-758.

McDermott, J. F., Robillard, A. B., Cher, W. F., Hsu, J., Tseng, W., & Ashton, G. C. (1983). Re-examining the concept of adolescence: Differences between adolescent boys and girls in the context of their families. *American Journal of Psychiatry, 140,* 1318-1322.

McLemore, C. W., & Benjamin, L. S. (1979). Whatever happened to interpersonal diagnosis? *American Psychologist, 34,* 17-34.

Mamay, P. D., & Simpson, R. L. (1981). Three female roles in television commercials. *Sex Roles, 7,* 1223-1232.

Mann, A. H., Jenkins, R., & Belsey, E. (1981). The twelve-month outcome of patients with neurotic illness in general practice. *Psychological Medicine, 11,* 535-550.

Marder, S. R., Van Kammen, D. P., Rayner, J., & Bunney, W. E. (1979). Predicting drug-free improvement in schizophrenic psychosis. *Archives of General Psychiatry, 36,* 1080-1085.

Margolin, F., Talovic, S., Fernandez, V., & Onorato, R. (1983). Sex role considerations and behavioral marital therapy: Equal does not mean identical. *Journal of Marital and Family Therapy, 9,* 131-145.

Marks, I. M. (1969). *Fears and phobias.* London: Heinemann.

Marks, I. M., & Herst, E. R. (1970). A survey of 1,200 agoraphobics in Britain. *Social Psychiatry, 5,* 16-24.

Marsh, G. N. (1977). "Curing" minor illness in general practice. *British Medical Journal, 2,* 1267-1269.

Masterson, J. F. (1976). *Psychotherapy of the borderline adult.* New York: Brunner/Mazel.

Mavissakalian, M., & Michelson, L. (1982). Agoraphobia: Behavioral and pharmacological treatments, preliminary outcome, and process findings. *Psychopharmacology Bulletin, 18,* 91-103.

Mayo, J. A. (1979). Marital therapy with manic-depressive patients treated with lithium. *Comprehensive Psychiatry, 20,* 419-426.

Meissner, W. W. (1978). The conceptualization of marriage and family dynamics from a psychoanalytic perspective. In T. J. Paolino & B. S. McCrady (Eds.), *Marriage and marital therapy.* New York: Brunner/Mazel.

Merriam, S. B., & Hyer, P. (1984). Changing attitudes of women towards family-related tasks in young adulthood. *Sex Roles, 10,* 825-835.

Miller, R. D., Strickland, R., Davidson, J., & Parrott, R. (1983). Characteristics of schizophrenic and depressed patients excluded from clinical research. *American Journal of Psychiatry, 140,* 1205-1207.

Mills, C. J., & Bohannon, W. E. (1983). Personality, sex-role orientation, and psychological health in stereotypically masculine groups of males. *Sex Roles, 9,* 1161-1168.

Milton, F., & Hafner, R. J. (1979). The outcome of behavior therapy for agoraphobia in relation to marital adjustment. *Archives of General Psychiatry, 36,* 807-811.

Murphy, H. M. B. (1976). Which neuroses need specialist care? *Canadian Medical Association Journal, 115,* 540–543.

Murphy, J. M., Sobol, A. M., Neff, R. K., Olivier, D. C., & Leighton, A. H. (1984). Stability of prevalence: Depression and anxiety disorders. *Archives of General Psychiatry, 41,* 990–997.

Murstein, B. I. (1970). Stimulus–value–role: A theory of marital choice. *Journal of Marriage and the Family, 32,* 465–481.

Myers, J. K., Weissman, M. M., Tischler, G. L., Holzer, C. E., Leaf, P. J., Orvaschel, H., Anthony, J. C., Boyd, J. H., Burke, J. D., Kramer, M., & Stoltzman, R. (1984). Six-month prevalence of psychiatric disorders in three communities. *Archives of General Psychiatry, 41,* 959–967.

Oakley, A. (1972). *Sex, gender and society.* New York: Harper & Row.

O'Connor, P. (1981). *Understanding the mid-life crisis.* Melbourne: Sun Books.

Orlofsky, J. L. (1982). Psychological androgyny, sex-typing, and sex-role ideology as predictors of male-female interpersonal attraction. *Sex Roles, 8,* 1057–1073.

Parelman, A. (1983). *Emotional intimacy in marriage. A sex roles perspective.* Ann Arbor: UMI Research Press.

Parker, G. (1979). Sex differences in non-clinical depression. *Australian and New Zealand Journal of Psychiatry, 13,* 127–132.

Parker, G. (1983). *Parental overprotection.* New York: Grune & Stratton.

Patterson, J. M., & McCubbin, H. I. (1984). Gender roles and coping. *Journal of Marriage and the Family, 46,* 95–104.

Pilkonis, P. A., Imber, S. D., Lewis, P., & Rubinsky, P. (1984). A comparative outcome study of individual, group, and conjoint therapy. *Archives of General Psychiatry, 41,* 431–437.

Pilowsky, I. (1978). A general classification of abnormal illness behavior. *British Journal of Medical Psychology, 51,* 131–137.

Planansky, K., & Johnston, R. (1967). Mate selection in schizophrenia. *Acta Psychiatrica Scandinavica, 43,* 397–409.

Pleck, J. H. (1981). *The myth of masculinity.* Cambridge, MA: MIT Press.

Prochaska, J., & Prochaska, J. (1978). Twentieth century trends in marriage and marital therapy. In T. J. Paolino & B. S. McCrady (Eds.), *Marriage and marital therapy.* New York: Brunner/Mazel.

Quadrio, C. (1983). Rapunzel and the pumpkin eater: Marital systems of agoraphobic women. *Australian Journal of Family Therapy, 4,* 81–85.

Quadrio, C. (1984). Families of agoraphobic women. *Australian and New Zealand Journal Psychiatry, 18,* 164–170.

Rabins, P., Pauker, S., & Thomas, J. (1984). Can schizophrenia begin after age 44? *Comprehensive Psychiatry, 25,* 290–293.

Rabkin, J., Quitkin, F., Stewart, J., McGrath, P., & Puig-Antich, J. (1983). The dexamethasone suppression test with mildly to moderately depressed outpatients. *American Journal of Psychiatry, 140,* 926–927.

Rachman, S. J., & Hodgson, R. J. (1980). *Obsessions and compulsions.* Englewood Cliffs, NJ: Prentice-Hall.

Radloff, L. S. (1980). Depression and the empty nest. *Sex Roles, 6,* 775–781.

Rapp, M. S., & Thomas, M. R. (1982). Agoraphobia. *Canadian Journal of Psychiatry, 27,* 419–425.

Rice, E. (1974). The compulsive companion: A case study. *International Journal of Psychoanalytic Psychotherapy, 1,* 183–194.

Roberts, R. E., & Vernon, S. W. (1982). Depression in the community. *Archives of General Psychiatry, 39,* 1407–1409.

Robson, B. E. (1983). And they lived happily ever after: Marriage concepts of older adolescents. *Canadian Journal of Psychiatry, 28,* 646–649.

Rogers, E. (1969). *Modernization among peasants.* New York: Holt.

REFERENCES

Rosenbaum, J. F., Woods, S. W., Groves, J. E., & Klerman, G. L. (1984). Emergence of hostility during alprazolam treatment. *American Journal of Psychiatry, 141,* 792–793.

Rotter, N. G. & O'Connell, A. N. (1982). The relationships among sex-role orientation, cognitive complexity, and tolerance for ambiguity. *Sex Roles, 8,* 1209–1220.

Rounsaville, B. J., Weissman, M. M., Prusoff, B. A., & Herceg-Baron, R. L. (1979a). Marital disputes and treatment outcome in depressed women. *Comprehensive Psychiatry, 20,* 483–490.

Rounsaville, B. J., Weissman, M. M., Prusoff, B. A., & Herceg-Baron, R. L. (1979b). Process of psychotherapy among depressed women with marital disputes. *American Journal of Orthopsychiatry, 49,* 505–510.

Roy, A. (1982). Suicide in chronic schizophrenia. *British Journal of Psychiatry, 141,* 171–177.

Ruble, T. L. (1983). Sex stereotypes: Issues of change in the 1970's. *Sex Roles, 9,* 397–402.

Rudden, M., Sweeney, J., Frances, A., & Gilmore, M. (1983). A comparison of delusional disorders in women and men. *American Journal of Psychiatry, 40,* 1575–1578.

Sager, C. J. (1976). *Marriage contracts and couple therapy.* New York: Brunner/Mazel.

Schoeneman, T. J. (1982). Criticisms of the psychopathological interpretation of witch hunts: A review. *American Journal of Psychiatry, 139,* 1028–1032.

Schwartz, L. S., & Val. E. R. (1984). Agoraphobia: Multimodal treatment approach. *American Journal of Psychotherapy, 38,* 35–46.

Scutt, J. (1983). *Even in the best of homes: Violence in the family.* Penguin Australia.

Seaman, L. C. B. (1981). *A New History of England 410–1975.* New York: Barnes & Noble.

Segal, H. (1973). *Introduction to the work of Melanie Klein.* London: Hogarth.

Sheehan, D. V., Ballenger, J., & Jacobsen, G. (1980). Treatment of endogenous anxiety with phobic, hysterical, and hypochondriacal symptoms. *Archives of General Psychiatry, 37,* 51–59.

Sims, A. (1975). Factors predictive of outcome in neurosis. *British Journal of Psychiatry, 127,* 54–62.

Singh, B., Nunn, K., Martin, J., & Yates, J. (1981). Abnormal treatment behaviour. *British Journal of Medical Psychology, 54,* 67–73.

Slevin, K. F., & Wingrove, C. R. (1983). Similarities and differences among three generations of women in attitudes towards the female role in contemporary society. *Sex Roles, 9,* 609–624.

Smail, P., Stockwell, T., Canter, S., & Hodgson, R. (1984). Alcohol dependence and phobic states: 1. A prevalence study. *British Journal of Psychiatry, 144,* 53–57.

Stolk, Y., & Brotherton, P. (1981). Attitudes towards single women. *Sex Roles, 7,* 73–78.

Sturdivant, S. (1980). *Therapy with women.* New York: Springer.

Tennant, C., Bebbington, P., & Hurry, J. (1982). Female vulnerability to neurosis: The influence of social roles. *Australian and New Zealand Journal of Psychiatry, 16,* 135–140.

Tinsley, E. G., Sullivan-Guest, S., & McGuire, G. (1984). Feminine sex role and depression in middle aged women. *Sex Roles, 11,* 25–32.

Tyrer, P. (1984). The classification of anxiety. *British Journal of Psychiatry, 144,* 78–83.

Vaughn, C. E., & Leff, J. P. (1976). The influence of family and social factors on the course of psychiatric illness. *British Journal of Psychiatry, 129,* 125–137.

Vose, R. H. (1981). *Agoraphobia.* London: Faber & Faber.

Wadeson, H. G., & Fitzgerald, R. F. (1971). Marital relationships in manic depressive illness. *Journal of Nervous and Mental Disease, 153,* 180–196.

Wallace, A. F. C. (1970). *Culture and personality.* New York: Random House.

Watson, J. P., Elliot, S. A., Rugg, A. J., & Brough, D. I. (1984). Psychiatric disorder in pregnancy and the first postnatal year. *British Journal of Psychiatry, 144,* 453–462.

Webster, A. (1953). The development of phobias in married women. *Psychological Monographs, 67,* 1–18.

Weissman, M. M., & Akiskal, H. S. (1984). The role of psychotherapy in chronic depressions: A proposal. *Comprehensive Psychiatry, 25,* 23–31.

Weissman, M. M., & Klerman, G. (1977). Sex differences and the epidemiology of depression. *Archives of General Psychiatry, 34,* 98–111.

Weissman, M. M., Klerman, G., Prusoff, B. A., Sholomskas, D., & Padian, N. (1981). Depressed outpatients: Results one year after treatment with drugs and/or Interpersonal Psychotherapy. *Archives of General Psychiatry, 38,* 51–55.

Weissman, M. M., Myers, J. K., & Thompson, W. D. (1981). Depression and its treatment in a U.S. urban community—1975–1976. *Archives of General Psychiatry, 38,* 417–421.

Williamson, R. C. (1972). *Marriage and family relations.* New York: Wiley.

Wolpe, J. (1970). Identifying the antecedents of an agoraphobic reaction: A transcript. *Journal of Behavior Therapy and Experimental Psychiatry, 1,* 299–304.

Zinner, J., & Shapiro, R. (1972). Projective identification as a mode of perception and behaviour in families of adolescents. *International Journal of Psychoanalysis, 53,* 523–530.

Zitrin, C. M., Klein, D. F., Woerner, M. G., & Ross, D. C. (1983). Treatment of phobias: 1. Comparison of imipramine hydrochloride and placebo. *Archives of General Psychiatry, 40,* 125–137.

Author Index

A

Ackerman, N. W., 47, 60, 231*n*.
Adams, B. N., 60, 231*n*.
Akhter, S., 50, 56, 231*n*.
Akiskal, H. S., 123, 238*n*.
Al-Issa, I., 186, 187, 231*n*.
Andreasen, N., 104, 234*n*.
Andrews, G., 121, 152, 231*n*.
Anthony, J. C., 124, 237*n*.
Ashton, G. C., 62, 236*n*.
Ashton, H., 109, 231*n*.

B

Badenoch, A., 223, 226, 231*n*., 234*n*.
Ballenger, J., 112, 238*n*.
Barlow, D. H., 114, 212, 231*n*.
Barnes, G. E., 123, 231*n*.
Barnes, R. D., 62, 235*n*.
Barrett, J. E., 123, 124, 231*n*.
Beaber, R. J., 115, 231*n*.
Bebbington, P. E., 38, 63, 78, 79, 126,
    231*n*., 238*n*.
Beck, J. G., 212, 231*n*.
Belsey, E., 115, 236*n*.
Bem, S. L., 53, 232*n*.
Benjamin, L. S., 43, 236*n*.
Bennett, S. K., 37, 235*n*.
Benson, B. A., 156, 232*n*.
Berg, I., 78, 232*n*.
Berkovitz, R., 193, 236*n*.
Berman, E., 105, 108, 232*n*.
Bird, H. W., 73–75, 232*n*.
Birley, J. T. L., 189, 232*n*.
Birtchnell, J., 116, 232*n*.
Blowers, C. M., 112, 232*n*.

Bohannon, W. E., 23, 236*n*.
Bothwell, S., 123, 126, 232*n*.
Bowen, R. C., 112, 232*n*.
Boyd, J. G., 189, 233*n*.
Boyd, J. H., 124, 237*n*.
Brehony, K. A., 156, 232*n*.
Briscoe, M., 78, 126, 232*n*.
Brodaty, H., 121, 231*n*.
Broderick, P. C., 37, 235*n*.
Brotherton, P., 16, 238*n*.
Brough, D. I., 77, 238*n*.
Broverman, D., 18, 232*n*.
Broverman, I. H., 18, 36, 232*n*.
Brown, G. W., 63, 189, 190, 232*n*.
Buglass, D., 112, 118, 153, 159, 232*n*.
Bunney, W. E., 106, 236*n*.
Burke, J. D., 124, 237*n*.
Burns, L. E., 153, 159, 232*n*.
Butler, A., 78, 232*n*.
Byrne, D. G., 63, 235*n*.
Byrne, J. P., 50, 231*n*.

C

Canter, S., 164, 238*n*.
Catalan, J., 112, 121, 232*n*., 235*n*.
Chambless, D. L., 107, 112, 154, 156, 232*n*.
Chapman, J., 44, 232*n*.
Cher, W. F., 62, 236*n*.
Childs-Clarke, A., 112, 232*n*.
Christensen, H., 121, 231*n*.
Clancy, J., 112, 232*n*.
Clarke, J., 112, 232*n*.
Clarkson, F., 18, 232*n*.
Cobb, J. P., 112, 213, 232*n*.
Cochrane, N., 215, 232*n*.
Collins, G., 186, 236*n*.

Crisp, A. H., 105, 234n.
Cross, J., 44, 232n.

D

D'Arcy, C., 63, 78, 232n.
Davidson, J., 111, 236n.
Davidson, L. R., 67, 232n.
Dean, D., 104, 232n.
Dicks, H. V., 50, 57, 82, 233n.
Doctor, R., 153, 233n.
Duncan-Jones, P., 63, 235n.
Dunn, G., 118, 233n.
Dupont, R. L., 196, 200, 233n.

E

Eberlein-Vries, R., 193, 236n.
Edmonds, G., 121, 232n.
Edwards, S., 106, 233n.
Eisenstein, V., 47, 60, 233n.
Elliot, S. A., 77, 238n.
Elpern, S., 63, 233n.
Ennis, J., 121, 232n.
Epstein, R. S., 151, 235n.
Erikson, E. H., 48, 56, 233n.

F

Faegermen, P. M., 194, 233n.
Falloon, I. R., 111, 189, 190, 233n.
Fernandez, V., 45, 236n.
Fisher, J., 223, 231n., 234n.
Fisher, S., 209, 233n.
Fitzgerald, R. F., 151, 238n.
Fitzgerald, R. G., 151, 235n.
Fodor, I. G., 156, 233n.
Fowler, R. C., 196, 233n.
Fox, R. E., 209, 233n.
Frances, A., 185, 238n.
Frank, G., 104, 233n.
Franks, V., 43, 233n.
Fry, W. F., 112, 156, 233n.

G

Garanki, H., 42, 233n.
Gath, D., 121, 232n.

Gelder, M., 112, 235n.
Gibbons, J. L., 184, 233n.
Gibbons, J. S., 184, 197, 233n.
Gilderman, A. M., 190, 233n.
Gilmore, M., 185, 238n.
Gold, D. D., 185, 194, 233n.
Goldberg, D., 113, 115, 121, 233n.
Goldberg, S., 27, 233n.
Goldman, J. D., 18, 61, 62, 233n.
Goldman, N., 124, 133n.
Goldman, R. J., 18, 233n.
Goldstein, A. J., 107, 112, 154, 156, 234n.
Goodstein, R., 112, 156, 234n.
Gordon, M., 11, 234n.
Greene, B. L., 225, 226, 234n.
Grove, W., 104, 234n.
Groves, J. E., 90, 238n.
Grunebaum, H. U., 196, 200, 233n.
Guidano, V., 160, 236n.
Guntrip, H., 49, 234n.
Gurman, A. S., 209, 234n.

H

Hadley, S. W., 210, 234n.
Hadzi-Pavlovic, D., 121, 231n.
Hafner, R. J., 21, 45, 105, 112, 118, 120,
    121, 153, 154, 156, 161, 163, 169, 211,
    213, 215, 222–225, 231n., 234n., 236n.
Hagnell, O., xiii, 234n.
Haley, J., 168, 169, 235n.
Hallam, R. S., 112, 235n.
Hare-Mustin, R. T., 37, 45, 48, 235n.
Harris, T., 63, 232n.
Harrison, F., 8, 9, 11, 235n.
Harvey, P. R., 121, 231n.
Hatton, P., 222, 234n.
Heins, T. J., 126, 132, 235n.
Henderson, A. S., 112, 232n.
Henderson, S., 63, 79, 235n.
Herceg-Baron, R. L., 116, 238n.
Herst, E. R., 153, 236n.
Hodgson, R., 164, 238n.
Hodgson, R. J., 168, 237n.
Hoenk, P. R., 112, 232n.
Holden, N., 106, 235n.
Holmes, J., 112, 156, 235n.
Holzer, C. E., 124, 237n.
Hoover, C. F., 151, 235n.
Horn, S. H., 184, 232n.
Horwitz, A. H., 63, 235n.

Houston, J., 78, 232n.
Hsu, J., 62, 236n.
Hurry, J., 38, 63, 231n., 238n.
Hurvitz, N., 24, 91, 108, 208, 210, 235n.
Huxley, P., 115, 232n.
Hyer, P., 37, 236n.

I

Imber, S. D., 225, 237n.
Ickes, W., 62, 235n.

J

Jackson, D. D., 10, 235n.
Jacobsen, G., 112, 238n.
James, K., 44, 235n.
Jannoun, L., 112, 235n.
Janowsky, D. S., 151, 235n.
Jenkins, R., 115, 236n.
Johnston, R., 187, 237n.

K

Karp, S. A., 63, 233n.
Kay, F. G., 6, 235n.
Kedward, H., 118, 123, 235n.
Keller, M., 104, 234n.
Kennard, J., 116, 232n.
Kern, J. W., 190–192, 235n.
Klein, D., 42, 112, 233n., 239n.
Klerman, G., 122, 124, 239n.
Klerman, G. L., 90, 238n.
Kniskern, D. P., 209, 234n.
Kohl, R. N., 107, 210, 235n.
Kohout, J., 112, 232n.
Kramer, M., 124, 237n.
Krause, N., 38, 235n.
Kreitman, N., 112, 232n.
Kuipers, L., 193, 236n.
Kumar, V., 106, 233n.

L

Lanke, J., xiii, 234n.
Larkin, F., 222, 234n.
Laslett, P., 2, 7, 235n.
Last, C. G., 212, 231n.

LaTorre, R. A., 187, 235n.
Lavine, L. O., 62, 236n.
Lazarus, A. A., 110, 212, 235n.
Leaf, P. J., 124, 237n.
Lederer, W. J., 10, 235n.
Lee, R. R., 225, 234n.
Leff, J., 151, 189, 193, 194, 197, 235n.,
   236n., 238n.
Leighton, A. H., 125, 237n.
Lesser, A. L., 149, 151, 236n.
Levi-Strauss, C., 27, 236n.
Lewis, P., 22, 237n.
Lieberman, S., 105, 234n.
Lief, H., 105, 232n.
Lindsell, H., 6, 236n.
Liotti, G., 160, 162, 236n.
Lombardo, J. P., 62, 236n.
Loranger, A. W., 184–186, 194, 236n.
Lorenz, K., 25, 236n.
Lucas, C. J., 186, 236n.
Lustig, N., 225, 234n.

M

Mamay, P. D., 71, 236n.
Mann, A. H., 115, 116, 118, 152, 236n.
Marder, S. R., 106, 236n.
Margolin, F., 45, 236n.
Marks, I. M., 153, 159, 160, 211, 234n.,
   236n.
Marsh, G. N., 116, 120, 236n.
Martin, J., 102, 238n.
Martin, P. A., 73, 232n.
Masterson, J. F., 49, 236n.
Mathews, A. M., 112, 232n.
Mattick, R. P., 121, 231n.
Mavissakalian, M., 112, 236n.
Mayo, J. A., 110, 150, 236n.
McCubbin, H. I., 64, 237n.
McDermott, J. F., 62, 236n.
McDonald-Scott, P., 104, 234n.
McGill, C. W., 189, 232n.
McIntyre, D., 44, 235n.
McGrath, P., 104, 237n.
McGuire, G., 45, 238n.
McGuire, R., 78, 231n.
McLemore, C. W., 43, 236n.
Meissner, W. W., 50, 52, 236n.
Mendel, D., 209, 233n.
Merriam, S. B., 37, 236n.
Michelson, L., 112, 236n.

Miller, R. D., 111, 236n.
Mills, C. J., 23, 236n.
Milton, F., 112, 213, 236n.
Moss, H. B., 190, 233n.
Munby, M., 112, 235n.
Murphy, H. M. B., 118, 237n.
Murphy, J. M., 125, 164, 168, 176, 237n.
Murstein, B. I., 60, 65, 237n.
Myers, J. K., 122, 124, 152, 153, 164, 237n., 239n.

N

Neff, R. K., 125, 237n.
Noyes, R., 112, 232n.
Nunn, K., 102, 238n.

O

Oakley, A., 60, 237n.
O'Brien, G. T., 212, 231n.
O'Connell, A. N., 57, 238n.
O'Connor, P., 148, 237n.
Öjesjö, L., xiii, 234n.
Olivier, D. C., 125, 237n.
Onorato, R., 45, 236n.
Orlofsky, J. L., 58, 68, 237n.
Orvaschel, H., 124, 237n.

P

Padian, N., 122, 239n.
Park, S., 44, 232n.
Parelman, A., 62, 237n.
Parker, G., 48, 124, 237n.
Parrott, R., 111, 236n.
Patterson, J. M., 64, 237n.
Paulker, S., 185, 237n.
Pilkonis, P. A., 225, 237n.
Pilowsky, I., 102, 237n.
Piper, W. E., 187, 235n.
Planansky, K., 187, 192, 237n.
Pleck, J. H., 54, 237n.
Powell, J. M., 184, 233n.
Presley, A. S., 112, 232n.
Prochaska, J., 61, 237n.
Prochaska, J., 61, 237n.
Prosen, H., 123, 231n.
Prusoff, B. A., 116, 122, 238n., 239n.
Puig-Antich, J., 104, 237n.

Q

Quadrio, C., 112, 156, 237n.
Quitkin, F., 104, 237n.

R

Rabins, P., 185, 237n.
Rabkin, J., 104, 237n.
Rachman, S. J., 168, 176, 237n.
Radloff, L. S., 81, 237n.
Rapp, M. S., 122, 237n.
Ravid, R., 124, 233n.
Rayner, J., 106, 236n.
Razani, J., 190, 233n.
Rice, E., 168, 237n.
Roberts, R. E., 123, 237n.
Robillard, A. B., 62, 236n.
Robson, B. E., 61, 237n.
Rodney, W. M., 115, 231n.
Rogers, E., 5, 237n.
Rorsman, B., xiii, 234n.
Rosenbaum, J. F., 90, 109, 238n.
Rosenkrantz, D., 18, 232n.
Ross, D. C., 112, 239n.
Ross, M. W., 118, 234n.
Rothblum, E. D., 233n.
Rotter, N. G., 57, 238n.
Rounsaville, B. J., 116, 126, 213, 238n.
Roy, A., 205, 238n.
Ruble, T. L., 16, 66, 238n.
Rubinsky, P., 225, 237n.
Rudden, M., 185, 186, 194, 238n.
Rugg, A. J., 77, 238n.
Ryder, R. G., 196, 232n.

S

Sager, C. J., 60, 238n.
Sainsbury, R., 186, 236n.
Sashidaran, S., 104, 232n.
Schoeneman, T. J., 100, 238n.
Schuham, A., 73, 232n.
Schwartz, L. S., 112, 156, 238n.
Scutt, J., 133, 238n.
Seaman, L. C. B., 1, 2, 238n.
Segal, H., 49, 50, 238n.
Shapiro, R., 104, 112, 234n., 239n.
Sheehan, D. V., 112, 238n.
Sholomskas, D., 122, 239n.
Simpson, R. L., 71, 236n.

Sims, A., 116, 238*n.*
Singh, B., 102, 238*n.*
Slevin, K. F., 37, 238*n.*
Slyman, D. J., 112, 232*n.*
Smail, P., 164, 238*n.*
Sobol, A. M., 125, 237*n.*
Stewart, J., 104, 237*n.*
Stockwell, T., 164, 238*n.*
Stolk, Y., 16, 238*n.*
Stoltzman, R., 124, 237*n.*
Strickland, R., 111, 236*n.*
Strupp, H. H., 210, 234*n.*
Sturdivant, S., 23, 46, 238*n.*
Sturgeon, D., 193, 236*n.*
Sturt, E., 63, 231*n.*
Sullivan-Guest, S., 45, 238*n.*
Surtees, P., 104, 232*n.*
Sweeney, J., 185, 238*n.*
Swift, H., 223, 231*n.*
Swift, K., 112, 234*n.*

T

Talovic, S., 45, 236*n.*
Tennant, C., 38, 63, 78, 79, 121, 126, 238*n.*
Thomas, J., 185, 237*n.*
Thomas, M. R., 112, 237*n.*
Thompson, W. D., 122, 239*n.*
Thorpe, G. L., 153, 232*n.*
Tiller, J., 121, 231*n.*
Tinsley, E. G., 45, 63, 238*n.*
Tischler, G. L., 124, 237*n.*
Tseng, W., 62, 236*n.*
Tsuang, M. T., 196, 233*n.*
Tyrer, P., 114, 238*n.*

V

Val, E. R., 112, 238*n.*
Van Kammen, D. P., 106, 236*n.*
Vaughn, C. E., 189, 238*n.*
Vernon, S. W., 123, 237*n.*
Vogel, S., 18, 232*n.*
Vose, R. H., 153, 154, 238*n.*

W

Wadeson, H. G., 151, 238*n.*
Wallace, A. F. C., 37, 238*n.*
Watson, J. P., 77, 238*n.*
Webster, A., 112, 156, 238*n.*
Weissman, M. M., 116, 122–124, 126, 152, 153, 213, 214, 237*n.*, 238*n.*, 239*n.*
Williamson, R. C., 64, 239*n.*
Wing, J. K., 189, 232*n.*
Wingrove, C. R., 37, 238*n.*
Woerner, M. G., 82, 239*n.*
Wolpe, J., 110, 239*n.*
Woods, S. W., 90, 238*n.*

Y

Yates, J., 102, 238*n.*

Z

Zinner, J., 82, 239*n.*
Zitrin, C. M., 42, 112, 239*n.*

Subject Index

A

Adjustment problems, marriage and, 228
Affective disorders, 122–151
  primary, studies of, 226
Age
  at marriage, in preindustrial England, 7
  and schizophrenia onset, 185, 186
  and sex-role issues in married women, 81,
    82
Aggression, and female sex-role
    stereotyping, 25–27
Agoraphobia, 153, 154
  behavior therapy for, 211–213
  in men, 160–164
  simple versus complex, 154, 155
Alcohol dependency, and phobias in men,
    164
Ambivalence, of patient to therapist, 217,
    218
Anglican church, in preindustrial England,
    5–7
Anniversary reactions, abnormal grief and,
    166
Anxiety disorders, 152–183
Anxiety states
  and abnormal grief, 165–168
  diagnosis of, 164, 165
Arrested grieving, 166, 167
Attractiveness, physical, see Physical
    attractiveness

B

Balance of power, changes in, 211, 212
Behavior therapy
  for agoraphobia, 211–213
  marital interaction and, 110, 111

Benzodiapines, marital interaction and, 109
Bethlem hospital, 101
Bipolar disorder, see Mania
Birth control, 12

C

Child rearing, after industrial revolution, 9,
    10
Chronic depression, 124
"Collapsible" man, 73–75
Community studies, of depression, 122–124
Companionship, as form of marriage, 61
Competition
  husbands and, 70–72
  women and, 77, 78
  with men, 75–77
  by proxy, 72–75
Competitive husbands, 70–72
Competitive marriage, 75–77
Competitive women, and sex-role conflict,
    77, 78
Complementary marriage, 72–75
  sex-role conditioning in, 80, 81
Complex agoraphobia, 156, 157
  in men, 161–164
  versus simple agoraphobia, 154, 155
"Compulsory marriage", 176
Conditioning, see Sex-role conditioning
Conflict
  marital
    denial of, 98, 99
    repercussions of, 116–118
  sex-role, see Sex-role conflict
Conjoint marital therapy
  for agoraphobia, 213
  limitations of , 214, 215
  with schizophrenic partner, 190–192

Conjoint marital therapy (*continued*)
  study results in, 213, 214
  see also Spouse-aided therapy
Courtship
  as preparation for marriage, 64, 65
  and intimacy, 66, 67
  process of, 65, 66
  and schizophrenia in men, 188
Cultural change, and female sex-role
    stereotyping, 27, 28

D

Dating, as preparation for marriage, 64, 65
Delusions, gender-related content
    differences in, 185, 186
Depressed men
  case study of, 21–23
  marital interaction and, 143–149
Depressed women
  individual therapy for, 213, 214
  marital interaction and, 126, 127
  renegotiation and, 214
  sex-role stereotyping and, 127–133
  and sex-role strain and conflict, 133–143
Depression
  community studies of, 122–124
  in men, *see* Depressed men
  in women, *see* Depressed women
Depressive position, identity and, 51, 52
Deterioration, *see* Marital deterioration
Diagnosis, psychiatric, 103–105
Diazepam, marital interaction and, 108, 109
Disintegration, *see* Ego disintegration
Displaced mourning, 166, 167
Division of labor
  after industrial revolution, 9, 10
  and marital economics, 4
Droit de seigneur, 19
Drugs, overvaluation of, 106

E

Education
  for marriage, 228
  in preindustrial England, 6
Ego disintegration
  and agoraphobia in men, 164
  identity and, 51

Empty nest syndrome, 130
Epidemiologic Catchment Area research
    program, 152
Expectations
  of marriage, 4, 5
  sex-role, in women, 37, 38
Extramarital sexual liaisons
  as negative marital repercussion, 208
  in preindustrial England, 7

F

"Failed parent", 217
False self, 56, and sex-role strain, 57–59
Family therapy, and sex-role research, 44–46
Father, stereotype of, 17, 18
Feminist therapy, and sex-role research, 46
Feudal system, 19

G

Gender identity, 53
  feminine, 55, 56
  masculine, 53–55
  and sex-role strain, 57–59
Grief
  abnormal, anxiety states and, 165–168
  biological basis of, 165, 166
  unresolved, anxiety symptoms and, 166, 167
  see also Mourning

H

"Hidden agenda", 219
Historical continuity, traditions and, 27
Hostility
  marital, *see* Marital hostility
  of spouse to therapist, 216, 217
Housework, 11
  labor-saving devices for, 12, 13
Husbands
  competitive, 70–72
  and denial of personal problems, 175, 176
  of psychotic women, 200–202
    indirect encouragement by, 202–204
  reaction to wife's behavior therapy, 211, 212

I

Identity, 47, 48
  consolidation of, 56, 57
  depressive position and, 51, 52
  of gender, 53
    feminine, 55, 56
    masculine, 53–55
    sex-role strain and, 57–59
  individuation and, 48
  intrapsychic structure development and,
    48–50
  and Oedipus complex, 52
  problems, object relations theory and, 52,
    53
  and theories of M. Klein, 50, 51
  see also Projective identification
Illness-confirming behavior, 117
  marital repercussions of, 118–120
Imipramine, for panic attacks, 41, 42
Individual therapy, 207
  for depressed married women, 213, 214
  and marital repercussions
    agarophobia and, 211–213
    negative, 208–210
    positive, 209
    research on, 210, 211
  and spouse-aided therapy
    combination of, 226, 227
    comparison of, 222–225
Individuation, 48
Industrial revolution
  child rearing after, 9, 10
  division of labor after, 10, 11
  effects of, 7–11
  marriage customs prior to, 1–7
  see also Preindustrial England
Institutionalization, mental illness and, 102
Internalization, identity and, 48–50
Interpersonal psychotherapy, 214
Intervention, therapeutic, 120, 121
Intimacy
  courtship and, 66, 67
  marital, 62–64
Intrapsychic structures, development of, 48–
  50
Introjection, identity and, 50

J

Jargon, psychological, 208

K

Klein, Melanie, theories of, 50, 51

L

Labor, division of, *see* Division of labor
Labor-saving devices, 12, 13
Late-onset schizophrenia, 185
Learning theory, 110, 111
Lithium carbonate, marital interaction and,
  110

M

Machismo, case study of, 83–87
Mania, marriage and, 149–151
Marital conflict, denial of, 98, 99
  repercussions of, 116–118
Marital deterioration, following therapy,
  209, 224
  causes of, 224, 225
Marital hostility
  and men with schizophrenia, 189, 190
  sex-role conflict as source of, 192–194
Marital interaction
  and abnormal grief, 167, 168
  behavioral therapies and, 110, 111
  and depressed men, 143–149
  impact of psychotropic drugs on, 108–110
Marital intimacy, sex-role stereotyping and,
  62–64
Marital repercussions, for individual
    therapy
  agorophobia and, 211–213
  negative, 208–210
  positive, 209
  research on, 210, 211
Marital status, schizophrenia and, 184, 185
Marital stress, psychosis and, 194–196
Marital system, and psychiatric system
  interaction, 105–111
Marital therapy
  and sex-role research, 44–46
  see also Conjoint marital therapy;
    Spouse-aided therapy
Marriage
  adjustment problems and, 228
  competitive, 75–77
  complementary, 72–75
  sex-role conditioning in, 80, 81

Marriage (*continued*)
"compulsory", 176
dating and courtship as preparation for,
64–67
and depression, 124–126
effects of industrial revolution on, 7–11
effects of technology on, 11–15
and mania, 149–151
in preindustrial England
economics of, 2–4
expectations of, 4, 5
and religious context, 5–7
and psychiatric disorder, 107, 108, 111–
114
as psychological institution, 206
schizophrenia and
in men, 187–194
in women, 194–204
status-oriented, 70–82
symbiotic, 82–98
Marriage customs, in preindustrial England,
1–7
Marriage resource therapy, *see* Spouse-
aided therapy
Married women, *see* Wife; Women
Married Women's Property Act (1882), 9
Mate selection, 59, 60
dating and courtship and, 64–67
emotional intimacy and, 62–64
sex-role stereotyping and, 60–62
Medicine, psychiatry and, 103–105
Men
agoraphobia in, 160–164
depression in, *see* Depressed men
phobias and alcohol dependency in, 164
schizophrenia in, 187–192
see also Husbands
Mental health, personal responsibility for,
227, 228
Mental illness
clinical effects of stereotypes about, 102,
103
historical attitudes to, 100–102
and male sex-role stereotyping, 21–25
preventative approaches to, 228, 229
"Mid-life crisis", 148
Mortality, in preindustrial England, 5
Motherhood, sex-role expectations and, 37,
38
Mourning
displaced, 166, 167
rituals of, 165

N

Nationalism, and male sex-role
stereotyping, 20

O

Object relations
integration of, 56, 57
theory of, 52, 53
Obsessive compulsive disorders, 168, 169
in men, 176
case study of, 176–183
in women
case studies of, 169–173
marital contributions to, 174–176
Occupational stereotype, 16, 17
Oedipus complex, 52
Oxazepam, effects of, 109

P

PAD, *see* Primary affective disorder
Panic attacks
preagoraphobia and, 159
sex-role conflict and, 39, 40
Parish, 1, 2
Passivity, schizophrenia and, 188
Patient
and ambivalence to therapist, 217, 218
and permission for spouse involvement,
218, 219
preserving hope in, 107
Personal fulfillment, 14
Personal relationships, in preindustrial
England, 5
Phobias, 153
in men, and alcohol dependency, 164
see also Agoraphobia
Phobic disorders, 153
Physical attractiveness
as status symbol, 10
and marriage expectations, 4, 5
Poor Law Act (1601), 2
and mentally ill, 101
Power, balance of, 211, 212
Preindustrial England
economics of marriage in, 2–4
expectations of marriage in, 4, 5
parishes in, 1, 2
religion in, 5–7

Primary affective disorder, studies of, 226
Primary care physician, 114–116
Primogeniture, 2, 3
Projective identification
  identity and, 50
  and marriage preservation, 94–98
  and reluctant nurturing, 91–94
  and sex-role conflict, 87–91
  and sex-role stereotyping, 83–87
  in symbiotic marriages, 82, 83
Prostitution, 8
Protective rituals, and sex-role stereotyping, 25
Psychiatric diagnosis, 103–105
Psychiatric disorder, marital context and
  denial of, 107, 108
  lack of research into, 111–114
Psychiatric system, and marital system
  interaction, 105–111
Psychiatrist
  preserving hope in, 105, 106
  see also Therapist
Psychiatry
  and medicine, 103–105
  and sex-role research, 43, 44
Psychoanalysis, and sex-role stereotype
  reinforcement, 23–25
Psychological problems, marital intimacy
  and, 62–64
Psychological symptoms
  and illness-confirming behavior, 118–120
  and marital conflict denial, 116–118
  primary care physician and, 114–116
  from status-oriented marriages, 70–82
  from symbiotic marriages, 82–98
  therapeutic interventions and, 120, 121
Psychosis
  husbands of women with, 200–202
    and indirect encouragement, 202–204
  impact on marriage, 196, 197
  and marital stress, 194–196
  marriage and, 184–205
  see also Schizophrenia
Psychotherapy
  individual, see Individual therapy
  interpersonal, 214
  sex-role conflict and, 42
  and sex-role stereotype reinforcement,
    23–25
  and treatment goals, 220–222
Psychotropic drugs, impact on marital
  interaction, 108–110

R

Religion, in preindustrial society, 5–7
Renegotiation , depressed married women
  and, 214
Revolving door policy, 107
Rituals
  of mourning, 165
  protective, 25
Role conflict, see Sex-role conflict
Role reversal, schizophrenia and, 193
Role strain, see Sex-role strain

S

Schizophrenia, 184
  men with, 187–189
    and hostility in marriage, 189, 190
    and intervention in marriage, 190–192
  sex differences in
    and age of onset, 185, 186
    and marital status, 184, 185
  sex-role issues research in, 186, 187
  women with, 194
    enduring marriages of, 200–202
    and marital stress, case studies of, 194–
      196
    psychiatric treatment and, 197–200
Schizophrenic disorder, see Schizophrenia
Selection bias, psychiatric research and,
  111–114
Self-esteem, and female sex-role
  stereotyping, 27
Self, false, see False self
Self-starvation, case study of, 29–32
Sex-role conditioning, in complementary
  marriages, 80, 81
Sex-role conflict, 36–38
  case study of, 38–43
  competitive women and, 77, 78
  and depressed women, 133–143
  marital hostility and, 192–194
  and obsessive compulsive disorders, 174,
    175
  practical help for, 229
  simple agoraphobia and, 157–160
  see also Sex-role strain
Sex-role expectations, in women, evidence
  and effects of, 37, 38
Sex-role issues
  in married women, 81, 82
  in schizophrenic disorder, 186, 187

Sex-role research
 feminist therapy and, 46
 marital therapy and, 44–46
 psychiatry and, 43, 44
Sex-role stereotyping
 depressed women and, 127–133
 female, 25–32
  obsessive compulsive disorders and,
   173, 174
 male, 18–20
  and mental illness, 21–25
 marital intimacy and, 62–64
 and mate selection, 60–62
 mutual dependence of, 32–36
 occupational stereotyping and, 16–18
 schizophrenia and, 204, 205
Sex-role strain
 and depressed women, case study of,
  133–143
 in men, 59
 Pleck's theory and, 54, 55
 in women, 57–59
 see also Sex-role conflict
Sex-role strain paradigm, 55
 and object relations integration, 56, 57
Sex-role tyranny, and agoraphobia in men,
  161–164
Sexual feelings, towards therapist, 208
Sexual intercourse, religious guidelines for,
  6
Sexuality
 depressed men and, 143–149
 schizophrenia and, 205
 Victorian era and, 10
Shorter working hours, 13–15
Simple agoraphobia
 overrepresentation in clinical research,
  155, 156
 and sex-role conflict, 156–160
 versus complex agoraphobia, 154, 155
Social distancing, and sex-role stereotyping,
  26, 27
Social status, marriage and, 12
Social stigmatization, professional help and,
  206
Splitting, identity and, 50
Spouse
 and hostility to therapist, 216, 217
 preliminary interview with, 219, 220
 reaction to partner's therapy, 210, 211
Spouse-aided therapy
 and individual therapy
  combination of, 226, 227

 comparison of, 222–225
 process of, 218–222
 theoretical basis of, 215–218
 see also Conjoint marital therapy
Status
 marital, schizophrenia and, 184, 185
 social, marriage and, 12
Status-oriented marriages, psychological
  symptoms from, 70–82
Status symbol
 marriage as, 11
 physical attractiveness as, 10
Stereotype
 defined, 16
 of father, 17, 18
 of mentally ill, 100–102
  clinical effects of, 102–103
 occupational, 16, 17
 sex-role, see Sex-role stereotyping
Submission gestures, and sex-role
  stereotyping, 26
Suicide, in schizophrenics, 205
Symbiotic marriages, psychological
  symptoms from, 82–98
Symptom bearers, young married women
  as, 78–80
Symptoms, see Psychological symptoms

T

Taboos, 26, 27
Tamashiro Marriage Concepts
  Questionnaire, 61
Technology, effects on marriage, 11–15
Territorial boundaries, and sex-role
  stereotyping, 25, 26
Territoriality, case study of, 33–36
Test Act (1673), 5
Therapeutic intervention, psychologic
  symptoms and, 120, 121
Therapist
 negative marital effects and, 209, 210
 patient's ambivalence to, 217, 218
 sexual feelings towards, 208
 spouse's hostility to, 216, 217
 see also Psychiatrist
Therapy
 family, 44–46
 feminist, 46
 marital, 44–46
 see also Behavior therapy; Conjoint
  marital therapy; Individual therapy;

Psychotherapy; Spouse-aided
therapy
Totems, 26, 27
Traditions, historical continuity and, 27
Treatment goals
establishment of, 220, 221
implementation of, 221, 222

V

Valium, *see* Diazepam
Victorian era, ideal wife in, 10

W

Warfare, and male sex-role stereotyping, 19,
20
Weight loss, and marriage stabilization, 32
Wife
idealization of, 9–11

of men with schizophrenia, 188, 190–192
role in preindustrial society, 3, 4
in Victorian era, 10
see also Married women
Wife abuse, constraints on, 3
Women
age and sex-role issues in, 81, 82
as symptom bearers, 78–80
and competition
with men, 75–77
by proxy, 72–75
sex-role conflict and, 77, 78
depressed, *see* Depressed women
religious status of, 6
sex-role expectations of, 37, 38
see also Wife
Work, changing hours of, 13–15

Y

York retreat, 101